The
THREE WARS
of
ROY P. BENAVIDEZ

The
THREE WARS
of
ROY P. BENAVIDEZ

Roy P. Benavidez and Oscar Griffin

Corona Publishing Company
San Antonio 1986

THIS BOOK IS RESPECTFULLY DEDICATED TO:

My family: Lala, Denise, Yvette, Noel, my Aunt Alexandra
and Uncle Nick, and my brothers and sisters.
They have always been at my side.

My brothers-in-arms who fought in Vietnam and their families.
They truly understand the meaning of "Duty, Honor, Country."

My friends—especially Ab Webber and Fred Barbee—
and all those whose encouragement and support
sustained me in my quest for the Medal of Honor.

Our nation's young people, tomorrow's leaders.

ACKNOWLEDGMENTS

Many individuals have contributed their time and expertise toward this book. A few were called upon to give more than their fair share when they were asked to make (often painful) recollections of events they would rather have left buried in their past. We are, of course, indebted to them all.

Special thanks, however, must go to Lt. Col. Ralph Drake, Warrant Officer Roger Waggie, and particularly Brian O'Connor. Their knowledge of the event surrounding the action in Cambodia on May 2, 1968, were especially helpful. A grateful acknowledgment is accorded to Lt. Col. Charles Kettles for his assistance in locating valuable witnesses. SGM Eldon A. (Buddy) Gee, U.S. Army (Ret.), helped with technical advice and photographs. But the person who deserves the medal for this work is Jerry Grisham, whose insightful interviews and amazing work on the manuscript truly made this book possible.

ROY P. BENAVIDEZ
OSCAR GRIFFIN

CONTENTS

PART III   THE GREEN BERET

PART IV   NO PERMISSION TO DIE

PART V   PURSUIT OF HONOR

CONTENTS

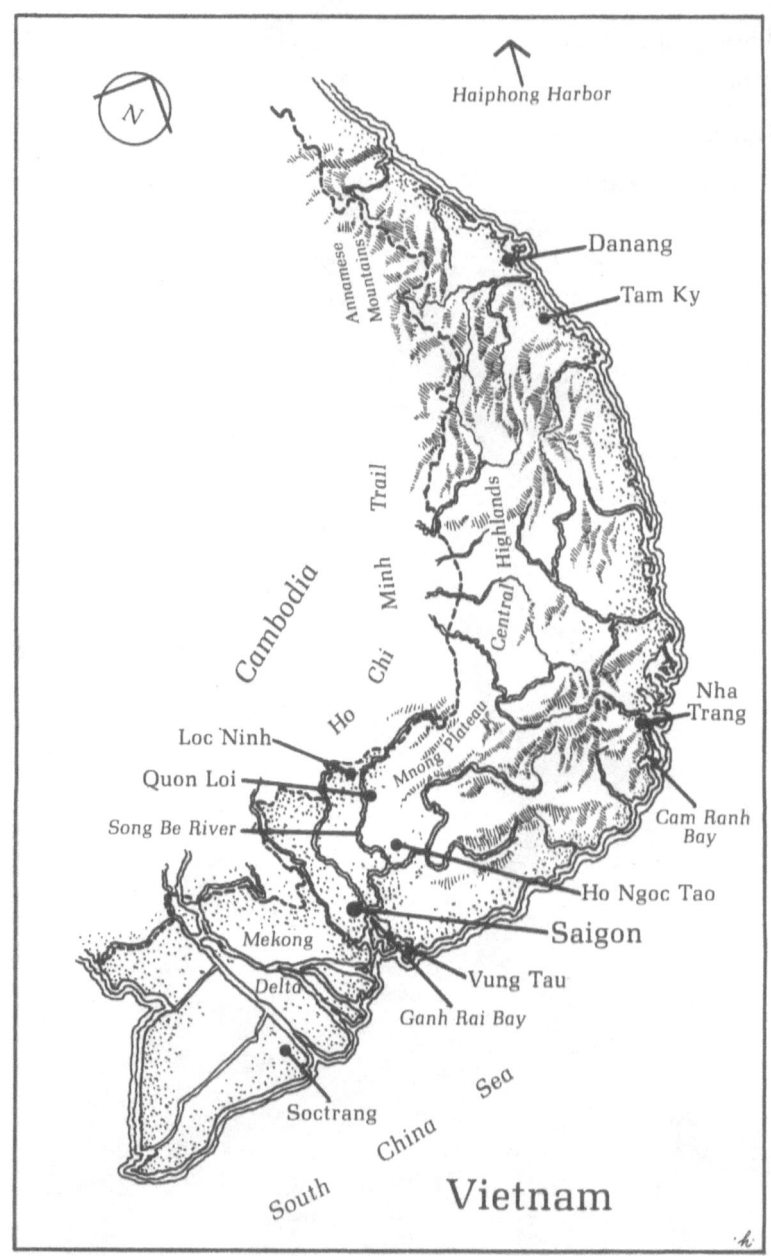

Map by Paul Hudgins

PROLOGUE

I FLASHED "THUMBS UP" to the crew members who hauled me aboard and then collapsed in a boneless heap on the deck. The whine of the rotors switched to a ratchedy chop and the helicopter staggered into the air. As if on cue, the firefight raging around and below the craft intensified as the North Vietnamese regulars realized their prey was escaping.

From where I lay crumpled behind the pilots, I could feel the chopper shake as it clawed for altitude and freedom from the jungle deathtrap below. Above the sound of the rotors, the howl of the turbine, and the chatter of the door guns, I could hear and feel the clatter of bullets against the hull below—like hail in reverse.

I watched the blistering Cambodian sunlight lance through the holes appearing overhead as bullets ripped through the deck and chewed through the ceiling. I winced at each addition to the deadly light show, hoping the next bullet wouldn't first pass through me.

That day, I think, I was truly terrified for the first time in my life. Safety, and all that the sweet music of those rotors signified, was finally within reach. But it could all be snatched away with one lucky shot by a NVA stumbling around in the clearing below, squinting into the sun, and firing blindly at our retreating chopper.

That possibility was dramatically demonstrated as one of the door gunners suddenly was flung backward, arms flailing, to fall inches from where I lay.

Already in a fetal position, I curled into an even tighter ball, offering as small a target as possible.

The firing soon slipped behind us, and I was able to turn my attention to the shape I was in. I couldn't move; I was paralyzed. Or perhaps I was just scared stiff. Now I was no longer afraid of catching that final bullet. God knows, I had already been hit enough. Now, the fear that I would not live stole into my mind. There seemed to be enough evidence to back up the thought, judging from what I could tell on my own. Breathing was almost impossible; the pain was unbearable.

God, the pain! What felt like a punctured lung made each ragged breath an ordeal in agony. I closed my eyes in a futile attempt to find refuge in the darkness.

Minutes, or maybe it was seconds, into the flight, I forced open my blood-caked eyelids and squinted into the half-light of the cabin. A medic moved about in what little room was available. Bodies were piled in the rear, heaped like sandbags. A few of the wounded had been placed on top of them and the medic was adjusting tourniquets and changing dressings. There didn't seem to be much else he could do.

"What about him?" said an unseen voice near my head.

"I don't think so," the medic answered. "He's pretty bad; better leave him alone."

They seemed to move away. Apparently I was near enough to death to be beyond help, and it probably wasn't worth the effort to place me on the charnel pile in the rear.

Getting enough air into my lungs was becoming a greater problem. I could only suck in small amounts through my nose. And my mouth was so full of blood I might as well have tried to breathe under water. It flowed through my ruined lips onto the deck, coursed from my slashed arms, and streamed from my punctured belly and the bullet holes in my legs. Countless shrapnel wounds on my back and arms turned even the sweat that stained my clothing a frothy pink.

"Jesus, am I floating in my own blood?" I wondered.

From my floor-level perspective, the deck seemed awash with blood. It flowed like hillside springlets from the pile of corpses. And like a miniature crimson sea, its tides governed by the tossing of the buffeted helicopter, the blood flowed back and forth, around and through the spent shells, ripped clothing, scattered equipment, and outstretched dead and dying arms and legs. It spilled out the open doors in rivulets, showering the jungle below as the wash from the rotors ripped it into millions of droplets.

I drifted into shock. Impressions from my body and what I could tell of my surroundings came to me at times in distinct but separate fragments—bright, sharp, and jagged as a shattered mirror. And then softly, like a dream, thoughts and even pain would dissolve into quiet grayness.

But always the pain would return—unyielding, uncompromising. My head ached and I knew my jaw was broken. A rifle butt square in the mouth had taken care of that. An earlier swing by the same weapon to the back of my head had left it ringing like a bell. And the vibration of the crippled chopper had set off the bell's clapper again.

At that moment, the only satisfaction I could take was that the club-wielding NVA son of a bitch who had tried to take off my head, knock out my teeth, and then gut me with his bayonet was in worse shape than I. He was lying dead in the jungle below, my knife still sticking from his rib cage. I prayed to God I wasn't soon going to join him, wherever he was now.

My right arm was snug against my right side. Like my left, the enemy's bayonet had laid it open, but I needed it to hold my intestines in place. With every shallow breath, my entrails squirmed, warm and moist, beneath my fingers, working to spill free into the blood-lake on the chopper deck.

The only sounds I heard were the racket of the chopper through the muggy Southeast Asian sky and the murmurs from the rear as the wounded were tended. I could blot that out, just as I could the sight of what remained of my buddies.

But the smell assaulted me, pulling me repeatedly from my shock-induced reverie. I can still call up that unforgettable stench—an assortment of odors composed of the warm, salty metallic smell of blood overlaid with that scorched-bacon aroma of human flesh seared from the bone and spiced with excrement, urine, gunpowder, napalm, sweat, and, of course, fear.

The trip back to the Loc Ninh Special Forces base in western South Vietnam took about twenty minutes. The rough thump of the chopper landing brought me alert. Thank God, I made it this far; now if I can just make it to the hospital in Saigon, I'll be alright, I thought.

"Holy shit, look at this!" I heard as the first outsiders took a look inside our flying butcher shop.

"Get those stretchers over here, on the double."

I waited, eyes closed, and listened as men clambered into the chopper and began handing the wounded out the door.

"Hey look," someone called. "These three ain't ours. Somebody was throwing NVAs on too."

I struggled to look toward the voices. Two soldiers were standing near the dwindling cache of bodies. One pointed at three remaining corpses.

"Must not have had time to check IDs," the other said as he tugged at an arm.

I retreated to the darkness behind my eyelids. Soon, I felt arms lifting me and sensed the sunlight fall across my face as they handed me through the doorway.

"Just put him over here with the other three on the ground," said the voice belonging to the arms holding my legs.

The other three? "Oh, Christ, No!" my mind cried as realization dawned. Half of the blood I had just dumped over Southeast Asia belonged to the Yaqui Indian nation. More than once my native American features had been mistaken for Oriental. Now, by God, they were going to get me dumped with the enemy dead.

And there didn't seem to be much I could do about it. I couldn't move or talk and could barely open my eyes.

They laid me on the ground in the sun beside my new comrades—men whom I had mistakenly loaded on the helicopter in the confusion of getting the hell out of that death-dealing Cambodian jungle.

Fortunately for my sanity, the irony of the situation was short-lived.

"Hey! That's Benavidez," I heard a familiar voice cry out. "That's no damn Gook. That's Sergeant Benavidez, that's Roy right there," he said excitedly. I still couldn't see him, but I recognized the voice as that of Master Sergeant Jerry Cottingham, a reconnaissance team leader I knew well. However, Cottingham's recognition did not distract the medical officer examining the casualties. In the short time I had been lying there, the three enemy soldiers had been stuffed into rubber body bags. And I had already heard the sharp crackle at my feet as another was shaken out.

As my heels were lifted, a face swam into view. A doctor stared at me, a look of professional assessment about him. I felt hands grab my knees as the body bag was pulled over my feet and up my calves.

What had become an unrelenting nightmare had to come to an end, I thought. One way or the other. If the medical officer failed to realize I was still alive, the black airtight bag would finish the job begun by the enemy. Designed to protect the sensitivities of the people charged with the duty of handling bodies, it would cut off all oxygen once it closed over my head. I would suffocate within minutes.

The rattle of the body bag grew louder and I could tell it was already up to my thighs.

"There's nothing I can do for him," said the medical officer, as his face began to recede from my view.

"What do you mean, nothing!" The silent scream flashed through my mind. And with all the energy I could summon, I spat at him as he started to rise from his knees. I say spat, but actually, I sprayed a mixture of blood, spittle, and mucus into his startled face.

"What the hell!" he sputtered. "Stop," he ordered, turning toward my feet.

The ominous crackle of the body bag ceased, and my heels were lowered to the ground.

"He's alive," the doctor said. "Get him onto a stretcher; he's going to Saigon."

PART I

THE NINE-RULE WAR

CHAPTER 1

"THE CAPTAIN HAS turned on the 'No Smoking' and 'Fasten Seat Belt' signs. We are now beginning our descent into Saigon's Tan Son Nhat Airport. Please bring your seats to an upright position in preparation for landing."

The stewardess's voice roused me from the exhausted half-doze I had managed for the last three or four hours. Bringing my seat forward, I stretched and yawned. I knew the routine and began checking the immediate area around my seat, putting up the tray, inventorying my personal belongings, and in general trying to put in order the debris of almost twenty consecutive hours in the air and over two days total travel time.

Houston, Texas, was a long way away at the moment. I had begun this marathon trip there two—or was it three—days before, flying to Travis Air Force Base in California, then on to Anchorage, Alaska, followed by an endless Pacific flight to Hawaii, and now this killer of a run to South Vietnam.

Somewhere along the way had been a layover or two, but at the moment, the trip's length and the accompanying jet lag made it tough to remember whether it was in Alaska or Hawaii. A man is definitely tired if he can't remember if the last time he slept in a real bed was in Alaska or Hawaii.

Well, Vietnam, here I am, I thought. Roy Benavidez is here to save you from the Red Peril. I looked up at the pretty flight attendant standing by me in the aisle with her hand outstretched, palm up. And he will get right to it as soon as he finds those plastic cups piled somewhere under his seat, I amended.

Thinking back on the stewardess, I later wished I had taken a closer, more appreciative look at her fresh-scrubbed, round-eyed, American Beauty face. It would be a while before I'd get another look at an American woman.

As the Military Air Transport Service (MATS) plane banked for its final approach, I glimpsed the city of Saigon through my window. It could have been any metropolitan area in the world viewed through any airliner window. Large, industrious, populated with people intent on pulling themselves up the economic ladder or just hanging tight where they were, making a living for themselves and their families.

But Saigon was not such a place. At least, not now—not in December, 1965. It ranked at the top of anybody's list of the most confusing, frustrating, and dangerous places to be in the world. I had been briefed before leaving the States on the conditions to expect in South Vietnam, and newspapers and magazines picked up along the way had added to the evolving picture of a nation bent on suicide.

Even as the aircraft settled into the hot, humid soup that serves as air in Southeast Asia, the South Vietnamese leaders were again playing their version of musical chairs. Another general, Nguyen Van Thieu this time, was the new chief of state while the flamboyant Air Vice Marshal Nguyen Cao Ky, he of the black flight suit and pink scarf, was the new prime minister. It marked a return to

4

military rule after an interval of civilian attempts to govern the increasingly ungovernable.

One of my fellow passengers, a civilian dressed in corduroy slacks and a flowered sports shirt, said "You want to head the government here? Just take a number and stand in line. They'll get to everybody sooner or later." If he had not been aboard a military aircraft, he could have been a businessman from Cleveland. More likely, he was a CIA operative.

I was certainly arriving on the scene at a historic time. I was not the only American seeing South Vietnam for the first time. Earlier that year, the Viet Cong had launched their long-awaited summer offensive and had staggered the south's forces with its size, precision, and ferocity. The Central Highlands, an area I was soon to know intimately, had suffered badly.

Now six more battalions of U.S. combat troops, totaling 8,000 men, along with 13,000 support personnel, were moving into the country, bringing to 75,000 the number of American soldiers there. It was more than triple the number that had been there less than a year earlier. No, I was far from alone.

I was going in as an advisor. After a brief orientation at Military Assistance Command, Vietnam (MACV) headquarters, I would be assigned to an Army Republic Viet Nam (ARVN) unit somewhere in the countryside. Considering the rapid buildup of American combat personnel, the advisor role in South Vietnam was rapidly becoming a thing of the past. I was afraid my new job would be out of date before I could get to it.

But no need to worry. I would find more than enough for an advisor to do. The war still had a way to go before becoming an all-out American affair.

The thump of terra firma, squall of tortured tires, and howl of reversed jet engines announced the arrival of Sergeant Roy P. Benavidez in the "Paris of the Orient." I looked around at my fellow passengers, wondering again for the hundredth time who the civilians were. Only about half of the men wore military uniforms.

We filed off the aircraft, tired but grateful the trip was over. As we moved toward the front of the plane, the two flight attendants took up their customary positions at the door to wish us goodbye.

"Pray for us," I said, passing them on my way out.

"We will, Sergeant," said the tall redhead. "Be careful." She knew. She had watched other advisors disembark and she had seen them loading coffins into the cargo bay for the return flight. But neither of us knew the trickle both ways was forerunner of a future flood.

Stepping through the door into the late afternoon sunlight, we were greeted by the heat. Heavy and dank, it flowed over us.

"How about that," I said to the guy behind me, a fat man already sweating as he fought to balance a suitcase and a duffel bag, "it's just like home." He looked at me like he thought the heat had already sucked out my brains.

But I was telling the truth. Summer in South Texas around my hometown of El Campo can be murderous. The heat and humidity in Southeast Asia, even in December, is not all that different from the lower reaches of Texas. But where the weather of South Vietnam has it over Texas or any other part of the U.S. is in its monotonous and debilitating character.

Even in El Campo, fall, winter, and spring meant a respite from the frying pan of summer. Not along the belly of Asia. There it is hot—period. It would soon lose its nostalgic appeal for me.

CHAPTER 1

An Army bus, its motor idling, waited below. The civilians trudged off toward the terminal entrance while the military personnel gathered around the open door of the bus. About fifteen of us trooped aboard, taking care to maneuver around the sandbags piled at the top of the steps and around the driver, an enlisted man.

The rear of the bus bounced as our baggage was thrown through the rear door and piled haphazardly on the back seats. Within a few minutes we were all aboard and began the drive into the city.

Through the wire mesh that covered the windows, installed to discourage terrorists from tossing grenades into the vehicle, I got my first closeup view of Saigon. The city was bustling. People were everywhere; the streets were clogged with trucks, taxis, and motor scooters. They surged around the bus. From a seat two rows behind him, I watched our driver. Although he drove straight through the traffic, his body moved, shifting from side to side, away from the masses of people in the narrow streets and at the corners as they appeared first on the left and then the right. He reminded me of a halfback doing a nifty bit of open-field running.

I doubt he was aware of his actions. They were unconscious response to the press of humanity; people who he knew could change from innocent pedestrians, shopkeepers, or cyclists into bomb-throwing guerrillas in the blink of an eye. The bus was conspicuous and its cargo of fresh military advisors a tempting target.

He seemed to relax when we picked up speed on the boulevards—but not much.

In 1965, Saigon had not decayed to the extent it would at the height of the war, but already there were signs. Many of the people in the street were children, most of them orphans; their numbers would become legion as the savagery grew. Cripples and beggars were in abundance, and the black market was a thriving enterprise. Supplied by the goods arriving from the U.S., the trafficking in contraband would grow to dominate life in the squares in the years to come.

Before leaving the U.S.—"The World" as grunts learned to call it—I managed to get in some extracurricular reading on South Vietnam and Saigon. Most of it spoke of Saigon as the perfect French provincial city. I had read of the lovely, wide boulevards, beautiful squares, the small shops and sidewalk cafes that snuggled together along its tree-shaded streets, the lush tropical vegetation of bougainvillea, mimosa trees (just like back home in Texas), jasmine, and acacias that turned each residential area into a tropical garden.

But the beauty I had read about was fading fast and would much too soon vanish altogether.

CHAPTER 2

WE ARRIVED AT our destination, the Capital Hotel in the Cholon District, the ethnic Chinese enclave within the city. Waiting there was a captain who herded us together in the lobby. Pointing to the South Vietnamese guards at the entrance, he assured us that the building was secure.

"I want you all to get some rest this evening," he said. "We expect you to be ready for orientation come tomorrow. There'll be a bus waiting for you out front at 0800." No time was going to be wasted in beginning our education.

"Oh, by the way," he continued as we began to break up, heading toward the stairs, "it would probably be a good idea to spend your evening here in the restaurant and bar. I don't think any of you are ready for Saigon nightlife. Good evening."

The hotel was a rather seedy affair, but it was relatively clean. And the bar was open. After securing my belongings, I wandered into it, and found the other two members of my division, the 82nd Airborne, sitting at a table.

The captain and sergeant, whose names I have long forgotten, asked me to join them. We drank and talked about the strangeness of our being in Southeast Asia while our division was in

the Dominican Republic, part of President Johnson's attempt to stabilize that island republic's government.

Before being assigned to Vietnam, I had been pulling easy duty. For the previous six months, I had been an army recruiter at Fort Ord in California. After that stint, I went back to Fort Bragg, North Carolina, to find that my outfit, the 325th, Second Battalion, had already pulled out for the Caribbean. Waiting for me were orders to go the other way—to South Vietnam.

It was disconcerting but orders were just that—orders. In a way, my assignment as an advisor should not have come as a surprise. At the beginning of 1965, the army was looking for men to serve as advisors. Their ranks had been thinned by the increased tempo of the war in Vietnam. And a part of our training at the 82nd had been in counterinsurgency warfare.

We soon called it an evening and went to our rooms. The next morning, we were up at 0700 and went to breakfast. A bus waited at the front door and four of us, aspiring advisors all, trooped between the guards, got in, and headed for MACV.

We worked hard for two weeks. It wasn't long, but we were given basic information about the Vietnamese culture and told we were expected to acquire more once we entered the field.

We were taught the language like tourists—learning key phrases from "Good morning, how are you?" to be put to use in polite conversation, to "I'm wounded and need help" for the more practical job of communicating in the field. It wasn't much but, again, we were expected to supplement our vocabulary once we were assigned.

We were issued a small 2-1/2 x 3-1/2-inch card upon which were printed nine rules that were to govern our conduct while in

South Vietnam. Looking back on them, the naiveté involved in their preparation is phenomenal. When it comes to etiquette, they serve as a perfect model for any American visiting a foreign country. But putting them to work in the midst of a vicious civil war could prove to be difficult, if not downright foolhardy—especially when it was often impossible to tell who the enemy was.

NINE RULES

For Personnel of U.S. Military
Assistance Command, Vietnam

The Vietnamese have paid a heavy price in suffering for their long fight against the communists. We military men are in Vietnam now because their government has asked us to help its soldiers and people in winning their struggle. The Viet Cong will attempt to turn the Vietnamese people against you. You can defeat them at every turn by the strength, understanding, and generosity you display with the people. Here are nine simple rules:

1. Remember we are guests here: We make no demands and seek no special treatment.
2. Join with the people! Understand their life, use phrases from their language and honor their customs and laws.
3. Treat women with politeness and respect.
4. Make personal friends among the soldiers and common people.
5. Always give the Vietnamese the right of way.
6. Be alert to security and ready to react with your military skill.

7. Don't attract attention by loud, rude, or unusual behavior.
8. Avoid separating yourself from the people by a display of wealth or privilege.
9. Above all else you are members of the U.S. Military Forces on a difficult mission, responsible for all your official and personal actions. Reflect honor upon yourself and the United States of America.

I suppose every man handed a copy of the Nine Rules asked himself the same question: Why only nine? We all could think of at least one or two more. Probably because one more and the temptation to refer to them as the Ten Commandments would have been irresistible. And that would have been bad public relations.

Speaking of public relations, I was also introduced to civic and psychological operations during orientation, all part of the program of "nation-building" within South Vietnam—an effort to raise the living standards of the people, to develop their identity with and loyalty to the Saigon government, and to enlist their support in defeating the rebels. In cooperation with U.S. civilian agencies such as United States Operations Mission (USOM) and CARE, military advisors were expected to (when combat duties did not take precedence) help in the distribution of relief supplies to refugees, build and repair schools, dispensaries, playgrounds, marketplaces, pagodas, latrines, orphanages, and leprosariums; dig wells, clear land, carry out irrigation and drainage projects; construct and repair roads, bridges, and culverts; distribute tools, fertilizer, and seed; work for rodent and insect control; improve the grade of chickens and pigs with breeding stock provided by USOM; build ponds and stock them with fish, also supplied by

USOM; distribute schoolbooks, pencils, notebooks, blackboards, and chalk; and conduct classes in English for Vietnamese troops and, in some instances, local officials.

This litany of good deeds was outlined to us by one of the civilian instructors. He was a small gray-haired man with glasses which constantly slipped down as the heat of the small unairconditioned room which served as our classroom greased his nose. He didn't seem to notice how many times he put his forefinger to the bridge of his nose and pushed the spectacles up.

"All of these tasks," he informed us during our time with him, "have long been the domain of Special Forces personnel. But they also are part and parcel of your stay here in South Vietnam."

A lieutenant sitting next to me, a gunnery expert who was later assigned to advise a company of artillery south near Soctrang, leaned over and whispered in a voice dripping with a Mississippi drawl and sarcasm, just loud enough for half the room to hear: "Goddamn, this is great. I thought when I joined the army that all that time in high school I spent raising pigs for FFA projects was gonna be wasted."

But, we were candidly informed, it was far easier to outline these extra-military duties than to actually carry them out. Why? "Because," said Spectacles, "you will get little assistance from the Vietnamese themselves. The army cannot or will not provide adequate protection to the local population against Viet Cong attacks and terrorism. And you will learn that wherever you find yourselves, the local government representatives are as poorly motivated."

We were faced with the prospect of inviting enemy acts of terrorism by helping to improve the lives of the people. A new school, church, or even outhouse symbolized to the Viet Cong not only American attempts to win the loyalty of the people but also that Vietnamese civilians were cooperating with the Americans.

Retribution would almost always follow, and almost always there was no one to provide protection. For the average Vietnamese villager, the most prudent course to follow was to remain impoverished and alive.

Our role as advisors to our South Vietnamese allies was constantly reinforced by the instructors, civilian and military alike. We were allowed to suggest actions to be taken, but we were not expected to initiate any. We were expected to defend ourselves, that went without saying, but we were not to be found at the head of a charge against any enemy.

They were directives I would try to follow as best I could once I went to the field, but even as they were being outlined to us in that hot Saigon classroom, the rules of the war were changing.

CHAPTER 3

D URING THE ORIENTATION program we took a couple
of field trips outside Saigon to get a firsthand look at "genuine"
Vietnamese village life. Finally, I was told to pack up and head for
my post in the countryside.

My limited access to the "big picture" (whatever that was) was
ending. After a cab ride to Tan Son Nhat, I boarded a military
transport and headed north. I was jumping with joy because our
first stop would be Da Nang, and I knew that Bob Hope and his
Christmas Show were due there at the same time.

Even from a height of several thousand feet I was impressed
with the geographical diversity of the country. Our flight took
us quickly out of the watery world of the Mekong Delta, up onto
the Mnong Plateau, and into the heart of the Central Highlands.

The Highlands, varying in elevation from around 600 feet to
more than 3,000 and averaging around 100 miles in width, stretched
from Bao Loc in the south, about 100 miles northeast of Saigon,
to the Ngoc Ahn Peak on the Laotian border, only some 60 miles
southwest of Da Nang. North of the Highlands and extending to
the Demilitarized Zone (DMZ) were the Annamese Mountains,
an extremely rugged and heavily forested chain with many peaks

topping five thousand feet. Through its vertical wilderness of rain forests, raging rivers, and insurmountable ridges, at least two branches of the Ho Chi Minh Trail poured arms, materiel, and soldiers into the South.

One of my traveling companions, another advisor who was returning to duty by way of Da Nang, pointed out the window to a clearing below. "That's Montagnard country," he shouted above the roar of the engines. "There's one of their villages to the right. Probably Rhade."

I was able to make out the collection of characteristic longhouses, each inhabited by one or more families. The inverted "V" shaped roofs rested upon the elongated outer walls and the floor was some four feet above the ground, built upon posts. Like most Montagnard longhouses, these were constructed with a north-south orientation, following the axis of the valley.

The word "Montagnard" is a loosely used term for one of the largest minority ethnic groups in Vietnam. Like the word "Indian" in North America, it covers many tribes. Estimates put the number at more than a hundred, totaling anywhere from six hundred thousand to a million people in all of Indochina. In South Vietnam, there were about twenty-nine tribes with a population of more than two hundred thousand.

The Rhade mentioned by my companion is one of the tribes in the central part of the country west of Nha Trang. I didn't need him to tell me why we were avoiding getting too close to the village. The Montagnards had been a high-priority subject during orientation. No outsiders could successfully operate in the Highlands without the cooperation of the Montagnards. Both sides had courted the tribes' favor for years—and both had met with success. Montagnards were fighting with the VC and they also were aiding the South Vietnamese government. The pilot could not assume that any village over which we flew was friendly, so he treated it as if it were hostile. Already the watchword in South Vietnam, General Westmoreland's Nine Rules to the contrary, was: Only trust another American.

At the end of the flight, I made my way to the transit hotel on the base. It was what the name implied: a facility where travelers could rest. Many advisors coming in or out of the country stopped there before continuing on. Also, when the rigors of the jungle got to be too much, a trip in to Da Nang, to the hotel was welcome R&R.

After an evening of shooting the bull at the noncommissioned officers club, dubbed the Take-10 Club, I hit the sack. A small, portable fan hummed away on the dresser at the foot of the bed as I faded off to sleep.

The early morning sun heralded the arrival of Hollywood to Da Nang. The little fan continued to hum. As I lay in bed watching the dust motes dance in the sunlight, I thought about how that small appliance symbolized all that was alien about the environment in which I found myself.

It was December, Christmas was upon me, and I was lying in a room relying on a common fan to keep me cool. Without it, the heat in the room would have been uncomfortable, perhaps intolerable. Even in South Texas at this time of year, long-sleeved shirts were in order. A fan definitely was not. Yet here, halfway around the world, it was a necessity if comfort was desired. Well, Merry Christmas anyway, I thought as I climbed from the last real bed I would lie in for many days.

The site for the Bob Hope Christmas Show was the middle of a dry rice paddy. Thousands of Marines shoehorned themselves into every available space. By the time I got there, clouds had gathered and a light drizzle had begun to fall. I saw only a few Army infantrymen, most of them advisors like me, as I walked among the sitting and reclining Marines. I was struck by the youth around me. I would never have told them—I valued my hide too highly—but it looked more like a Boy Scout jamboree than a gathering of warriors.

Directly in front of the stage (which was nothing more than two deuce-and-a-halfs backed end-to-end) was another truck which held one of the television cameras and its crew. The spectators to the sides and in front of it and the stage had reaped the rewards of arriving early and were jealous of their positions. There was no room to sit and none of the men made a move to make any room for me.

I looked up at a man standing beside the camera, earphones draped around his neck. Sudden inspiration hit me.

"Say, mister," I called to him.

"Yeah, Sergeant," he said, "whatcha need?"

"Maybe you can help me," I replied, stepping between two Marines who grudgingly leaned aside to let me pass. I wanted to get closer because I didn't want anyone to hear me but the man with the earphones. "There's going to be trouble here if I have to sit with these Marines. I'm Army and, you know, we have a little problem getting along with them."

He got the point immediately. A brawl in front of the stage where cameras couldn't avoid it would create quite a problem, a problem the tired Hope crew could do without.

"Okay," he said after a second's hesitation. "Climb up here. Sit on the edge there and stay out of the way of the camera and those cables."

Within seconds I had one of the best and most comfortable seats in the house, only thirty or forty feet from the stage. The camera lens jutted out over my head. I would see exactly what that unblinking eye would see. I had written my wife, Lala, and told her I would be in the audience at the Hope show. She wouldn't be able to see me, I realized, but she could watch the show over my shoulder. It was a comforting thought.

Security was tight, with sentries stationed at all points of the compass around the paddy. Some guards were even in the trees. Just before Les Brown and his Band of Renown struck up the opening number, a firefight erupted over a hill to the side outside the base fence. We could hear the rattle of small-arms fire and the thump of mortars. Helicopter gunships were the only visible signs of the battle we could see from our position. They whipped and darted around the hill like angry wasps, spitting death into the jungle below.

The struggle was still going on when Hope made his entrance. He cracked a few jokes about "Charlie" and their reaction to his visit. The fatigue-clad throng howled its appreciation of his humor. The show went on and the furor at the edge of the jungle took a backseat to Joey Heatherton and her sexy undulations. It was marvelous. For a few precious hours, it really was Christmas.

When the last bow was taken, I made my way back to the hotel, grabbed my duffel bag, and headed for the airstrip. This would be my first night as an advisor in a combat situation. Even as I hummed a few of the Les Brown songs still running through my mind, I began to wonder about what I was getting into.

As we were airborne, I leaned against the fuselage of the Huey, listened to the "whup-whup" of its blades, and felt my apprehension and anxiety grow.

CHAPTER 4

THE DARKNESS WAS complete when the craft came to rest for the day at my new duty post, Tam Ky. As I swung down from the chopper, I heard a jeep pull up. A silhouette got out of the vehicle. "You Benavidez?" he asked, walking toward me.

"Yeah, that's me," I replied, finally picking up the sergeant's stripes on his fatigue jacket.

"Welcome to the 26th Battalion, Sergeant. And Advisory Team One. My name is LaChance. Call me Clarence if you have to go by first names, but I prefer LaChance."

"Okay, LaChance, I'm Roy." I looked around at the surrounding darkness. "Looks like I didn't make it in time to get a good view of the town," I added.

"Don't worry," he said, grunting as he pitched my bag into the rear of the jeep and climbed behind the wheel, "you're seeing the place at its best right now."

On the bumpy ride to battalion headquarters, over potholed roads hardly deserving the name, LaChance gave me a preliminary briefing on what life was like as an advisor to an ARVN infantry battalion.

"You got to understand," he said, "the last thing a Vietnamese soldier wants to do is fight. Especially his relatives and neighbors.

And that's what the VC are. The Viet Cong, with the exception of the northerners who come through here on their way south, are all local people. And so are the soldiers. Hell, they're not much more than a glorified local militia anyway."

As I listened, I tried to pick up what impressions I could pull out of the darkness slipping by. No one was out, although it couldn't have been dark for more than an hour. The night, I knew, belonged to the little soldiers in the black pajamas. Our presence was unusual and, when I thought about it, dangerous. I found out in due time that LaChance's trip to the airstrip was highly unusual. Unless it was on a specific combat mission, the Vietnamese soldiers, and especially the Americans, almost never ventured outside the battalion compound after dark. But it was the unusual nature of the trip which LaChance was relying on to protect us.

The importance of never establishing a pattern to our behavior was drummed into us during orientation. A daily, routine trip to the airstrip would have been an invitation the VC would find hard to turn down. A quick unscheduled run made it virtually impossible, short of just being in the right place at the right time, to set up an ambush.

Halfway through the drive, LaChance's rambling narrative petered out and he kept his eyes fixed on the fan of light which we were following down the rutted road. He relaxed noticeably as a gate came into view just as we topped a low knoll. As we skidded to a stop, a Vietnamese guard walked from the shadows and swung open a wood and barbed wire gate just wide enough for the jeep to squeeze through.

Minutes later I found myself in battalion headquarters, such as it was. It was no more than a tin-roofed shack which served as living quarters for the Vietnamese officers and their American advisors. It looked like a set for a John Wayne movie. Bare, low-wattage light bulbs provided what little illumination there was. Army cots were in the corners and a rickety table covered with maps completed the scene.

LaChance watched my face as I took in the decor. "Once you've spent a few nights in the jungle," he smiled, "this will seem like the Hilton. If nothing else, it's fairly secure. Remember, I said fairly."

"Actually, it's pretty much what I expected," I said. "The briefings in Saigon and back in the States made it pretty clear what we were going to find out here in the boonies."

As I found myself thinking of those briefings, I realized that not many American soldiers had ever been in the position I found myself. Here I was one of a relatively few thousand Americans assigned to assist the Army of the Republic of Vietnam (ARVN) overcome Communist aggression and invasion. The history and politics of the war didn't mean much to me at the time. They still don't.

I am a soldier! Soldiers do as they're told! I had been ordered to offer combat advice to a pitifully weak army of a nation allied with the United States against the threat of Communism. It was that simple, to me at least. Back in 1965, Americans were just becoming aware that there was a war going on, and only a handful of experts spoke of it as a Vietnamese civil war.

But survival, not politics, was what I was thinking about as LaChance pulled up a chair to the map-covered table and motioned for me to do the same. He pulled out a pack of Winstons, and reached for a thermos to pour us each a cup of coffee.

"If you get tired of hearing nothing but Vietnamese," he said between puffs, "you can always go into Tam Ky to the American compound there. It's the Payne Compound, named after a Marine corporal who got killed here a couple of years ago."

The compound, he told me, was also a good place to pick up information.

Americans from Da Nang were in and out of Payne Compound regularly. Some of them, perhaps as many as twenty-five, were advisors to the villagers on subjects ranging from agriculture to medicine.

"All of them, most likely, are CIA," LaChance said, "and can be excellent sources of intelligence. And we need all the help we can get. I think they realize that. They are as aware as we are that we're sitting here right off a branch of the Ho Chi Minh Trail.

"Trail, shit—it's more like a damn highway out there, a redball. They're pouring into here out of Laos and we're supposed to stop them with these gun-shy Vietnamese sons of bitches."

We turned in that night without my meeting my fellow advisors. One was on patrol and the other two, including the captain, were over at the Payne Compound.

CHAPTER 5

THE NEXT DAY I met Captain Creech, our commander, Warrant Officer Dickie, an Australian who was an accomplished jungle fighter, and Lacy, another noncom like myself and LaChance.

"I don't know what they told you back in Saigon about life out here, but you should know that most of it is bullshit," the captain told me five minutes after we were introduced.

"First off, despite the fact that you have been sent here to help these people fight against Communist aggression—at their request, I might add—you can't trust a single one of them. Every one of the men you will be going on patrol with probably has a brother, cousin, or uncle out there on the other side. Either they don't want to fight against their relatives or they are actually sympathetic to them. If you want to stay alive, Benavidez, I suggest you develop a healthy case of paranoia."

The South Vietnamese, when they did fight, I learned, relied exclusively on American technology and firepower to do the job—and to save themselves, if possible, from getting involved in actual combat. It was not long before I would see this characteristic for myself.

Two days later I headed out of the compound on my first mission, a patrol headed by a Vietnamese sergeant, with about fifteen soldiers, myself, and Warrant Officer Dickie. I was looking at the people I was traveling with every bit as hard as I was scanning the hillsides for VC. The seeds of paranoia had fallen on fertile soil.

Most days it was walk out, take a tour of the countryside, see nothing, hear nothing, and return to camp. As an advisor, I had no authority to do more than suggest we head across the rice paddies for the woods or check out a hillside that might make a convenient observation point for the enemy. Most of the time I might as well be speaking Greek instead of halting Vietnamese.

Evenings were spent back at the compound, talking, and playing cards. Whenever we could, we'd head for Payne and the company of other Americans who could tell us what was going on in the rest of the country.

My first encounter with the Viet Cong came close to being my last. And it was a solitary sniper who almost did the trick. During a patrol with Dickie, about six kilometers out of Tam Ky, we entered what was marked on the map as a village sympathetic to the VC.

It was a bright sunny day with the humidity hovering at the soggy mark. The village itself was almost empty; everybody was either out in the fields or, just as likely, hiding in the hills, waiting for us to take our look around and leave. We stopped for lunch beneath a monstrous tree near the village's edge.

I was well into my rations when Dickie, who up to then had been sitting quietly next to me having a smoke before digging in, said in a low voice, "Just keep eating, chap. Don't pay me any mind. We're not alone."

Despite his muttered command, my fork hesitated halfway to my mouth, and I stared up at him as he rose with his weapon casually swinging at his side. Pulling my thoughts together, I completed the motion of bringing the food from the plate to my mouth. I had forgotten to swallow the bite it was supposed to replace and I sat there in the shade with my cheeks puffed with rice like a chipmunk.

Despite a mouthful of food, the saliva suddenly dried up in my mouth, and I felt like I was chewing sawdust. The message was clear: There were VC somewhere nearby.

I managed to swallow and at the same time look natural as I tried to figure out what the hell was going on. I looked around the group, my eyes taking in the squad of ARVN soldiers crouched about, eating, looking past them to the tranquil village, and beyond that to the rice paddies that stopped at the edge of the forest more than three hundred yards away.

Nothing seemed to be the slightest bit out of the ordinary. But there Dickie was, walking among the lounging soldiers, seemingly as unmindful of danger as they, stopping to say a word here and there. I swiveled my head again, forgetting for a moment how such action might appear to some mysteriously concealed enemy.

I was about to convince myself that I had misunderstood Dickie's parting comment when behind me the roar of his automatic rifle shattered the afternoon silence.

Automatically, I dove ahead toward the tree trunk, rolled over on my back, brought the muzzle of my M-16 up and pointed it in the general direction in which Dickie was firing.

South Vietnamese soldiers were flying in every direction, cursing and looking for anything that would serve as shelter. In an instant, food, utensils, and whatever other gear had been loose went sailing through the air.

"What is it? What is it?" was all I could get out. Dickie was standing quietly in the middle of the pandemonium, his rifle still pointed upward. He stared intently into the tree above our heads.

"Oh my God!" I whispered as it dawned on me what he had done. I climbed to my feet beside him. "I don't believe it." In direct contradiction to my voiced skepticism, the clatter of metal on wood overhead in the canopy of leaves told of the approach of a falling object. With a last rattle, an AK-47 popped out of the foliage and fell at my feet.

I stared at it a moment, along with the rest of the squad, most of whom were still lying prone in the grass and in a small nearby ditch half full of stagnant water. The shock of the moment was broken by more commotion from above. Crackling branches, louder this time, notified us that the owner of the weapon lying at our feet was on his way to join it.

He tumbled into view; his heels caught the last limb and spun him into a grotesque caricature of an Olympic dive the last fifteen feet. The body hit the ground hard. I heard the snap of bones breaking.

Dickie prodded the corpse with the toe of his boot as he casually reached to replace the cigarette he had stubbed out when he had first become aware of the sniper's presence. The body rolled loosely over onto its back, one leg bent at an unnatural angle to one side.

I stared at the face, scratched and battered from the rough passage through the treetop. He was a young man, almost indistinguishable to my western eyes from the friendly soldiers who now crowded around.

CHAPTER 5

"I had to shoot a little sooner than I wanted," Dickie said. "I'm afraid, chap, he was taking dead aim at you. Probably figured you were getting a little nervous."

He said it quietly, no assertion of blame in his voice. But I could feel the heat gather at the base of my neck and creep upward. The others didn't know anything was up. I did and I had not acted properly. The sniper likely could tell from the way I was looking around that I suspected something. If he could get me, possibly the rest would panic and ignore his presence in the tree.

I stared up into the almost impenetrable mass of foliage. With his black pajamas on, there didn't seem to be any way he could have been detected in the shadows near the trunk.

"Fighting in the jungle," said Dickie, reading my expression, "you either learn some things or you die." He was a jungle fighter of the first order, a veteran of Malaysia. I decided right then and there to stay close to this Aussie.

I would have preferred to learn the ropes of jungle tactics a little slower, but by the very nature of the action, that was impossible. There were no enemy lines and no safe havens, not even in our own quarters.

We took special care during the night to sleep on our stomachs and made sure that others did the same. No snoring allowed. The Vietnamese, it was said, didn't snore, so anyone heard sawing logs in the darkness was assumed to be an American.

On one occasion, a Catholic priest visited us for an evening. After talking late into the evening with him, we retired to our bunks. Within fifteen minutes, just as I was drifting off and dreaming of a South Texas meal of fried chicken and mashed potatoes, a loud snore yanked me straight up in bed.

In the darkness, I could see the rest of the team doing the same, with the exception of one lone horizontal figure, singing away and sounding like a foghorn. It was the priest.

"Father! Father!" LaChance said, shaking him. "Wake up."

The elderly priest snorted, coughed, and finally awoke, thoroughly confused. "What's wrong?" he asked groggily. When we told him, he seemed surprised, adding that he wasn't aware that he snored. Being a priest, I suppose, had a lot to do with that—nobody to reach over in the night, shake you, and tell you to shut up.

Instead of returning to bed, we sat up the remainder of the night, talking of home with our visitor.

Often during the spring and summer in Texas, especially along the Gulf Coast, southern winds send water-saturated clouds sailing off the ocean to dump their soggy loads on the land. For days, the rains continue without letup. In that respect, South Vietnam also felt like home.

During a particularly violent rainstorm one evening, as LaChance, Dickie, and I sat playing cards at our rickety table, I watched the lightning flashing outside, lighting the empty compound. Through the flap that separated the Vietnamese commandant's quarters from ours, I could see the major sitting at his own table, writing.

"Major," I said, "you better have your men put something over anything shiny you got lying around. And make sure your men who have gold teeth keep their mouths shut."

The major, a man named Khanh, pushed his chair back, and came to the opening. Pushing the canvas aside, he peered in and asked, "Why is that, Sergeant Benavidez?"

"Because," I said, keeping a straight face and hiding a wink to the others, "I'm half Indian and we Indians believe that lightning reflecting off a bright surface can still strike and kill. It's bad medicine."

"Truly, Sergeant, you are an American Indian? I was not aware of that. It will be taken care of immediately."

He dropped the flap and went back into his room. We heard him speak sharply to his aide who had already turned in.

"I don't believe it," said LaChance, who was the linguist of the bunch and could pick up conversations between the Vietnamese better than the rest of us. "He's telling him to go down to the aid station and get sheets to cover all the mirrors."

"I'll be damned, Benavidez," roared Dickie, laughing as the Vietnamese sergeant stumbled out into the slop toward the medical tent, "That's the craziest thing I ever heard. You never cease to amaze me, mate." We all had a good laugh, but the final one was on me.

A week later, during a break in the weather, I was preparing to leave with the company on a search-and-destroy mission into the countryside. Major Khanh walked up to me as I prepared to take my position toward the rear. Advisors always stayed well to the rear. It was a questionable procedure, at best, since there was never any way of telling from which direction an attack might come.

"Sergeant Benavidez," he said, "you will go on point," indicating I was to lead the way for the patrol.

I had no desire to be on point. While the VC could attack at any position along the line, they were more likely to hit the force the hardest there. Anyway, the guys on point were the ones most likely to trip any one of a whole array of nasty booby traps. No sir, I didn't belong on point.

"But Major," I said, "that is not normal procedure for advisors. I would have to check with my senior advisor," meaning Captain Creech who was standing by me.

"Sergeant, we are fortunate to have you," the major continued. "You are an American Indian. I am aware of the formidable scouting abilities of your people. You will be a great help on point."

I couldn't believe my ears. This guy had seen too many John Wayne movies. And he wanted me up front stalking the trail of the VC. No way, Jose.

"Captain," I said, turning to Creech, "please explain to the major that . . ."

Creech was already twenty feet away, his back to me, and his shoulders shaking. I didn't think he was crying over my fate.

"Thanks, Captain," I shouted after him as I gathered my gear and headed toward the point patrol. "I'm taking you out of my will, and it's a sure bet now that someone's going to cash in on it."

CHAPTER 6

FROM THAT POINT on, I was the unofficial Indian guide of the battalion. Being near the head—I absolutely refused to be the first man—of a column of soldiers is risky business at best. An American up there was sure to set the saliva glands of the VC to working overtime.

Fortunately, I didn't fit the mold of a typical GI. Short and slight of build—I weighed about 140 at the time—I was no larger than the other soldiers around me. My Mexican and Indian ancestry, the Indian part I was not quite so proud of at the moment, gave me a complexion that could be mistaken for oriental.

To make the illusion complete, I learned to avoid slapping at insects which plagued us at every step. The Vietnamese ignored them, and every American learned to do the same to avoid calling attention to himself. Also, I made it a point to improve my sense of balance, so that I could walk the narrow levees separating the rice paddies without using my arms for balance. The fulfillment of a sniper's dream was to draw a bead on a patrol in the middle of a paddie and find one of them flailing away like a windmill, trying to avoid falling into the water. It was a sure sign he had found a round-eye.

Three days before Captain Creech was due to rotate back to the States, I went with him on what was scheduled to be his last action before leaving for Saigon. Within the hour after leaving the compound, the patrol left the road and headed across a flooded field, checkered by levees.

To our left, and at least four hundred yards away, a village nestled at the foot of a forested hill. We had passed that way a number of times and had never encountered any hostility. I was shading my eyes from the sun's reflection when the placid water ahead of us erupted in a half-dozen sprays. A fraction of a second later, the rifle reports followed, their sound slowed in the humid atmosphere.

By that time, the entire patrol was diving for what little cover the levees provided. I lay beside the captain, our lower bodies submerged in the water, our weapons cradled in the mud above the waterline.

"I think it came from the village, or near it, Captain," I said, spitting mud and grass out of my mouth.

We lay there for about fifteen minutes, but no further fire was forthcoming.

"Let's see what's going on," the captain grunted. "Keep your eyes on that tree line near the village, Sergeant. I'm going to try and draw some more fire." He started to rise.

"Captain," I said, grabbing his sleeve, "I don't think that's a good idea."

"Good," he replied, "give me a better one."

I stared at him. Something had to be done; we couldn't lie out there in the mud all day. We had to find out if the snipers were still there or had hauled ass when they realized they had missed.

Neither of us considered ordering any of the ARVN soldiers to check out the situation. The captain was about the only one of the advisors who could do it, but he would have to override the authority of the Vietnamese sergeant who was nominally in command of our patrol. An attempt to do so might or might not succeed. The sergeant was lying to our left and was making no effort to initiate any action. He was staring at Creech, eyes wide.

"Let me do it, Captain," I heard myself say. I swallowed the lump in my throat. My impulsiveness had gotten me into trouble before in my life, would do so in the future, and was hard at work in this rice paddy.

But it made sense. The man was going home in three days. I couldn't live with myself if I let him put himself in danger without making an attempt to change his mind. I also knew he wouldn't buy it. Creech was one of those rare breeds who really believed you didn't ask someone to do something you wouldn't do yourself. And he believed a leader led by setting an example.

"Stay here," he said, crawling to his knees and ignoring my comment. "Don't move and see if you can pick up where they're firing from."

He jumped to his feet, kicking up mud, and taking off across the paddy to our right. The snipers had not fled. He got no more than ten feet before they opened up. Another ten feet, with the water churning around him from his own pounding and the chop of the bullets, was all he made before he fell.

I heard him grunt in pain as he fell, followed by a moan. I turned to the Vietnamese sergeant. "There, to the left of the tree with the split limb. Fire!" How many were there I didn't know, but I had seen the wisps of smoke from the underbrush as they opened up on the captain.

As our patrol began firing, I jumped to my feet and ran to the captain. I splashed down beside him and grabbed his shoulder.

"Captain, are you hit?"

He turned a mud-splattered face toward me. I couldn't see any blood on him or in the water.

"Benavidez, you stupid son of a bitch. I thought I told you to hold your position. Don't you know how to follow orders?"

Well, he obviously wasn't shot. He had only tripped in the muck and fallen. Embarrassed by his pratfall, he turned his anger on me.

The return fire stopped, and after a few minutes, we crawled out of the mud. We finished the patrol. Covered with stinking sediment from the bottom of the field, we didn't look too much like fighting men. And as the sun dried it into crusts on our clothes and skin, we didn't feel too much like it either. After his initial outburst, the captain didn't say much to me the rest of the day. But that evening he took me over to the Payne Compound and bought me a drink—all without one word about the day's activities. By the end of the week he was gone, just another drop in the seemingly endless stream of personnel flowing into and out of South Vietnam.

The American advisors in South Vietnam were professional soldiers. No one was drafted and sent there. Many volunteered to serve; others like myself who found themselves ordered to Southeast Asia considered it a compliment to our level of training that we were considered for the job. It was a chance to put to the test the things we had learned. And besides, we thought we were helping a nation stave off Communist aggression.

The Vietnamese were either apathetic or hostile toward us. Their army was a joke. We American advisors felt as out of place as Alice at the Mad Hatter's tea party. We were encouraged to participate in the rescue of the nation as long as we didn't get in the way.

The point was driven home to me less than a week after Captain Creech left for the U.S. There was an ARVN first lieutenant in the company named Wag—due to make captain soon. He had been trained in an infantry school in the States and was executive officer of our battalion. He spoke pretty good English. And in a South Vietnamese army full of crazy officers, Wag stood out as a super crazy.

Slim and tall for a Vietnamese at about five feet ten inches, Wag didn't seem to fit in with the rest of his countrymen. I think he was ethnic Chinese. I know he was feared because, it was said, he was a hothead with an affinity for cruelty toward civilians and Viet Cong prisoners.

A few days after the sniping incident involving Captain Creech, another patrol was sent to the area to check it out. LaChance and I were the Americans sent along. As we gathered with the platoon that morning to set out, I noticed that Lieutenant Wag was present in full battle regalia, obviously going along.

"What's he doing here?" I asked LaChance, who was checking his canteen.

"Who?" he replied.

"Wag. There he is over there by the gate."

"Oh shit," he moaned. "The last thing I need this morning after last night at Payne is to go on patrol with that crazy bastard." The night before, LaChance had been overserved at the Payne Compound as he celebrated his birthday.

"He's probably along just to observe," I noted hopefully. The ARVN officers did that occasionally.

By midmorning we were near the village where we had taken sniper fire that day. I saw Wag stop the sergeant in charge of the platoon and point toward the collection of huts. There had been no plan to enter the village, I knew, but the lieutenant had his own idea. LaChance and I exchanged glances. Neither of us cared too much for the change in objectives—especially when it was made at Wag's insistence.

The sergeant didn't argue, and we headed up a small rutted road, actually a pathway, toward the tiny hamlet. As we approached the first house, Wag stopped and pointed again, this time toward one of the rice paddies that surrounded the village on three sides.

Three Vietnamese peasants, dressed in the traditional black pajamas, were squatting, silent, and unmoving in the calf-deep water. They were less than 150 feet away. Wag called to them to come forward; they stayed put. Nothing particularly unusual in that. The peasants had learned that, as far as the army was concerned, a peasant running away was a VC escaping and one advancing was a VC attacking. The safest tactic was to remain quiet and unmoving.

When they didn't obey his command, Wag pulled his .38 revolver—a favorite among the South Vietnamese officers—and fired at them. He missed, but they came running.

The lieutenant began yelling, ordering everyone in the village to assemble immediately before him. Soon, about thirty to thirty-five villagers stood in the clearing in the center of the houses, joining the other three.

"I don't know what's going on, but I don't like it," I muttered to LaChance. "Ask Phan." That was our interpreter who helped us at times over the rougher linguistic humps.

CHAPTER 6

LaChance turned back to me after putting the question to Phan and getting an answer. He didn't look like he enjoyed the answer.

"He's accusing them of being VC and attacking our patrol the other day. He says those three are VC."

"He wants to know who fired at his friend," Phan said, leaning around LaChance toward me.

"That's right," LaChance nodded, as if it all made sense now. "Wag and Captain Creech were friends; I've seen them drinking together at the compound."

Apparently Wag was taking the opportunity to seek revenge for the attack on our patrol and his American friend. Of course that was all bullshit. The pompous little ass had simply found a convenient excuse to bully these people.

Wag was parading up and down before the villagers, waving the pistol, and berating them. Suddenly, before La-Chance and I could get a translation of his tirade, he reached forward and dragged a woman out of the crowd by her hair.

Screaming, she stood on tiptoe as he held her high by her long black hair. It took only a moment to realize she was pregnant—about seven months I supposed.

I finally made out a bit of what he was saying.

"You are pregnant by VC; you have a VC baby inside you. If you want it to live, tell me who here is VC."

The woman continued to scream, mostly inarticulate, but denying she was VC.

"Oh, Jesus," I said, looking at LaChance. He only shook his head. We both knew there was nothing we could do. If we objected, the lieutenant would either ignore us or order his men to restrain us. I had never felt so helpless in my life.

Wag threw the woman to the ground and began viciously kicking her in the stomach with the toe of his boot, screaming at her that he would kill the little VC before it could murder any more of his men. The villagers stood stoically, watching the atrocity without emotion.

I thought I was going to be sick. LaChance's face was ashen; I figured it was a mirror of my own.

Leaving the woman in the dirt, curled into a ball and holding her stomach, Wag dragged forward one of the three peasants we had encountered as we entered the village.

Holstering his pistol, he pulled out his bayonet and began stabbing the man in the arms and his upper torso. It wasn't enough to mortally wound him, but his pajamas were soon soaked with his blood. The man flinched and cowered but made no move to run.

With each plunge of the knife, Wag seemed to work himself into an even greater rage, if that was possible.

I felt LaChance's hand on my shoulder. "Let's get out of here," he said in a low voice. "They already think we're too much a part of this." And he was right. Several of the men in the frightened group were staring right at us. The mighty Americans. They had no idea of the restrictions under which we operated. All they knew was that the soldiers carried American arms, were supplied entirely by the Americans, and were accompanied by Americans. Surely anything done, any atrocity committed, was carried out under the directions of, and with the blessings of, the Americans.

But before we could move, Wag threw down the bayonet and drew his .38. He placed its muzzle against the temple of the man he had been torturing, and blew his brains out.

Time seemed to almost stop. So distinctly etched in my mind's eye that it appeared almost in slow motion, I watched the spray of gray matter shower the villagers, their own eyes wide in shock at what they were witnessing. The man fell to his knees, then forward onto his face. The woman lay near his head, still curled in the same position as before, staring into the dead eyes of the corpse before her.

I backed away, wanting to get away from that village, wanting to be anywhere that some sanity ruled. LaChance and I both turned on our heels and led the way out of that picturesque little village in the midst of a rice paddy.

I knew then that as long as there were men like Wag, it didn't make any difference if we built a thousand hospitals and schools and installed a million miles of sewer lines, the people would remember us standing there and watching while a madman murdered their neighbors.

CHAPTER 7

THE PRESENCE OF the Payne Compound was a blessing. When the hassle of dealing with the Vietnamese soldiers reached the hair-pulling stage, it was a welcome relief to retire to that tiny American oasis. The small club was often filled with civilians whose exact job among the Vietnamese populace was not quite spelled out to the rest of us. But often they would have tidbits of information which proved useful to the advisors.

During one of these forays to Payne, I found myself sipping a whiskey poured over real ice and listening to one of those civilians talk about reports of a North Vietnamese staging area some twenty kilometers west of our position.

There was nothing really new about the information. We knew the North Vietnamese were increasing their infiltration of the south, virtually in lockstep with the American buildup. And our location was too close to one of the off ramps of the Ho Chi Minh Trail not to have some rather large enemy concentrations somewhere close.

"The little slanty-eyed bastards got a whole battalion up in them hills outside of this town," the talkative civilian told his small, but attentive, audience. He had put away more than his share of booze during the course of the evening, and he had wandered from his initial lucid analysis of the movements of the North Vietnamese forces pouring into the area through the mountain passes to the west.

He began to curse the North Vietnamese and their VC allies. "The goddamn VC have turned those hills into a fucking ant bed. You can't step anywhere without the little assholes crawling over you."

When I left, he was giving his assessment of ARVN soldiers, calling them, among other things, ". . . a bunch of pussies afraid of the dark." The tiny group gathered about him, all about as drunk as he, were nodding assent in unison as I walked out.

Later that evening, lying in my bunk, I thought of just what might be out there not much more than two or three days march away. Frustration, the identifying stigmata of every American in South Vietnam, regardless of his role, washed over me, every bit as black as the surrounding tropical night.

Listening in the quiet to the scrabble of insects foraging about the room for whatever tidbits we may have dropped during the day, it occurred to me that maybe, just maybe, there was something I could do. Not much in the way of making any difference in the way this war was being run, but possibly enough to do some good for me and begin to feel maybe half-assed useful to these people and myself. I drifted off to sleep with a vague idea taking shape in my brain.

In the morning I told Captain Lewis, Creech's replacement—on the job for only a couple of weeks—of the poop I had picked up over at Payne the night before.

"So," said Lewis, "there's nothing new about stories of North Vietnamese units in those mountains." He spat out a wad of chewed-up sewing thread. He was repairing a rip in a pair of pants.

"I know that, Captain," I replied, trying not to sound too exasperated. I knew what I wanted to do and why, but I wasn't sure I could get it across to the captain.

We were in the shade of the shack we called home. By midmorning, it was already too hot to be inside. I pulled up a box and sat down beside him as he continued to mend his clothing.

"Part of our job is to gather intelligence," I continued. "And as far as I can tell, it doesn't get done. All we do is go for walks in the countryside and wait for the VC to take a shot at us.

"We return the fire, and then hotfoot it into the nearest village to interrogate the old men and women. On one hand you hear how everybody is related to someone on the other side and not too keen on fighting each other, and then you have to stand by with your finger up your ass while a squad beats the shit out of some local or pours water down his throat until he chokes. I'd hate to see what would happen if they were strangers."

The captain looked up from his lap and spat out another piece of string.

"What do you want, Sergeant?" He was losing patience fast. I could tell what he was thinking. He'd heard all this bullshit before. If I wanted results, I'd better get through this quick.

"Let me have a couple of men, Captain; and let me just get lost in those mountains west of here. Maybe I can come up with some concrete information that might be useful to someone."

He was quiet about a minute, concentrating on the twin tasks of sewing and dealing with a mouthy sergeant. "I'll have to clear it with battalion," he said. I relaxed; despite what I had said about getting lost, I knew we didn't set foot out of those gates on any mission without the Vietnamese brass being briefed on what we were up to.

"Thank you, sir," I replied, getting to my feet, not wanting to push my luck.

The captain and I talked on a Tuesday. He put in a request that afternoon to battalion for me to take a squad on an intelligence-gathering mission into the VC-infested mountains. The okay came at the end of the week through Captain Tran, a fellow churchgoer and S-2 security officer for the battalion.

Right after I had arrived at Tam Ky, some of the Vietnamese officers learned I was Roman Catholic. They were from Saigon and, being members at one time of the late President Diem's ruling class, also Roman Catholic. I soon found myself riding in the jeep with them into town on Sundays to a tiny Catholic chapel for Mass. The officer who had initially invited me was Captain Tran.

Tran came over on Friday from battalion headquarters to deliver personally the authorization for my little expedition. "You must understand," he told Captain Lewis and me, "your mission, with its somewhat ill-defined objective, cannot be awarded a top priority. You may put together a squad to leave next Wednesday. Until then, other duties take precedence."

Obviously well-educated, Tran spoke excellent English.

As he was leaving, he turned at the door and asked, "Benavidez, do you wish to go to Mass with us Sunday?"

"Yes sir," I replied. Church seemed to be in order if I was going off into the hills to play cat and mouse with the North Vietnamese.

Walking to the opening, Lewis watched Tran's retreating back.

"Sergeant, may I suggest you reconsider the captain's invitation," he said, turning back to me.

"Sir?"

"Well, Sergeant, it looks to me like you've been setting a pattern, going into town every Sunday like that. And if I've noticed it, chances are somebody else has."

Avoidance of setting a pattern in your daily activities was not one of The Nine Rules, but right there near the top. Especially if you wanted to survive long enough to go home.

"What really bothers me," he went on, "is that Tran, who should know better—after all he is the security officer—has made no effort to alter the pattern."

I stared at him for a couple of seconds, not quite understanding what he was getting at. Suddenly . . .

VC agent! The thought leaped full-blown into my head. I knew it was already turning round in the captain's. To a civilian who never experienced Vietnam, such thinking must smack of paranoia. Even now, as the war slips farther back into the vaults of history, it begins to seem so to me also. Back then such suspicion had its roots in the desire for survival. The American tendency to take an individual at face value cost the lives of many men in South Vietnam. And many with a suspicious nature lived to return home.

There wasn't much more to say on the matter. There certainly wasn't enough upon which to act. Maybe Tran was an enemy agent, and then again, maybe he wasn't. He might just be a lousy security officer. A spy or an incompetent. The South Vietnamese army seemed to have its fair share of each; and it was often impossible to separate the two. The captain and I both stashed our thoughts on the subject in our mental files under Tran: proceed with caution.

Early Sunday morning, a jeep honking outside awoke me. I went to the door and told the two officers sitting in the vehicle I wouldn't be attending church this morning.

Ordinarily, Tran's absence in the jeep would not have attracted my attention. But since he had invited me, I thought it of passing interest that he also was not going into town this morning. Perhaps he was either sick or too busy. I thought no more of it and went back to bed.

Later that afternoon Captain Lewis looked me up. I was sitting beneath a tree reading a three-week-old copy of *Time* magazine.

"Glad to see you decided to sin today and skip church," he said pointedly.

I looked up at him, squinting in the bright shade. There was a tone in his voice that indicated more than an interest in my relations with the church.

"A bomb," he went on. "It was planted under that second bridge you go over. Wasted them all."

"Thank you, sir; I guess I owe you one." It was all I could think to say. Tran, that son of a bitch, had set me up. He didn't go, but he thought I was going to be along for the ride.

Or was it just another ambush, the kind that went on all over the cities of South Vietnam as regular as clockwork? If it was the work of Tran, was he just taking the opportunity to blow an American advisor away or did it have to do with my upcoming intelligence-gathering mission? My head began to hurt and it wasn't from the heat. You could go crazy trying to figure it out.

"Yeah, Sergeant, I know," Lewis said, reading my expression. "And they wonder back in Washington why we get so goddamned frustrated."

Well, I decided, if I was paranoid, I might as well get into it. Of all the possible explanations for the bombing, the one that appealed to me the most was the one which had VC agents scrambling to keep me, Roy Benavidez, from taking off into their mountain stronghold to gather information—information which would prove disastrous to their cause.

Then again, maybe my mission was just a scrap tossed my way to keep me quiet. Maybe someone up the ladder realized that occasionally the American advisors needed to be allowed some slack in the tight rein of restrictive regulations that threatened to strangle us.

CHAPTER 8

I WOULD LEAD the patrol, along with LaChance. We selected a squad of the men we figured to be the most reliable. On Wednesday, before dawn, we set out with the squad toward the west and the foothills of the rugged Annamese Mountains.

Travel at first was easy, but by early afternoon we were leaving the narrow sliver of coastal plains behind and heading up into the foothills. We were soon expending all our energy in climbing vertical slopes, using the lush vines and whatever tropical vegetation was at hand to pull ourselves up the embankments and ease our descent on the other side.

More than once I lay on my back, pushed my rucksack above my head, and with heels digging into the spongy soil, wormed my way up the steepest slopes. Progress was slow. The extra exertion made up for any decrease in temperature due to the higher altitude. The humidity seemed as high as ever, and we sweated just as much as if we were slogging through the rice paddies of the lowlands. Most of all I remember my thirst. In almost no time, I emptied the two canteens I carried; mountain streams supplied water the remainder of the trip.

Insects swarmed about in clouds. As usual, the Vietnamese members of our little troop ignored them. LaChance and I gritted our teeth and did our best to pretend they weren't there.

We were on a reconnaissance mission and had no desire to attract attention. We had foregone regulation military apparel and were all dressed in the uniform of the Vietnamese peasant, the traditional black pajamas. To protect ourselves from the sun as much as possible, we all wore the conical hats which were also the peasant's trademark.

On the second day out, it began to rain—not hard, but a steady drizzle that soaked us and raised our misery index a few points more. Higher in the mountains, and some twenty miles from the relative security of Tam Ky, we found signs of the enemy's presence—abandoned campsites, some fairly recent and others long deserted.

There had been no effort to hide the camps. The Viet Cong, (or North Vietnamese, as the case might be) saw no point in being particularly cautious in this wilderness. They knew they had nothing to fear from the South Vietnamese Army so long as they stayed close to their fortified bases.

We listened carefully to every noise that reached us, acutely aware that the jungle's muting of all sounds would give us little advance warning if anyone approached. We ate our noonday meal of rice in silence; at night, the same provisions were devoured in pitch darkness. No fire also meant we spent the night in wet clothes, the cool night air of the Highlands sending shivers down our spines.

On the third night out, I lay wrapped in my poncho liner trying to forget my discomfort and get some sleep. I felt sure the next day would finally bring some results. A few hours earlier we had heard voices due north of our position. Though we could not pick out words, we felt certain we were now near active enemy positions. A deep gully prevented our heading directly toward the sounds, and by the time we had negotiated a detour around the obstacle, we could no longer hear them. However, we continued in the general direction from which they came until dark.

As I lay there, a hand suddenly grabbed my left forearm, clamping down with such force that I felt the fingernails dig in. Shocked by the suddenness of the attack, I momentarily froze, but when no knife came stroking across my throat, I tried to think, through the alarm of adrenaline flooding through me.

Who had bedded down beside me when we made camp? The darkness was absolute; I could not see beyond the end of my nose.

I was suddenly released and heard the hand, apparently a fist now, slamming over and over into the ground between us. I was completely baffled; my alarm began to subside. Again, my unidentified companion—I at least thought of him now as one of our own—seized my arm, and this time the other hand followed, first to my shoulder and then to my head where he proceeded to stick a finger in my ear.

I finally yanked away, eyes wide and staring, trying to pierce the blackness. The guy was either crazy, queer, or both. What the hell was going on? I thought. A low moan came from the darkness beside me, followed by more hammering on the ground.

The hand brushed my sleeve again as he reached for me; the moan became a throaty squeal, moving up the scale a few octaves.

Instinctively, I reached for the knife at my belt. If the son of a bitch was crazy, he was going to bring the VC down on us, and if he was queer . . .

I got no further with the thought as I sensed the presence of someone else squatting at my side.

"What the fuck is going on here?" the voice of LaChance whispered. "Sounds like you're killing a pig over here."

"Don't ask me," I replied, whispering also. "Whoever this is over here is going crazy or something."

LaChance stepped over me, almost tripping over the thrashing body beside me. I heard him whispering in Vietnamese. LaChance's linguistic talents to the rescue.

"Give me your canteen, Benavidez," his voice came out of the darkness.

I fumbled in my rucksack, locating the canteen by feel. I held it out in the general direction from which LaChance's voice last came, sloshing the contents so he would know where it was.

The sound of the cap being unscrewed and water pouring from it followed. Within a few seconds, the moaning and movement ceased.

"Bug," LaChance said as he shoved the canteen against my shoulder. I took it.

"Bug what?" I whispered back, not understanding.

"He had a bug in his ear. I guess it crawled in there while he slept and started buzzing around trying to get out again. That can just about drive you off your nut."

"What did you do?"

"I poured water in his ear and it floated out. He's okay now."

A thought hit me. "Why didn't he tell me what was going on? He almost got his throat cut."

"He said he didn't want to make noise and give our position away."

"Shit," was all I could say. I turned over and tried to go back to sleep. To think, I was about to knife some poor bastard because he had a bug in his ear.

In the morning, dawn crawled up to our position from the coastal plains below—only a few miles away but now another world. The faceless nighttime attacker became just another of the soldiers in the squad, although he was somewhat shamefaced when he saw me looking at him over breakfast—rice, of course.

If there was one thing about the soldier's life in South Vietnam I could say I found difficulty in adjusting to, it was the monotony of the food.

My taste buds, accustomed to the bite of picante sauce, spicy enchiladas, and fajitas rolled in tortillas and served with guacamole, not to mention good old American cheeseburgers, found the blandness of a strict rice diet awful. To my rescue had come the small PX at the Payne Compound. I had bought up every bottle of Tabasco sauce in the place. One of them went with me on every mission.

Following our simple meal, we set out toward the northwest, the same heading we had been on when dark overtook us the day before. Mist clung to every leaf and vine, giving a smoky unreality to our surroundings. The forest was quiet; the animals of the night were now asleep and only a few birds were up to meet the sun.

By midmorning, we had seen nothing; there had been no repeat of the voices of the previous day. I called for a rest at the escarpment. The squad, all out of breath, sank to the ground. I decided to scout ahead a bit.

There was heavy undergrowth and trees in all directions, spilling over the edge of the slope we had just climbed and cascading to the valley floor we had occupied only a few hours before. Vision ahead was limited but it seemed we were on a relatively level plateau.

I moved into the brush for a dozen or so steps until, suddenly, my foot came down on what I thought was solid ground, only to find no footing at all. I threw my hands up trying desperately to get a handhold as I crashed through the veil of vines which concealed a sharp drop-off.

To anyone watching from behind, it must have appeared that the ground had swallowed me up. Actually, I fell only a few feet and skidded down the slope on my butt until the dense foliage slowed and then stopped my descent.

I lay there on my back, hugging the incline, uncertain in my confusion whether a sudden move on my part might send me plunging downward on another, more dangerous fall.

Taking stock of my surroundings, I realized I was in no danger. Above me, I saw a small overgrown embankment, the bushes extending well over the side, except where I had ripped a section out as I fell through. I had come to rest some twenty feet below the base of the embankment, tobogganing over the thick grassy mat.

The hill, not nearly as steep as my first panicked reaction had thought it to be, fell away below my feet to a small stream some three hundred yards away where . . .

I froze. Suddenly, I felt as naked as a fly on a glass coffee table. There along the stream, covering both banks—Gooks as far as I could see. A whole camp of the bastards.

My heart in my throat, imagining any minute the alarm would sound below signaling the sighting of the intruder, I scrambled back up the slope, scratching and clawing until I was securely hidden. I was shaking like a rabbit. After a few minutes to give my heartbeat a chance to slow down, I removed my binoculars from the rucksack and surveyed the scene below.

The pajama-clad soldiers were everywhere, moving about on a thousand tasks. With all the activity going on down there, I realized that, unless guards were posted, the chance of anyone glancing up and spotting me had been remote. Swinging the glasses in an arc covering the camp and hillsides, I saw no evidence of sentries. They must feel secure, I thought. Shit, I would, too, out here.

That drunk over at Payne was right. About these hills being like an anthill, I mean. Those little black figures, scurrying about, looked just like a nest of pissants stirred up by a stick on a hot summer day down around El Campo.

Although I couldn't make out how far around the two bends in the creek the encampment extended, it had to be battalion size at least—eight hundred or more troops. And a unit of that size out here along the general route of the Ho Chi Minh Trail had to mean only one thing—they were North Vietnamese regulars, not Viet Cong as I first thought.

After closer scrutiny through the binoculars, I realized I was right. Despite their peasant gear, they had to be NVA. The clothing, intended to identify the wearers as VC, was not convincing—at least not yet. Clean, and obviously new, the material had recently come off sewing machines in the north.

At this stage of the conflict, Ho Chi Minh was still concerned with appearances. The North Vietnamese wanted the struggle in the south to appear as a civil war. Radio Hanoi said repeatedly that no outsiders except the Americans were involved. So, as NVA soldiers approached the border of Laos, the jumping-off spot for the first leg of their journey south along the serpentine Ho Chi Minh Trail, each gave up all personal belongings identifying him as anything but a loyal member of the resistance. Even family photos were confiscated. In return, the "volunteers" were outfitted with new black pajamas and Ho Chi Minh sandals—rope and rubber-tire thongs, another trademark of the rebels.

A few more weeks of wear and travel, I thought, and the humid south would give the apparel the threadbare look of any Viet Cong veteran. Although I couldn't be certain from where I was perched, I was also pretty sure each of the soldiers below was considerably better fed than the average VC. And they had not yet taken on the cave pallor of the VC who were forced to spend so much of their time underground.

Another indication that they were regular army was the unmistakable signs of discipline. Ordnance was stacked neatly throughout the camp. Soviet AK-47s and mortars were in abundant supply. In time, I knew, much of the equipment below, as it was lost or destroyed, would be replaced with American supplies. The camp was clean and looked like it had been there for a while. Probably a permanent way station along the trail.

Suddenly, I remembered the squad on the plateau behind me. If they came looking for me, they just might come crashing through the canopy of brush over me, sending us all tumbling down the hill. Even the most inattentive of the enemy might find that act hard to ignore.

Crawling back to the top and retracing my steps, I found them still sitting where I had left them. I had not been gone more than ten minutes; it had certainly seemed longer.

Minutes later, we were all in place some thirty feet to the side of where I had fallen through. The undergrowth provided plenty of protection for us all, and we had an excellent view of the goings-on below. For most of the afternoon, we just observed, trying to pick up any usable information from the activity below.

One thing was obvious—their morale was high. There was a crispness to the movement about the camp. None of the lackadaisical spirit that seemed to be such a part of the South Vietnamese army was evident. Troops training on a small, flat, dusty plain, trampled bare by thousands of feet, shouted and sang as they went through their maneuvers. True, they were untested in combat; a few weeks in the south could put a damper on their spirits. But for now, they seemed enthusiastic.

As we watched them, LaChance and I joked with our men, daring first one and then another to go down and scout the enemy. Finally, Tho, a private first class, said in broken, but understandable English, "I go, Sergeant."

"What'd you say?" I asked, turning to look at the diminutive soldier. The idea that one of them would take LaChance and me seriously hadn't occurred to us.

"I go find out what NVA do."

"Don't be stupid, Tho," LaChance snorted. "You get killed." We had a tendency, when talking with the Vietnamese in English, to fall into their pidgin version of the language.

"I no get killed," was Tho's reply. "I know these people."

LaChance looked at me; I shrugged. What the hell, why not, I thought. We hadn't learned an awful lot sitting up here. Maybe it was worth a chance.

I knew a little bit about Tho. He was an orphan, his mother and father supposedly killed by either the Viet Cong or North Vietnamese, I don't remember which. He was just a kid, somewhere in his midteens. LaChance and I had even talked of sending him to the States to go to school.

From what I knew of him, he seemed intensely patriotic, never hesitating to voice his hatred of the VC and North Vietnam. But I also knew that more than one patriotic son of a bitch had turned out to be a VC sympathizer or agent. So it was with intense reservation that I looked Tho in the eyes, trying to read some clue as to what was going on in his mind.

"Okay, boy, you go down there, but double-cross us and you one dead duck. You understand?"

He solemnly shook his head, his eyes never leaving mine. "I no doublecross you, Sergeant."

"You better not. Now, get on down that hill."

CHAPTER 9

A S WE WATCHED the small black-clad figure make his way down the hill, I heard LaChance chuckle at my side.

"You know, if he does screw us around, it's gonna be tough carrying out that threat of yours while you're haulin' ass as fast as you can back to Tam Ky."

"Yeah, I know," I replied. "And believe you me, the first sign I see of any movement up this hill, that's exactly what I'm doing."

"Think we could make it?"

"Beats me. Just pray we don't have to try."

LaChance and I were not the only ones concerned about Tho's loyalties. The four soldiers behind us carried on a lively discussion of the subject as they followed Tho's progress down the slope. We were all nervous.

Below, Tho walked into the camp. That's all; he just ambled right in, past the outer perimeter of tents, picking his way around the equipment piled here and there. And as far as we could tell, there was no challenge. Even now I find hard to believe the lack of suspicion on the part of the Vietnamese. Their indifferent attitude toward security drove many an advisor to distraction. Now here was evidence that this lack of concern was not limited to ARVN troops. I shook my head in wonder.

We soon lost sight of Tho in the crush of the camp. For the next four hours, we anxiously watched each swirl of activity in the encampment, especially any near the edge nearest our position. At any moment, we anticipated a charge up the hill, a move calculated to overrun us before we could react.

But nothing happened. Then we saw a figure leave the circle of tents and makeshift huts and head up the hill at an angle that would take him to our level considerably to the left of where we lay concealed. It was Tho. When he was well into the underbrush and out of sight of the camp, he veered toward us.

Back in our midst, Tho wore a smile that threatened to split his face in half. He was terribly proud of his feat. We sat him down, and while one of the others kept an eye on the enemy below, LaChance and I debriefed our spy.

Following intelligence-gathering procedures recommended when using a Vietnamese as an agent, we had permitted Tho to go on his mission with no guidelines from us. There was a reason for it. Tho was a receiver, a blank tablet upon which was written his experiences in the camp. We didn't want him to have any idea of what we wanted to know—because that's exactly what he would have told us.

Theory aside, perhaps we should have loaded Tho up with questions. As it was we got precious little usable information out of him. He squatted on the ground beside us and with a self-satisfied nod, told us that there was "No problem. Everything taken care of."

I stared at him. "What does that mean?" I asked, glancing at LaChance who looked as puzzled as me.

"North Vietnamese think army soldiers are scared—too scared to fight. They think Americans scared too."

This wasn't getting us anywhere.

"Well, we not scared," I said, getting to my feet. "We attack." LaChance covered his mouth with his hand to stifle the laughter I knew was about to break through. Our Vietnamese comrades-in-arms suddenly became agitated and appeared to be looking for the nearest exit.

"No! No! We not attack." Tho was on his feet with me. "They think army soldiers on the run."

"You make any sense out of this shit?" I asked LaChance.

"Only that their morale is as high as we figured," he replied. "They're feeding them a heavy dose of their own superiority before they send them down the trail."

I looked around at the fidgety members of our little squad. "Well, I can't say I find that much to disagree with in what they're telling them."

According to Tho, no one had paid much attention to him, accepting him as just one of their own. He had come and gone as he pleased in the camp. Apparently, all he picked up was idle chatter. He was too frightened to ask pointed questions about units or destinations. Actually, it was no more than we had expected. Too much inquisitiveness would undoubtedly have roused even this outfit's suspicions.

We spent the night overlooking the NVA camp, and in the morning, after an hour or two of light, headed back the way we had come. Upon our return to Tam Ky, I reported to the captain what we had seen.

I know the captain made his report to the South Vietnamese brass. But from that point on, the results of our hike into the mountains become lost in the red tape and outright indifference of the ARVN command. I do know that during what was left of my tour, no operation was mounted into those mountains.

I judged my attempt at materially altering the conduct of the war as being ineffective, so I settled back into the routine of just being a military advisor.

Not long afterward, Dickie saved my life again. We were entering another of those countless hamlets surrounding Tam Ky. I remember I was thirsty. We had walked across a number of rice paddies which were lying fallow with no water in them. We kicked up a lot of dust, and my throat was coated with it. Perhaps it was my discomfort, combined with the usual boredom of an uneventful day, that got me into trouble.

I was startled by a whimpering from the fence alongside the road at the edge of the village. Looking closer, I saw a puppy in a sack, hanging from a fence post. Only his head protruded; a drawstring which held the opening tightly around his throat also looped over a nail.

I walked over to him, wondering who would leave an animal out in the sun like that, helpless with no water.

"What's the matter, boy? Someone put you there for safekeeping and go off and leave you? Let's see what we can do for you."

I reached out to free the struggling animal. Behind me, a sudden burst from an automatic weapon erased the thought from my mind. I whirled to see Dickie, his rifle pointed to the sky.

"Just hold it there, mate," he said, before I could recover enough to ask what was going on. He walked over to the puppy, pulled his knife, and slit the little fellow's throat. I stood there, watching in shock as the tiny body twitched a half-dozen times, blood flowing down the canvas material and splattering in the dust. He didn't make a sound.

When the animal was dead, Dickie again took his knife and slit the bag lengthwise and removed the body. Attached to the dog's hind leg was a length of wire. At the other end, and secured to the bag itself, was a grenade.

"Pull the pup out, mate, and he pulls the pin. Both you and Rin Tin Tin here have bought it." He placed the small, still body on the ground beside the fence.

"Hated to do that to the little thing," he said pensively. "But I couldn't be sure how he was wired—wriggling around like that could have done me in if I'd tried to figure it out with him still alive. This way, only he goes."

The VC understood Americans. That dog was not there for Vietnamese soldiers. A Vietnamese would not have given the dog a second glance. Canines were no more than livestock. But to an American, it was a pet—man's best friend in need of rescue.

The event that followed a few days later made me long for a chance—no matter how brief—to put the war out of my mind for a few hours.

Refugees had become a problem around Tam Ky. They poured in from the countryside as North Vietnamese and VC activity grew in intensity. With no housing facilities for them, they posed a health problem for the local populace and themselves. There was also the question of security. Hundreds of homeless refugees wandering around provided an excellent cover for enemy agents or saboteurs, a medium through which they could move undetected.

In many ways, it made good sense to provide a central location for housing them. To that end, an area for a camp was set aside at the southern edge of town. About a mile and a half from our position, it was only about half that distance from the airstrip, and near the civilian aid encampment.

Fenced in, it was a pitiful excuse for a camp. The people themselves had built a few rough sheds, nothing more. Toilet facilities were nonexistent. From a handful, the numbers in the camp had grown to about three hundred.

Maybe it was the Christmas spirit, I don't know, but whatever the reason, someone in the civilian aid sector decided it would be a good idea if the Americans, military and civilian, pitched in to help erect housing and dig latrines. Our little group gathered whatever tin sheeting and lumber we could find to contribute to the construction of four barracks. People from Tam Ky worked hard to make life as bearable as possible for the refugees, almost all of whom had nothing but the clothes on their backs.

Three nights later, following completion of the camp, I lay on my bunk reading. I was still nursing a sore index finger I had hammered instead of a nail; it made turning the pages of my book difficult.

LaChance got to his feet from the desk where he had been writing and went to the doorway. After a moment, he turned. "Come here a minute," he said.

Captain Lewis, Dickie, Lacy, and I all joined him, stepping out into the night.

"Look yonder," LaChance continued, "over by the airstrip."

"It's the Jolly Green Giant," Dickie said. "What's he doing?"

The C-130 gunship was flying tight circles, its floodlights darting back and forth. We could also hear the "whoo-o-o-sh" of its Gatling guns as thousands of rounds chewed into something or someone.

Captain Lewis left us to call the strip from battalion headquarters. We continued to watch the show as the aircraft's lights and tracers lit up the sky. Within a few minutes, the captain returned, a gloomy expression on his face.

"It's the refugee camp," he said. "Looks like someone attacked it. The gunship's engaging them."

We were stunned by the news. For a long moment, there was silence among us. We all knew that the people in that camp had no way to defend themselves. Terror was a deft instrument in the hands of the VC. It was very effective in discouraging the Vietnamese from cooperating with the government. And the powerless refugees would make excellent examples for the locals to see and remember.

"You think we ought to get over there and see what's going on?" asked LaChance, putting into words what I'm sure the rest of us were thinking. I know I was.

"No use," the captain replied. "By the time we get over there, it'll be over."

Before any of us could argue the point with him, all hell broke loose in our own camp. Suddenly, throughout the area, mortar rounds began dropping, the explosions ripping the darkness into flaming fragments.

We hit the ground, all of us belly-flopping into the dirt in unison as the brilliant flashes momentarily blinded us. I flung my arms over my head, the toes of my boots digging at the topsoil; two rounds exploded not more than fifty feet from us. The whine of invisible shrapnel whipping through the air above us sang in my ears.

Over the teeth-rattling eruptions, I heard the popcorn snap of small-arms fire. It was coming from outside—snipers. Immediately, our outposts began returning the fire, although I doubted whether they knew where to aim.

Jesus! What was that smell? I peeked through my arms. Not more than six inches from my face was the latrine to the side of our shack. I thought about inching forward into it—any port in a storm—but hesitated. For the moment, the idea of lying up to my nose in shit appealed to me less than sticking it out where I was.

"It's just harassment," I heard the voice of Captain Lewis say over the sounds of the firefight. "Keep us pinned down until they get away from the refugee camp."

"Doin' a fuckin' good job of it," came Dickie's wry reply.

For the next thirty minutes, we stayed put. The small-arms fire soon dissipated, but our attackers continued to lob mortar shells into the camp. Finally, all was quiet, and we got to our feet. For all the sound and fury, very little damage was done. Like the captain had said, the main objective of the VC had been to harass us, keep us away from the other side of town and out of their hair. And that they had done.

In the morning, I suggested we make a run over to the refugee camp. Within minutes, the captain, LaChance, and I were on our way, bouncing along the rutted road in a jeep.

As we drove up to the entrance, we could see the place was in bad shape. The gates had been shot to splinters, just ragged bits of wood and wire hanging to the posts. The barracks were pocked by bullets; one was still on fire.

The only people we saw at first were a few old folks poking around in the rubble. Most of the others, I suppose, had run away. We got out of the jeep. There was no sign of South Vietnamese soldiers. Of course that was no surprise. The ARVN troops couldn't care less for the civilians—I had already seen that demonstrated enough. These poor bastards were catching it from both sides without the slightest idea why.

Walking beside one of the buildings, we heard crying—actually it was wailing—coming from around the corner. We followed the sound. Captain Lewis stopped short, LaChance and I almost piling into him.

"Goddam!" he whispered.

"What is it, Cap . . . ?" LaChance never finished the question. He didn't need to.

I crossed myself. It was all I could do.

There, on the wall of the barracks facing us, three children were nailed, crucified, the spikes in their hands and feet suspending them three feet above the blood-soaked ground. Three adults, two women and an old man, squatted on the ground. The old man held out his hand, holding in his palm each drop of blood which still dripped slowly from the toe of a little girl.

The two women cried and screamed, reaching hands first to one child and then to another. Two boys and the girl had been nailed in place and then shot repeatedly. Very little was left of one little boy's face.

The attack had been over for hours, but no attempt had been made to remove the bodies. We started to do it ourselves but thought better of it. This was their tragedy. They would take the small bodies down when they wished. There was really nothing we could do.

"Let's go," said Captain Lewis. We turned and walked away. God, I thought, there must be justice somewhere for men who would do this to another human being.

PART II

"DUTY, HONOR, COUNTRY"

CHAPTER 10

URMURING VOICES, CLEAN sheets, and white uniforms. Soft, gentle hands. Warm, swirling, bubbling waters, a body as impassive and unmoving as a log. Soft music, long narrow corridors, uncounted hours staring dumbly out windows at bright, sunlit lawns. And coolness—the absence of unrelenting heat. Without understanding why it meant so much, I basked in the comfort. In splintered moments of clarity, the realization I was in a hospital of some kind would emerge from the chaos of my mind. But the insight soon faded and I would return to confusion.

Just how long I had been coming out of it, I don't know. But suddenly one day I sat staring at the brightly colored jumble on the table in front of me. Alone in a tiny room, with only a table and chair to break the monotony of the unadorned walls, painted a soothing light green, I felt a different confusion.

What am I doing? I thought. This is crazy. There's only one way to do it—the round pegs go into the round holes, and the square pegs into the square ones. But I knew I had spent plenty of time figuring out just which ones went where—how many times I had sat there I didn't quite remember. But it was a lot.

When the nurse pushed my wheelchair into the doctor's office, I decided to tell him. "Someone's pulling something around here, Doc," I said after the door closed behind the nurse. "There's no way you can put those round pegs in anything but the round holes, and the square ones have to go in the square holes. It's stupid to sit in there and do that stuff." He leaned back in his chair, smiled and nodded.

"You're right, Roy, there's no need to do it anymore."

I didn't realize the implications of what I had said, but he did. The fog was finally lifting. I was returning to life. Even the space I had merely been occupying now had a name.

I was in the Beach Pavilion of the Brooke Army Medical Center. I was at Fort Sam Houston. I was in San Antonio. I was in Texas. I was home.

I was paralyzed!

From the waist down, I could not move. No feeling, no sensation, nothing. Questions raged through me. Most of them, I soon found out, would go unanswered. No one else knew the answers, and I simply could not remember.

I tried to remember, but there was an incredible blackness I could not penetrate. I recalled my arrival in Vietnam; I could call to mind the people, my buddies, the action we experienced together, even the Bob Hope Christmas Show. And there must have been a last recon mission . . . but . . . but . . . Nothing came to mind. Not one damned thing. It was unbelievable. I recalled a hospital bed, that's all.

A priest was bending over me, peering intently into my eyes. I screamed, crying "No! No! I'm not dead!" or something like that. The fright was at the thought he was administering last rites to me. At least I think that was at the root of my fear. Like all the memories of the events from that moment on until the day I stared incredulously down at the child's peg set before me, they are alternately sharp and hazy. And always confusing. My life was suddenly a movie in which the projectionist had completely omitted a reel in the middle of the feature and then thoroughly screwed it up by projecting the following reels out of focus.

Bit by bit I managed to piece together a frustratingly incomplete chronicle of my mysterious journey. A patrol of U.S. Marines had found me lying unconscious in the jungle. Since I was wearing black pajamas, there had been uncertainty about my nationality until they found my dog tags tucked into a split seam of my lapel and resewn.

Next, a trip to a hospital ship lying offshore. And then a flight to Clark Air Force Base in the Philippines and another hospital where I remained oblivious to my surroundings until my encounter with the chaplain. Elapsed time from my discovery until my awakening—anywhere from a week to two weeks. I was in no condition to keep tabs on events.

My wounds? Amazingly, not one drop of blood was spilled. A large bruise—a giant X branded on my right buttock—was the major one. Another bruise discolored my left knee. The best guess is the injuries resulted from the impact of a large piece of shrapnel, probably from a land mine. Why the metal didn't penetrate my body and why the Marines found an unconscious American and not a decomposed corpse, only God knows.

Apparently coming from below—another argument for a mine—the force of the impact telescoped my backbone, snapped my spinal cord like a whip and sent my brain hammering against the inside of my skull. Another miracle: nothing was severed and nothing was crushed. But the damage was considerable. In addition to the paralysis, I suffered significant loss of hearing in my right ear and a numbing of my sense of taste—conditions which persist today.

Now that I had finally come around in my head, a physical therapy regimen got underway. There was no encouragement in the process. There seemed to be more concern with teaching me to adapt to life in a wheelchair than to recover fully. There were no words of optimism about the life I would lead when I walked out of the hospital. That's because, I thought ruefully, they don't expect me to walk out of here.

One day ran into another. But there were worse places to be than Beach Pavilion. The hospital sits facing the street that runs the length of the parade field at the fort. Like most of the other buildings that adjoin it and the officers' housing across the field, Beach Pavilion's architecture reflects the Spanish influence that pervades San Antonio: beige stucco outer walls and red tile roofing. The building is in the shape of an H.

For an edifice that began as a cavalry barracks, it made the change to hospital quite nicely. However, the lengthy hallways that make up the long legs of the H are slightly narrower than those of most modern hospitals, and there is a makeshift look to the spaghetti strands of piping that crisscross the ceilings of the wards.

The wards themselves are pleasant enough. But nothing could cheer me up after the realization that the two-wheeled contraption in which they carted me off to hydrotherapy each day was going to be my primary method of transportation for the rest of my life.

When she could, my wife, Lala, made the 150-mile trip up from El Campo to keep me company. My brother, Roger, or my cousins, Leo Foisner and Rudy Martinez and his wife, drove her up each time. Lala would wheel me out of the sterile fluorescent glow of the ward into a sunny dayroom. During the time I was trying to figure out the puzzle of the pegs and holes, she had been allowed very little contact with me. I was kept pretty much in isolation. Later, she said that on the few times she did see me I would just sit quietly, not saying much. Frankly, I don't remember the visits at all.

Lala—her name is Hilaria but no one calls her that—had always put up with a lot being the wife of a soldier. It was a life of tiny post housing and long absences on my part. When I went to Vietnam, the army had moved our mobile home, which I had recently purchased, from Fort Bragg, North Carolina, back to El Campo. There, she had waited patiently until a telegram delivered one January morning had given her the dreaded news that I had been wounded in action. For days, she had waited anxiously for details.

From the beginning, Lala and I were quite a pair, a real contrast in appearance. I was dark complexioned with black hair, a swirling blend of Mexican and Indian ancestry. On the other hand, Lala's green eyes, fair skin, light brown hair, and height—she stands five foot seven, tall for an Hispanic woman—spoke volumes about the role of the Irish in her family's history. Fortunately, she escaped most of the discrimination in South Texas that haunted the rest of us who wore our Mexican ancestry on our skins.

Friends since I was in the sixth grade, she in the seventh, our courtship adhered to Hispanic customs. While our Anglo class- mates went on dates to the movies, we met at closely chaperoned gatherings, usually dances. By today's standards, it was a very subdued romance.

Not until I was in the army and overseas in Europe did we begin to write and discuss seriously the prospects for our future together; by then, we were both in our early twenties. Finally I made the big move.

In the best Mexican-American tradition, I dispatched the local Catholic priest, Father Altamira, and my adopted father (who was also my Uncle Nick), and my grandfather to the home of my intended. There, they informed Juan Coy, Lala's father, of my wish to wed his daughter and asked for her hand.

My request was granted, and I was allowed to call on Lala when I was home on leave. We would sit together in her parents' parlor or on the front porch, talking and looking at each other.

Finally, on June 7, 1959, we were married by Father Altamira at St. Robert's Catholic Church in El Campo. I had just returned from a tour of duty in Germany. Following a honeymoon in Mexico, we went to my next assignment at military police school in Fort Gordon.

But in that spring of 1966, not even Lala could raise my spirits out of the depths into which my mysterious injuries had plunged me.

CHAPTER 11

THE HUMAN DEBRIS of Vietnam was beginning to wash up on the shores of America. In Brooke and other military hospitals throughout the country, wounded soldiers were arriving daily. Each day, I saw human beings with wounds so severe it was unbelievable they were still alive.

The blessing and curse of the Vietnam war was that badly wounded men were snatched from the jungle by helicopters and flown immediately to hospitals where they were treated. Many lived who in any other war of the past would have died on the battlefield.

I watched them there at Brooke—like the Black man who was charred so badly from a phosphorous explosion that he was virtually unrecognizable, his hands burnt matchsticks. I saw multiple amputees by the score.

Strangely, the carnage around me made my situation more intolerable. I didn't look at my suffering comrades and give thanks for my good fortune in still being in one piece. Instead, when I stared down at the alien legs lying so quietly under the hospital sheets, they seemed to mock me.

I envied the man with no legs; he knew they were gone and would never return. Mine would remain to remind me of my first steps, running barefoot as a child through the fields to harvest the crops of West Texas and Colorado . . . launching me into the clear, chill air on my first parachute jump . . . cushioning my return to earth after that first wonderful experience of drifting through the cloudless sky.

Lying there, I tried to distract myself. I counted the ceiling tiles time after time—one by one, from the limit of my vision to right above my head. There were exactly 327 that I could see. The test was to arrive at that number each time, to prevent my mind from straying from its assigned task and miscount. When I tired of that game, there were always the floor tiles—scrubbed to a glossy shine—to inventory. Looking to either side of my bed, shifting my upper body a little, I could make out 280 of the little buggers.

But it was going to take more than mind games to save me from despair. What did I have to look forward to? The Army was certainly not going to keep me in uniform as a cripple. They would discharge me; they hadn't told me yet, but I knew it was only a matter of time. When they were certain I was not responding to therapy, they would wheel me out the door and send me home to El Campo.

I stared at the ceiling, not seeing the tiles or the pipe but a life as an invalid back in my hometown. I knew what that would be like. There was no sergeant from the 82nd Airborne back in El Campo. Instead, there was only a Mexican pepper-belly named Benavidez, a seventh-grade dropout, who used to work at the Firestone tire store. . . .

"Here they come, watch 'em," said the ticket taker at the door of the theater to the ushers. "Make sure they go upstairs."

The parade of Brown children filed past her, each handing her the tiny perforated tab, and then proceeding up the stairs to the balcony they shared with the Blacks. Well, we thought, at least we get to enter the show through the front door. The Blacks were even denied that. An outside stairway was reserved for them.

Once in the balcony, the division was down the middle—Blacks on one side, Mexicans on the other. Below, gringos milled about, sitting where they wanted.

Often, I edged past the usher and took my seat in the middle of the Whites. I was a small kid, a thin barefoot boy who couldn't hide the color of his skin, even in a darkened theater. Soon, I would feel the tap on my shoulder. "Okay, muchacho, get up. You don't belong down here. Go on upstairs where you belong."

I got into scores of fights just because I resented—and envied—the White kids who had new shoes or who could afford to buy an ice cream cone any time they wanted. There was no joy in being poor and no pride in my heritage. I was a spic, a tamale-eater, a greaser; nothing more—except angry. The rage and frustration were all there for the makings of a bully, and I went a long way toward getting there.

It was important to me to prove that I wasn't afraid of anything, much less anybody. I guess it was the machismo nature of the Hispanic male mingling with the Indian blood of my Yaqui mother. My mother was a member of an Indian tribe which settled in Mexico and then refused to bow to the Spaniards in the seventeenth century or the Mexicans in the nineteenth century. Defying army after army, only starvation had defeated them at the turn of the twentieth century.

"How about it, mister? Give me a quarter and I'll run in there and grab him by the balls." The cowboy looked at me and then at his companion. They were standing by one of the corrals at the stockyards in Cuero, Texas.

Before my mother died and my Uncle Nick took my brother, Roger, and me to live with him in El Campo, we lived in Cuero where I was born. I used to go down to the cattle auction barn and run errands for pennies. I was about seven years old at the time.

A half-dozen bulls stomped around in the enclosure. Next to their horns, their huge testicles, swinging in time with their swagger, were their most eye-catching feature. On impulse, I had turned to the man beside me.

The first man laughed. The fellow next to the one I'd spoken to leaned around his friend and looked down at me. "What're you talking about, boy? You mean go in there and yank the nuts of one of those bulls?"

"Yes sir."

This time they roared in unison. "Okay, you got a deal, kid," said the tall, lanky one who had questioned me.

"Now wait a minute," said his partner. "If he gets stomped by one of 'em, you're going in to get him."

They called others over and within minutes I had an audience. I crawled through the rails of the fence and edged along the inside, prepared to get out fast if one of the monsters charged me. A big one stood directly in front of me, facing the other way and rubbing his flank against one of the fence posts.

His huge testicles dangled invitingly just in front of his two back legs. I eased up to him. He never saw me coming. The rest was easy. I slipped a little to his side away from the fence, darted my hand under his massive belly and clamped my small fingers around his scrotum. And I yanked as hard as I could.

The beast bellowed, the foghorn blast accompanied by the lashing out of his rear hoofs. He swung around suddenly, looking to deal with his unseen tormentor with his horns. But it was too late. I had gone flying head first through the fence and into the dust outside.

When I got up, cowboys were leaning against the fence and sheds, howling with laughter. I was a hit. With the quarter in hand, I decided that maybe I had something. It became a regular feature around the cattle pens to pay a quarter to see the crazy little Mexican kid torment the bulls.

Outside of the schoolyard, my belligerent attitude got me nowhere—not that it earned me anything inside either. In the late 1940s and early '50s, El Campo was just like most Southern towns where discrimination was a way of life.

The difference, however, between my hometown and such Deep South cities as Birmingham and Jackson was that there were two ethnic groups at the bottom of the heap instead of one. Sometimes the rules—maybe because they weren't official—were confusing. Sometimes, it was more difficult for a Hispanic to buy a hamburger than a Black.

One sign I remember at the door of a cafe read "No Mexicans or Dogs Allowed." A friend of mine went to the back door of one such place, because he knew that's where the Blacks went to get served. It seemed logical to him that he could get served there. He was turned away by a cook, who pointed to another sign: "Can't you read? This door is for niggers."

How important was the color of your skin? Cousin Leo had a German father and his dad's brown hair and green eyes. My aunt's features came in second place to Leo. No doors were closed to him. Leo would go into a restaurant, take a booth, and wave to me through the window. He would also bring a hamburger for me when he came out.

In the 1950s, things began to change. Uncle Nick was appointed deputy sheriff for Wharton County! It was quite a step up for a Mexican American. It was progress. But it took time. Uncle Nick had seven kids, five of his own and my brother and me. My uncle could walk into any diner in town and be served. We never went with him because there was not enough money to take out a tribe like us. So I never got to see if the management would have kept the rest of us out. On an individual basis, they continued to do so.

By the time I was a teenager, the barriers were pretty much down. I could go into just about any eating establishment in El Campo. There was no civil rights legislation yet. Martin Luther King Jr. had yet to serve a day in jail. But times were just changing, I guess.

Lying there in that hospital bed, I thought about the changes. The civil rights movement had achieved results for all minorities. Things were much better back home—I knew that. But to go back there now—like I was—would be to admit defeat. I didn't think I was ready to do that yet.

CHAPTER 12

ONE EVENING AS my ward mates read or watched television in the dayroom, I rolled over to the edge of the bed. Holding to the rails, I wormed my way over the side. Like two logs, my legs crashed to the floor, pulling my hands loose and sending me to the hard tile.

"What the hell!" came the exclamation from across the room. "Benavidez—are you all right?"

"What's going on?" chimed in another questioning voice.

"I think Benavidez just fell out of bed," came the reply.

"I'm okay," I said from the floor.

"Call the nurse. His wheelchair is at the end of his bed. I don't think he can get to it."

"No! Don't call the damn nurse," I protested. "I'm gonna try some therapy on my own. Just leave me alone."

Rolling over on my stomach, I dug my elbows into the waxy-smelling tile and began to crawl across the floor toward the wall between my bed and the one beside it. The lower part of my body followed, dragging lifelessly behind me. Sitting with my back to the wall, I stopped to catch my breath. That's work, I thought.

But the real job lay ahead of me. Reaching up to the two night-stands, I managed to lever my body up, my legs swinging under me. It took almost five minutes, and I was exhausted, but I eventually stood upright, my back pressed against the wall.

"Well, kiss my ass. Look at that. Benavidez, you're going to break your neck and paralyze the rest of you."

I couldn't even take time to see who the speaker was. With palms pressed flat against the surface of the nightstands, my arms were all that held me up. While I felt nothing in my legs, the pain that sliced through my back made up for any lack of feeling below the waist.

Red hot pokers were laid across the middle of my back and electric shock spasms jolted every nerve end; the agony brought tears to my eyes. Like a pathetic rag doll, I stood there, teardrops rolling down my cheeks.

But I was determined to stand on my own two feet, strangers though they seemed to be. I released my hold on the nightstands and immediately slid down the wall like a drunk passing out in an alley. Taking a breath, I reached for the stands, determined to have another go at it. But two white shoes and a starched white dress stepped into view before I could move.

"Roy. Do you mind telling me what you think you're doing?" Looking up, I saw the pleasant Black face of Mrs. Smith, one of the nurses.

"Trying to walk, Mrs. Smith."

"Not tonight, Roy. Get back in bed."

She helped me up and heaved me back into the bed. "You're going to therapy, Roy," she said, an exasperated expression on her face. "If you can walk, they'll help you. Don't you be getting out of this bed anymore. You hear?"

CHAPTER 12

"Yes ma'am."

The next night was a repeat performance. Again, I made my way to the wall, inching across the floor. And again, I fell to the floor. This time, both Mrs. Smith and the other nurse on the floor, Mrs. Garcia, chewed me out before putting me back to bed.

But there was no thought of giving up. And each evening, I would make the short pilgrimage across the floor; the cracks and crevices in the linoleum beginning to look familiar like landmarks along a roadway. At some point—either the fourth, fifth, or tenth time, I don't know—the nurses no longer interfered. Instead, they would look in on me as I sat panting, my back to that wall, trying to gather strength to try it again, and ask if I needed help. All I had to do was shake my head and they would smile and walk on.

In their own way, the men in the other beds supported me. "There goes Roy," someone would say as I slid over the edge of my bed and thumped to the floor. "Bet you a beer he falls on his ass tonight."

"You're covered," would come a reply.

And each night, the winners were the ones who bet on my defeat.

Until one evening, I stood and did not fall. My legs held me— not very well and not for very long. But it was a victory. That night, the ever present tears were not all because of the pain.

From that point on, I concentrated on moving my feet. At first, nothing happened. I would stand like a totem pole for endless minutes, trying to concentrate through the curtain of agony on moving just one toe. Finally, I would crawl back to the bed, hoisting myself back up, sweating and straining, to fall into an exhausted sleep in which I dreamed of only one thing—walking.

It had been late January when they trucked me into San Antonio, as alert as a turnip. Now, May was half gone. I had no idea how long they would keep me now that I had returned to some form of sanity. I knew I had to hurry; when they finally rolled me through the front doors, I would probably have a medical discharge clutched in my hands. I didn't want that.

Finally, my toes began to respond. It was beyond belief. Standing at the spot I now called my own, I was able to wiggle them. Within a week, I was doing a simple little shuffle to the side, sliding a few inches along the wall, using my toes to pull me along. Progress came faster; soon, my ankles turned, and feet held together, I would turn my toes to the right, plant them and slide my heels after them.

The day I had been dreading finally came. Dr. Omar, a full bird colonel and head of orthopedics at Beach Pavilion, stood by my bed.

"Sergeant Benavidez, how are you feeling today?" he said in that voice they must teach all doctors in medical school, full of authority and confidence that they already know full well how you're doing.

"I'm feeling fine, doc," I replied, uncomfortable at his presence there.

"Sergeant, I've been getting some interesting reports on you. It seems you've been getting out of bed on your own and trying to walk." The authority in his tone was unmistakable.

"Yessir, I have." My reply was guarded. I didn't want to say too much before I knew which way the conversation was headed.

"Look, son, I understand how you must feel," he said, his face and voice softening as he sat down beside me. "But the truth is, I don't think there's a damn thing you can do to walk again."

"But sir . . ." he raised his hand to stop me.

"So, Sergeant," he went on, "I'm starting to process the paper-work to grant you a medical discharge. I really think it's the best thing for you."

"Please, doc, I know I've been a pain in the ass to the nurses, and I'm sorry." I was desperate. If I didn't think of the right thing to say, it was all over. I would be back in El Campo sitting in a wheelchair on the front porch.

"Look, doc, give me just a minute." I threw the sheets back and sat up in the bed. "It hasn't been for nothing. Just watch, doc . . . please."

I pulled my legs around until they dangled toward the floor. I pushed off the bed and stood upright beside it.

"See, doc, I can stand by myself. A month ago I couldn't even do that."

Clenching my jaw and trying with all my might to ignore the pain that clawed up and down my spine, I took one shuffling step, then two, and finally three along the bed, holding to it for support. I prayed that I wouldn't fall.

"Isn't that something, doc?" I said, the tears welling up and threatening any moment to spill over and down my cheeks. "I can walk, I can walk."

He looked down at the pad in his lap and back again to me. "Sergeant, even if you recover some mobility, what can you do? The army hasn't any assignment for someone with a disability like yours. I admire your courage, but I don't think there's anything else I can do."

"With more therapy I can walk, sir. Look at what I've accomplished so far."

Desperation was driving me now. I told him I was going to write General Westmoreland. "I know him, I used to drive for him. Maybe he can recommend some other doctors that can help me."

"Well, unless they're better doctors than I think they are, I don't think they'll do much good."

I realized I had offended him, but I really didn't care. "Look, sir, give me a break." I was still standing. "I can walk; you can see that."

We had the attention of the rest of the ward. "Yeah, doc, give him a break," came a voice from one of the beds behind me. "Let him go back to Nam and get zapped." Nurses Smith and Garcia had come into the ward and stood on either side of me supporting me; I was beginning to get wobbly.

The doctor took one last, long look at me, said, "Get back into bed, Sergeant," and walked out. The nurses helped me back into bed. I was sweating and wanted nothing more than to scream.

"I'll say one thing for you airborne boys," said Mrs. Smith as she pulled the sheet up over me. "You're tough."

"Yeah, hardheaded too," snorted Mrs. Garcia as she walked away.

There was no further mention of a medical discharge, and Dr. Omar didn't come around to see me again. Apparently, I was being left to my own devices. It was up to me.

CHAPTER 13

TIME WEIGHS HEAVY on your hands when you're confined to the hospital—especially when you're confined to that narrow bunk-sized bed that seems to harden with each passing day. What do you do when you've counted all the ceiling tiles, told your jokes until everyone is tired of listening to them, and threatened to throw up if the guy in the next bunk begins telling stories about his girl back home?

Hospital time, for me at least, was tedium time. I counted the hours, then the minutes each day as I waited for it to be time to roll out of that hospital bed and try to get those feet and legs moving again. Hospital time was also a time to think, to remember those events and those people who had influenced your life, for good or bad. In my mind, I returned to Germany.

I remembered the evening Frank Torres and I stepped out of the KBS Bar onto the West Berlin street. It was a beautiful night and we were feeling no pain. Somewhere along the way we had lost Ralph Gonzalez; we were too loaded to remember where. We had just returned to 6th Infantry Regiment headquarters from a week of exercises in the West German countryside, and we were tired and thirsty.

An overnight pass was going a long way toward taking care of the thirst. Tomorrow was Sunday—then we would rest. We were young. It was 1958, I was twenty-four, and I was going back to the States in less than a week to see Lala. Wedding bells were in my future for sure.

Outside the bar at the curb, two men—Americans—were arguing in loud voices. From the looks of it, they were servicemen. At the time, there were two ways to appear in public in Berlin—either in uniform or in civilian dress that included a coat and tie. We were emissaries of our government and were expected to dress as such. And behave as such. That's why the two men caught our attention.

Their clothing and haircuts marked them as U.S. servicemen. It was their behavior that was questionable. One was drunk out of his mind; the other was trying to persuade him to get into the taxi waiting beside them. The drunk was having none of it, cursing his companion in a loud voice for pulling him away from his fräulein in the bar.

The light fell on their faces as they swayed in an alcoholic rhumba, and I recognized them both as first lieutenants in our outfit. I walked over to see if I could help.

"Sir, can I give you a hand?" I asked the relatively sober one.

"Corporal," replied the lieutenant, apparently recognizing me despite my civilian dress. "Maybe you can give me some help with my buddy here."

"What the hell are you doing here, Corporal?" slurred the drunk, fixing me with what he thought was a withering stare. Instead, he looked cross-eyed.

"Nothing much, sir. Can I help you there?" I turned to see if Torres was nearby to assist, but he was standing well away from us. He was having none of it; Frank hated gringos anyway.

I turned back just as the lieutenant started swinging. "Get away from me!" he spluttered. "Take your hands offa me. Ain't no goddamn enlisted man gonna touch me," he screamed, getting louder and more violent. I grabbed one arm and held on, while his friend reached for the other. The incident was getting out of hand and we were drawing a crowd.

"Cold cock him, Benavidez!" Torres shouted from behind me. And without thinking, I did it, catching him with a solid right to the jaw.

He went down without a word, slumping into the back seat of the cab. I stared at him with my mouth open. I had just slugged an officer. The intoxicated man's fellow officer looked at me, the shock on both our faces blending nicely under the glare of the street lamp.

"Sir . . ." I said, not sure what to say, but knowing that there was nothing but trouble ahead.

"Come on, Ben, let's get out of here." It was Torres pulling on my sleeve.

Without another word to me, the lieutenant jumped into the taxi on top of his unconscious buddy and slammed the door as the cab pulled out into the traffic.

Torres was still pulling on my arm, eager to get away as quickly as possible. "Goddamn, Ben, you didn't have to hit him."

"What do you mean?" I said, stumbling after him. "You told me to hit him."

"Wait a minute, you're not going to blame me for you slugging an officer." We had stopped beneath a streetlight and were about to get into it not twenty feet from where I had just assaulted an officer. Reason returned to us before it went any farther, and we headed back to our unit. The fun had suddenly gone out of the evening.

I couldn't sleep that night. I just knew the shit was going to hit the fan when Monday came.

You've really done it this time, Benavidez, I thought. You've been getting into trouble ever since you got into this army. Now, it's going to be jail. They'll probably throw in a dishonorable discharge too.

Lying on my bed in the barracks, staring up into the night, I could see Uncle Nick the day I told him I was going into the army—going to be a soldier.

"You'll never make it, Roy," he snorted. "You're hardheaded and can't control your mouth. You won't even make it through boot camp."

But there had been no turning back. After two years of National Guard duty, including eight weeks at radio maintenance school at Fort Knox, Kentucky, I was convinced that army life was for me. At the school, I had seen up close men who carried themselves with pride and self respect—paratroopers. I wanted to be one of them more than anything I had wanted in my life.

Twenty years old, my mind was made up. Anyway, what was there for me if I spent the rest of my life in El Campo? Just another poor Mexican in a small Texas town full of them.

"Him? That's old Roy. He's the Mexican who works down at the Firestone place. Yeah, you can probably get him to clean up the brush on your place. Just give him a few bucks."

Unh-uh! No way was I going to settle for that. But it was close. I did pretty poorly on the tests the army insisted I take before they waived the results and took me anyway. They needed men who wanted to be there.

Lying there in that silent German night, I tossed and turned, forced to view each of the indictments of my past as each and every one flickered across the inside of my eyelids like old newsreels.

There I was—fighting in the Golden Gloves tournament in Fort Worth. At least, I'd managed to channel my combative instincts along more respectable lines. The school bully was now a boxer—an eleven-year-old fighter who had taken on everything in his class around El Campo.

But in that cow-town arena a White boy beat me to a pulp. It was no contest. Afterward, in the locker room, my brother, Roger, raged at the humiliation that I . . . he . . . hell, the whole Hispanic race had suffered at the hands of a gringo kid.

After basking in the glow of victory at ringside, my opponent walked into the room—alone. Without a word to me, Roger jumped the youngster and began working him over. The boy was tired, but I think he could still have given Roger all he wanted. My split lip was stark evidence of his ability.

Without thinking, I had jumped into the fight. Roger and I dragged the boy, kicking and screaming, into one of the toilet stalls at the end of the room. We plunged his head into the evil-smelling bowl; I reached for the handle and flushed it.

Then we panicked. Almost dressed, I snatched the rest of my clothes, and we ran. It was the end of my boxing career. And so much for good sportsmanship.

My first week in boot camp, I got into a fight with a cook. Standing at a sink, washing vegetables, I didn't hear my name called over the sound of the running water.

"Hey you! I'm talking to you!"

A hand on my shoulder spun me around. Without thinking, I slammed my fist into the man's chest and sent him flying onto the hot stove behind him. He wasn't badly hurt, but with less than a week in the service, I found myself in hot water. It was not a good beginning.

In the predawn darkness as the hands on my wristwatch toiled toward Sunday morning. I heard myself as I stood up in the middle of more than one crowded bar: "Anybody here think they can whip the ass of a good Indian?" There always seemed to be someone who thought they could.

"Booze, bad habits, and bad company are going to get you in trouble, Roy." That old saw of my Uncle Nick's played itself over in my mind as I lay there. It came back to me with the punch of a proclamation from God himself.

With the insight from a heavy dose of fear and remorse, I could see clearly how my behavior over the past three years had propelled me to this crisis in my life. I wouldn't even be in Germany if it hadn't been for my mouth.

In 1956, following my first tour overseas in South Korea, I returned to Fort Chaffee, Arkansas. I was due a thirty-day leave before reassignment. But before I left for home, I treated myself to a night on the town.

Before the evening was over, I found myself loaded in some little out-of-the-way honky-tonk mouthing off to some guy dressed in civvies. Considering the trouble the event caused me, I wish I could remember more of it. I do recall squaring off against the man but no blows were exchanged. The blow came the next day when I learned that I'd picked on a master sergeant in personnel.

CHAPTER 13

By the end of the day, I had orders in my hand to go to Germany. Goodbye, thirty-day leave. All it took for an assignment to be speeded up or delayed was for someone—a personnel sergeant?—to practice a little sleight of hand and switch paper from one pile to another.

I found myself in Augsburg in the Federal Republic of Germany with the 11th Airborne Division. All things considered, I was delighted. To be airborne had been my goal since joining the army. Now, although I was still a long way from being a paratrooper, I at least felt a bit nearer to my dream. The 11th even had a jump school; with a little luck, I might find myself enrolled as a student.

"Booze, bad habits, and bad company are going to get you in trouble, Roy."

How true. Only a week in Germany and Uncle Nick's warning proved to be just as valid.

Along with two airborne buddies, Ernie Trujillo and Frank Montoya, I made a stop at the Hillbilly Bar there in Augsburg.

"If you're ever going to be a trooper, Roy, you've got to learn that you don't take no shit off of nobody," Montoya had announced as we made ourselves comfortable at a table. The juke box was belting out "Fräulein," Bobby Helms's latest hit.

Trujillo pointed to a table of four enlisted men next to us, none of them wearing airborne wings. "Take those legs over there . . ." he said. A "leg" is any nonairborne-qualified soldier.

"Nobody in airborne buys the first drink when there's a leg around to do it for him," Montoya interrupted.

I was a "leg" myself, but hell, with my buddies I felt airborne.

I took the hint and when the waitress came over, I ordered: "*Drei brau, bitte*, and give the bill to those damn legs over there."

The "legs" in question ignored me—with the exception of one. "Hey," the biggest member of the group said, turning to look at me, "I ain't buyin' your damn beer." He continued to glare, the cross-eyed stare of a pissed drunk, for a moment longer before turning back to his buddies.

Our beer arrived, and the girl stood nervously waiting for someone to pay her. She looked first at me and then to the next table.

"Fräulein, I said the legs'll pay."

Almost before I got the words out, he stood over me. He was spoiling for a fight. I recognized a kindred soul.

"You little son of a bitch, I said I ain't buyin' no goddamn beer for you!"

I stood up too. He was big . . . six feet three if he was an inch. I was looking him square in the chest. Speaking of short, the situation had all the makings of a brief encounter.

I was overmatched, so I did the only reasonable thing: I kicked him as hard as I could in the balls. I had left sportsmanship gurgling down that toilet in Fort Worth.

He bent double, smooth like a well-oiled jackknife, an anguished gasp escaping his lips. Taking him by the shoulders, I spun him around, planted the sole of my boot on his butt, and sent him crashing back into the table with his buddies who had not moved.

"Drink up fast," I said, turning back to Trujillo and Montoya. "If we're still here when he gets up, he's gonna kill us." We were out in less than a minute.

I was on the carpet within twenty-four hours. I had put the man in the hospital. There was already enough bad blood between the airborne and regular troops before I had gotten involved, Sergeant

Villareal told me as I stood before him in his office. There had even been a number of fights between them.

"If you stay here, Benavidez, somebody may try to even things up with you," he said. Colonel Cassidy had ordered a halt to fighting among U.S. servicemen, Villareal went on. They had been making progress keeping a lid on things. I was not a good influence, he said, and shipped me off to Berlin. Since I learned later that the colonel had considered a court martial, I got off easy. But there went my chance at jump school. The airborne would have to wait.

And in the time I had been in Berlin, the only trouble I had been in was one or two missed bed checks. Now, with less than a week to go until I headed for home, I was finally in real hot water, if someone reported what went on outside that bar.

Sunday morning finally arrived. I had spent part of the night praying that nothing would come of last evening's encounter. I decided to follow up my prayers with some action. After dressing, I went to the chapel for early Mass and a last-minute confession, for good measure.

The priest, concealed by the privacy of the confessional, did not seem as disturbed as I by my recent transgression. Perhaps he was expecting the revelation of a rape or murder when I admitted at the outset that I had committed a terrible sin. Hitting an officer didn't measure up.

"I'm sure it's not as serious as you think, my son," he counseled, his voice quiet and reassuring. "Certainly it was only an accident."

"Accident! Like hell it was, Father," I blurted out. "I slugged the guy."

He still wasn't convinced of the seriousness of the situation. I had figured the whole deal was worth at least two rosaries, but he sent me away with a penance of only six "Our Fathers" and three "Hail Marys."

"Benavidez! Corporal Benavidez!"

It was the platoon sergeant. Monday morning was finally here, and it looked like it was going to live up to my expectations.

"Report to the first sergeant."

As I walked down the hall to his office, my last hope vanished. The previous evening outside the NCO club, I had passed the lieutenant I had popped Saturday night. I had given him the snappiest salute possible; he returned it casually without a hint in his expression that I was more than just any other soldier. Perhaps there was a chance this whole mess would pass without my seeing the inside of the stockade.

The futility of that thought struck home when I entered the orderly room and the first sergeant speared me with an icy stare. He looked like he couldn't believe what he was seeing.

First Sergeant Charlie Turner was an old World War II and Korean veteran. They called him the "Tiger," and at that moment, I felt like I was being stalked.

"You really done it this time, Benavidez," he said. "Come on, the company commander wants to see you."

As I followed him out, I whispered an aside to the company clerk seated at a nearby desk: "Why's he want to see me?"

"Don't talk to me, Benavidez," he muttered without even looking up. I shrugged and went on through the door. It was a dumb question anyhow.

Walking down that corridor to the CO's office, I knew how a condemned man felt on the last mile. I wished the priest was with me. Let him tell the company commander that it was "not as serious as you think, my son."

I stood at attention before my commanding officer. "Corporal Benavidez reporting as ordered, sir." I was scared stiff.

"Stand at ease, Corporal."

He sat at his desk and looked me over for a few seconds. It seemed like hours. I wondered if the first sergeant, standing at my side, could hear my heart pounding.

"I hear you had some fun Saturday night," he finally said, leaning forward.

I wasn't sure how to respond to that. What did he mean? "Yes, sir," I replied in as near a noncommittal voice as I could muster.

"Well, for a man going home in a few days, you sure don't look too happy."

"To tell the truth, Captain, I don't feel too good right now."

"Look, Corporal," he said, dropping the slightly mocking tone, "I'm aware there was some trouble Saturday night between you and someone else. I understand the situation, and I want to be fair."

"Yes, sir," I answered again, swallowing hard. I didn't look at him. Instead, I focused my eyes on the wall behind him—on a plaque hung there.

"You've been a pretty good soldier while here," he went on. "No trouble to really speak of." Not until now. I was making up for lack of quantity with a double dose of quality. I wished I were somewhere else. The words on that plaque. I had read them before someplace.

"Like I said, I want to be fair. So, I'm going to ask you a question, and I want a 'yes' or a 'no' from you. Understand?"

I pulled my attention back from the inscribed tablet behind the captain's desk. Fear can do strange things to a man. Rather than concentrate on a hopeless situation, my mind had actually wandered, seeking a safer place to light.

Now, I realized what he was saying. He's giving me a way out, I thought. At least, he seemed to be. I tried to gather my thoughts. If I read him right, he was willing to accept whatever answer I gave him.

"Did you strike an officer Saturday night, Corporal Benavidez?"

Well, there it was. My gaze shifted back to the wall behind his desk. Suddenly, I recognized the inscription there. The captain was a West Point graduate; the polished face of the plaque was stamped with the academy seal and the West Point code of honor. The words were there before me: "Duty, Honor, Country. I do not lie, cheat, or steal, or tolerate those who do."

The captain was waiting for my answer; at my side, the first sergeant stood, a frown beginning to crease his forehead.

It just kind of welled up inside me. I had wanted to be a soldier, a good soldier, the best soldier I could be. At least that's what I had been telling myself. But my actions said otherwise. Maybe it was time I took a stand.

God knows, I was no West Point graduate—just a semiliterate Mexican kid from South Texas who never even made it to high school. But if I really wanted my career in the service to ever amount to anything, those words needed to mean just as much to me as to the man sitting in front of me—even if believing in them meant the end of my career and maybe loss of my freedom.

The captain leaned forward, his hands clasped before him on the desktop.

CHAPTER 13

"Well, Corporal, did you or didn't you?" He spoke as if he couldn't understand the reason for my hesitation.

"Yes, sir." It was not much more than a whisper. I couldn't believe I was saying it. My guts balled up into a knot, and I thought I was going to be sick. Four days before I was to go home and I had just bought a ticket to the stockade and possibly a dishonorable discharge.

I heard the first sergeant's breath hiss through his clenched teeth; the sudden intake of air was the closest he would allow himself to a gasp of astonishment at my words. "What did you say, soldier?" The captain wasn't sure of his ears either.

"Yes, sir, Captain. I hit that officer the other night."

"Jesus Christ," muttered the sergeant at my side, unable to restrain himself any longer. I think he would have hit me if the captain hadn't been staring at both of us.

"Wait outside, Corporal Benavidez," the captain said, placing both hands palms down on the desk and pushing back. His words cracked with authority.

I was alone outside the CO's office in the hall for only a few minutes before the first sergeant joined me. He proceeded to chew me out, questioning every part of my character, parentage, and intelligence . . . especially my intelligence.

"You're a damn fool, Benavidez. I don't understand you. You could have walked right out of here without a problem. He gave you a chance."

"I know, First Sergeant." I didn't understand me either. But it didn't make any difference; it was too late to change my mind. It was going to be a long time before I saw Lala now.

I thought for a second I could hear the captain on the phone in his office. He was probably calling the MPs. Finally, the door opened and the captain looked out into the corridor.

"First Sergeant," he called, ignoring me. "The PFC can go now." He disappeared and the door closed.

I looked at the first sergeant; he stared back at me, shock on both of our faces. PFC. Private First Class. That was all, I thought. He'd busted me from corporal to PFC for knocking an officer cold. Relief flooded through me.

"You're a lucky Mexican, Benavidez, damn lucky," snorted the first sergeant. "Now, get out of here."

Unfortunately, my day with the captain was not over. I fell under his gaze once more. Standing outside the company office that afternoon, I was looking over the bulletin board when Torres rounded the corner and walked by. He'd heard of my morning encounter with the CO.

"Hey, I see you got KP from the captain, Ben," he called out in passing. I still felt resentment toward Frank; if he had given me a hand with that drunk in the first place, all this might have been prevented.

But then maybe it wouldn't have made any difference. I seemed to have the knack for saying and doing the wrong thing at the wrong time without anybody's help. I proceeded to demonstrate it as I called out to his retreating back: "I don't have KP; I'm going home." And louder as he moved on down the corridor, "So, you can just kiss my ass!"

I didn't hear the door to the orderly room open behind me. "What did you say, Private?" I turned. It was the captain.

Without thinking—a Benavidez trait—I answered the question. "Sir, I said you can just kiss my ass."

"You want to come in here, Benavidez?"

Oh my God, not again, I thought. I was back in trouble again. This was turning into a nightmare.

I followed him through the company office into his private one. Coming or going, he had the choice of using the door into the main office or the private entrance into the hall where I had sweated it out only that morning. If he'd come out the private door, he probably wouldn't have even noticed me standing there at the bulletin board. What luck.

The first sergeant was standing in the outer office when the two of us paraded through. His eyes widened in disbelief.

In the captain's office I tried to explain that it had not been him I was speaking to. I started to tell him that I wouldn't tell an officer to kiss my ass. Right, no more than I would strike one. I changed my mind.

"I didn't see anyone else, Private," he replied. "It was just you and me in that hallway."

"Aw . . . please, sir."

He began to laugh, and it dawned on me that things were not as bad as my paranoid mind thought them to be. He just couldn't pass up the opportunity to put me back on the hot seat for a few minutes. I wasn't sure I appreciated the captain's sense of humor.

I was only partly right about his motives for calling me in. After his laughter subsided, he revealed his curiosity. Why, he wondered, had I answered as I did and what was so fascinating about that plaque on the wall?

I did my best to explain my feelings to him. I had screwed up more than my share since joining the army. I didn't want to be a troublemaker. Maybe it finally occurred to me standing there before him that there had to be a point beyond which I was unwilling to go if I was to have a chance to be the soldier I had dreamed of becoming. Lying to my commanding officer was that point.

"I guess reading the words on that plaque brought it home, sir," I continued. "I may not be West Point material, but that's the kind of soldier I want to be."

He looked at me thoughtfully for a few moments, and then standing, offered me his hand. "Well, Benavidez, if you intend to make the army your career, and I hope you do, follow the lead of those words in that code and you'll make a good soldier."

I walked out of his office, and in a week I was back in the U.S.

CHAPTER 14

A FEW DAYS before the Fourth of July in 1966, I walked out of Beach Pavilion on my own two legs—shaky though they were. I was going back to El Campo—but not to sit in the shade on some porch. Lala and I were packing up and heading for Fort Bragg and reassignment to my old division, the 82nd Airborne.

I had been temporarily relieved of duty for some six months which meant I would probably be put in an office somewhere sorting papers. No lifting or physical exertion. I hated the whole idea of being indoors, having seen enough of four walls in the previous six months. But I thanked God that they thought I could do something and had not put me out to pasture on a disability.

Following that bedside chat with the doctor, I had worked even harder to prove to myself and anyone watching that complete recovery was just a matter of time. For hours I hobbled up and down the hallways, pushing my wheelchair ahead of me, holding to it for support. If I became too tired, I could always ride it back to my ward. Before long, I left the chair behind and edged along the corridors, keeping within arm's reach of the wall.

Even before I reached that stage, a favorite destination was the chapel on the ground floor. I would sit there in the tiny room, resting under the gaze of the saints standing silently on their pedestals along the cream-colored stucco walls. Those first visits were made more in a spirit of defiance than reverence. I wanted to confront God and let him see what he had allowed to happen to me. It was even better that I was confined to the chair; the effect was more dramatic, the self-pity a bit more sincere.

But as strength returned to my legs, my battered faith also renewed itself. Looking back over the events of the previous months, I was forced to admit that the fact that I was alive at all had the marks of a true miracle. And I was walking—despite the assurances of a number of doctors that I would never do so again.

Unfortunately, the pain which had been a constant companion remained—actually seemed to intensify as I pushed reluctant muscles to respond. Dogging my every step, it radiated from the small of my back in white-hot spikes of misery down into my legs and up through my shoulders. Medication only helped a little, but I began to rely upon it heavily for whatever relief I could obtain.

However, the best medicine was the morale boost I received the day I put my uniform on and walked down the steps of the hospital and into the waiting car. A bad dream was finally over and I was returning to the life I loved.

Lala and I spent the Fourth of July packing, and a few days later we pulled into Fort Bragg. An airborne buddy who was now in Special Forces, Tom Gloria, had arranged for our mobile home, (which the army had again moved) to be parked across the street from his in the Bonnie Doone trailer park off Bragg Boulevard only about three miles from Fort Bragg.

I went to work as the administrative assistant to the personnel sergeant of the 82nd. Where in my last assignment I had been advisor to ARVN troops as we combed the jungles of South Vietnam looking for "Charlie," I was now helping servicemen's wives as they waded through the army's maze of regulations in search of whatever benefits they were due.

There was plenty to do, for units of the 82nd were still on duty in the Dominican Republic, but I often dreamed of being back with LaChance and Dickie. Having heard nothing from them since my return, I didn't even know if they were still alive.

I also worked hard at masking the discomfort I still felt. Twice a day I downed a five-hundred-milligram capsule of Darvon; sometimes when the pain was particularly bad, I'd take three. The pills began to take their toll. I couldn't focus my thinking. I began to do my job in a fog.

When I stopped in at the NCO club after work, I was already walking sideways when I stepped into the room. After a couple of beers, I'd leave for home, and the car seemed to be flying. The benefits of the medication were now definitely being exceeded by the damage the drug was doing.

Eventually, I stopped in to see a doctor I knew at the dispensary. He was a friend and I managed to slip in to see him without a sick call slip. I didn't want attention drawn to my health.

"Roy," the physician said after examining me, "I think you'd better put those down." He pointed to the bottle of Darvon I had pulled out of my pocket when he asked what medication I was taking.

"Hey, I know they aren't doing me any good, doc, but I don't think I can make it without some help."

"The only way you're going to ease that back, Roy—short of becoming an addict—is to get on with your physical training. The only way to help the pain is to work it out."

I quit the pills cold turkey, and I began getting up each morning to run and work out at the gym. At first, the pain was unrelenting, but at least my head cleared and I could think without feeling that my head was stuffed with cotton. And finally, the pain eased. What there remained of it I eventually learned to ignore.

One brisk Indian-summer Saturday morning in September, I was retrieving the newspaper from the tiny patch of grass that served as our yard when Tom Gloria called to me from across the street.

"Come on, Hoss, hop in," he said as he walked toward his car. "Let's go jump." Tom had been away at school on temporary duty and needed a parachute jump to remain qualified. He was going to take care of it on the weekend.

"I can't jump, Tom, you know that."

"Hell, Roy, you're in shape now. You been through the refresher and got your release slip, haven't you?"

"Sure, I got it," I lied. We both knew there was no way I was going to find an officer to okay me to make a jump two months out of the hospital. But I piled into his '64 Ford with him, anyway, and we headed up Murchison Road thirteen miles to the Sicily Drop Zone.

When we got there, over a hundred jumpers were gathered around two helicopters. All of them were men who worked at administrative jobs in camp and didn't have time to jump during the week. They were there in order to earn that extra $55 a month a qualified jumper earned.

We got out of the car and walked over to the group milling around the Black jump sergeant who, along with another noncom, was waving his clipboard around and trying to organize the operation.

I stood aside as Tom went over to suit up. The rotors of the choppers began to turn lazily, the whine of the turbines absorbing the morning sounds. They would take the jumpers up to 1,300 feet. The men would sit on the deck, their feet hanging out in space, waiting for the tap on their shoulder that would send them over the side.

Roy P. Benavidez, MSG (ret), U.S. Army.

It was a beautiful way to jump, I knew. I had done it many times. With the chopper hanging there like a giant hummingbird, there was no prop blast kicking you sideways like there always was when you jumped from an airplane. There was no easier way to qualify.

At the thought of it, I could feel my palms begin to sweat, and the knives began to work their way into my back.

First Communion, Virgin of Guadalupe, Cuero; Seven-year-old Roy is fourth from left in the front row.

Roy as a migrant worker in Colorado sugar beet fields, age fifteen.

At Fort Ord, 1955, on his first liberty pass.

Lala and Roy, 1959.

Fort Ord, California, 1955.

At their wedding reception: (from left) Uncle Nick and Aunt Alexandra Benavidez, Roy and Lala, Lala's parents, Maria and Juan Coy; June 7, 1959

Ready for a ten-mile hike with backpack, 1957

MP School, Fort Gordon, Georgia, 1958

In Germany, February 1958, Co. A, 6th Infantry Regiment. Arrow points to Roy.

Roy at jump school, Fort Bragg, 1959

"Sicily" drop zone, Fort Bragg, 1963, Roy descending in left center

Jump school class, 1959. Roy is "3" in center of photo.

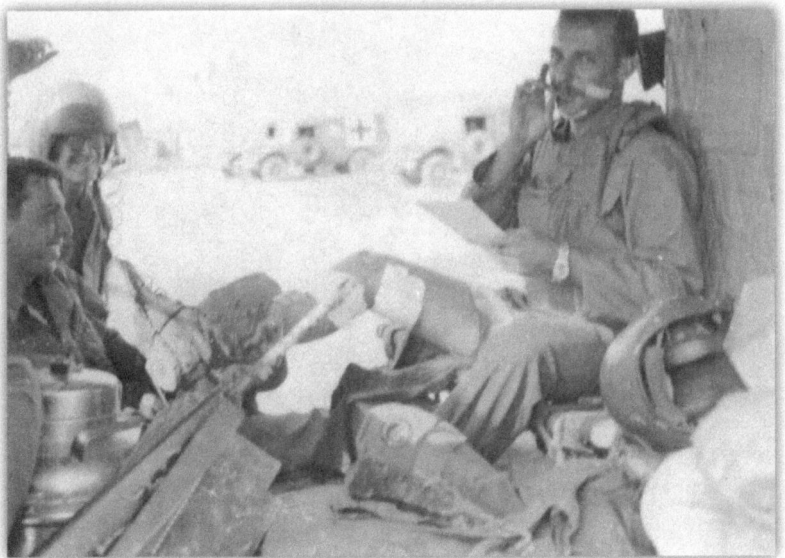

Roger Waggie (right), after chopper was shot down on 3/4/68 near Dong Tam

(From left) "Frenchy" Mousseau, KIA 5/2/68; W/O Dave Hoffman, KIA 6/12/68; unknown; Sp4 Mike Craig, KIA 5/2/68

A helicopter loads up for take-off.

Typical terrain in II Corps Tactical Zone, Binh Dinh province, Central Highlands
SFC Richard Scena

PART III

THE
GREEN
BERET

CHAPTER 15

"GET YOUR ASS out, boy! Move it!"

A boot, planted firmly on my backside, pushed me through the door, out of the shadowed interior into the bright North Carolina sunshine. It was 1960—the second week of jump school and my first jump from the tower.

Only it isn't the tower—rather it's "The Tower." Thirty-four feet high, thirty steps to the top. More men wash out of jump school when it's time to go off the tower than at any other point in their training. By the time you reach the top carrying full gear and it's your turn to go off the edge, you think you've climbed halfway to heaven.

Part of it is watching the ones ahead of you. Watching them get into the harness with only those two little straps between their legs keeping them from going straight down. As it is, the contraption drops fast enough. A tight body position is the key. Body rigid with arms tucked to the sides.

You know the ones that don't maintain the correct position without even watching. You can hear their jawbones pop as they reach the end of the slack and are jerked upright. They gasp, eyeballs popping, as the straps cut into their groin and drive their testicles all the way up to their navels.

Then they have to land. There's no soft sand or topsoil down there. The thousands who have preceded them have pounded that red North Carolina mud into something resembling reinforced concrete. Slamming into it after already being badly mistreated on the way down can and does make a number of individuals rethink their commitment to being a paratrooper.

I knew all about going out the wrong way, but I forgot everything I had learned as I went pinwheeling out of the tower on that first jump. I was jerked around like a fish on a line and then pounded into the ground.

As I lay in the dirt, the wind knocked out of me, I heard a voice laughing from the tower doorway: "Hey, boy, I think you forgot to do something. Better get back up here and try it again."

Jump school at the 82nd Airborne. It was hard—tougher than anything I had done since joining the army. Lala and I lived off base between Fort Bragg and Fayetteville. When I got home in the evening, I was exhausted. At 5 A.M. the next morning, I was back at the camp.

At times, I lay awake at night too tired to sleep, wondering what I was doing there. A few weeks before, I had been at Fort Gordon in Georgia with the softest job possible—chauffeuring a general's car. I had given that up for the hell of jump school.

Ironically, it was the driver's job that led to my being admitted to jump school. For four years, I had been applying for admission to that elite corps—the paratroopers, and I had been turned down every time. Following my return from Europe, I went to military police school at Fort Gordon and was eventually assigned to drive for General H. M. Hobson, commandant of the MP school. I regained the rank lost in Germany and finally made it to buck sergeant.

CHAPTER 15

I was there in 1959 when I found myself selected to drive for General Westmoreland when he visited Fort Gordon to speak at an officers' career course. Westmoreland had recently been named to command the 101st Airborne. Part of his purpose, I believe, in coming to Fort Gordon was to encourage the men to whom he spoke to consider joining the airborne. He was on the lookout for anyone with airborne potential; at the time, there was a move on to beef up the airborne divisions.

Finally, for once, I felt I was at the right place at the right time. Here's my chance to go airborne, I had thought. If he gives me half a chance, that's one officer who's going to hear just how I feel about being a paratrooper.

I picked up the general at Bush Field, the airstrip at Gordon, shortly after noon. He spoke to the assembly that evening, and the next morning I escorted him to his waiting plane.

While we drove about the base, he directed a few polite questions at me. I answered them just as politely and properly. Finally, he asked the question I'd been waiting for: "Sergeant, have you ever thought about going airborne?"

I took a deep breath. "Yes, sir, I've thought about it. In fact, it's all I've thought about since I joined the army. Sir, I'd pay my own way if I could get in." And I meant it.

"You must want to go pretty bad."

"Yes, sir. Pretty bad. I'm up for reenlistment in a few weeks; I'll give it another try."

He wished me luck as he left the car to board the waiting aircraft. I watched the plane taxi away. It had gone as I had hoped. At least, I thought it had. Maybe it was just wishful thinking on my part that he'd take time to deal with the wishes of an MP sergeant in Georgia.

Three months later I was jumping off the tower and eating North Carolina dirt. The only verification I ever received that the general opened some doors for me came in the resentment directed toward me by a few who accused me of cutting corners.

CHAPTER 16

SIX YEARS LATER, in 1966, I watched as the helicopters took off. The first group of jumpers sat three abreast in each of the two open doors, their legs casually dangling over the growing emptiness below them.

Tom had a six-pack of beer and a bottle of Jack Daniel's in the car—just something to settle the nerves and celebrate after a successful jump. I thought how good a nice stiff jolt would feel. My mouth was dry. Just the idea of going up and rolling off the deck of that chopper made me cringe. The jump itself didn't bother me. Like they say: It's not the fall that kills you, it's the sudden stop. I could picture myself in those last few feet coming in at sixteen feet per second. I shuddered.

"Are you gonna jump or what?"

The voice at my shoulder brought me back to earth and out of my reverie.

"What?" I turned. It was the noncom with the clipboard, a tough lifer by the name of Burns. I knew him. He had a reputation for being a rough customer. Everyone called him "Blood" Burns. There was a questioning look on his Black face.

"I said, what are you doin' here? You gonna jump?"

"Yeah, I was thinkin' about it." I hadn't realized it but, yes, I sure was. An extra fifty-five dollars a month would come in handy. And if I did it, I wouldn't have to qualify again for another three months. Just one jump. I could do that, especially if I was careful in my landing. Hit and roll on my left side. I wouldn't even have to let my right leg and hip take any of the impact. Nothing to it.

"Yeah, I think I will."

"Hey, get ready over there!" Burns shouted to a group shrugging into their harnesses. "Ya'll are goin' next. Move it." He turned back to me.

"Ain't you been on special duty?"

"I was. I'm okay now."

"Been through refresher?" he asked. "Got your slip?"

I needed a signed authorization from an officer that stated I was considered physically fit and had gone through a refresher course that included jumps from the tower. I knew Burns had no idea how long I was supposed to be out of action. Not that it made much difference. I didn't have the necessary slip. No officer was going to give me the go ahead. There was no way I could jump today.

"Sure, I got one," I lied. "Uh . . . let me look around a while. I'll give it to you when I get ready to go up."

"Hmmph . . ." he grunted, turning back to the men milling around him.

I started to figure out how to get up on one of those Hueys. At least, I thought, the mental exercise was making me forget my anxiety over jumping. My nerves . . . of course. A quick drink for the nerves—or just to take a break from a boring job.

I strolled over to the other sergeant. He held a similar clipboard.

"Wantta take a break?" I asked. "We got a six-pack and a bottle in the car over there."

"Yeah?" Immediate interest. I smiled.

Seconds later, I had the clipboard and was going through the papers secured to it. There they were, just as I knew they would be—a half-dozen refresher slips. It took less than a minute to fill one out, backdate it a couple of weeks, and sign the name of an officer I happened to know had just left for Vietnam. Then I sauntered over to "Blood" Burns.

"Here you go," I said, handing him the slip. "I guess I'll go for it."

Gloria walked up. He had finished his jump and was ready to go. He pulled me aside.

"What are you doing?" He looked suspicious.

"I'm going to jump."

"What! Are you crazy? You aren't supposed to do that."

"Like you said, I'm in good shape. Don't worry, I can do it."

"I don't care what I said. Go ahead, but I'm not responsible. You're doing this on your own." He cocked an eye at me. "How'd you get a refresher slip?"

Minutes later, he walked away, still muttering about his innocence in the matter.

I put on a chute. The nerves had returned in force. I tried to remain outwardly calm, but it felt like every inch of my body was sweating. Maybe Tom was right—maybe I was crazy. A couple of months ago, I was relearning how to walk. Now, I was going to jump out of a helicopter at an altitude of more than a thousand feet. If I screwed up, I was going to be right back in a hospital. And this time they would kick my ass out of the army—for stupidity if nothing else.

At that particular moment, I wasn't too pleased with my role as a male Latin. Being macho, I realized for the millionth time, could be a pain in the ass.

I took my place on the deck of the HU-1A and, along with the five others on board, secured my static line to the anchor line cable attached to the floor. As the ground was sucked away from us, I took inventory. Despite the intensive physical activity I had been putting myself through, there was still some pain in my back. In fact, from the moment I stepped out of Tom's car and the tension began to grow, the pain had steadily increased.

Now it pulsed along my back and down my right leg, keeping time with my thumping heart. I was no longer nervous—I was terrified. When was I going to learn not to act on impulse?

I didn't even feel the hand slap me on the shoulder—then begin to shake me. "Go!" came the voice in my ear over the slap of the rotors.

Instinct took over. I rolled forward and down . . . just like slipping off the edge of a swimming pool. Only instead of a splash, there's the wind in your face and the ground far below.

A tight body position, just like they teach in jump school. Not that day. Did I raise my elbow and allow the air flowing by to start me spinning? I was barely aware of where I was. I couldn't spare the time to evaluate my style.

Whatever the cause, I made two or three twists before my chute popped open above me. I continued to turn, winding up my lines like a kid spinning a tire swing. First left and then right, I revolved as I drifted down.

I was a "dirty leg." It would have been bad enough twisting like that if I had jumped from an airplane. But nobody made a jump like that out of a virtually stationary helicopter. Nobody.

As I came in, I could see Burns waiting, his hands on his hips. He had seen.

But first I had to land. Hit and roll. I hoped I could do that right. Normally, I would have come down feet first and rolled toward my right, letting my right leg, hip, and shoulder absorb the impact in a standard parachute landing fall. I had to come down on my left. If I landed on my right side and my leg wasn't able to handle it, I could end up breaking something—maybe my back.

For the first time in my jumping career, I hit and rolled on my left. And I made it look routine. There was no pain. It was anticlimactic—but I had made it.

Relief was short-lived. Burns was in my face almost as soon as I got to my feet.

"You damned leg! What kind of jump was that? What's the matter—scared?" He was furious.

I had no choice. There were still plenty of chutes. I had to go up again. Tom Gloria was over at the car. I could see the strained expression on his face. I imagine he was making use of the nerve medicine.

The second jump was better. I had over fifty jumps. I knew how to do it. There was no twist this time, but on the landing, I landed on my butt. Again, there was no problem with my back.

Most of the weekend jumpers had left. Burns looked around and shouted to the rest of us: "There's still some chutes here. Any of ya'll want to take an extra jump?"

"Wait a minute," I told Tom, heading for one of the packs.

"For Christ's sake, Benavidez . . ." I heard him exclaim as I walked toward the helicopter. "You're crazy!"

The third one's the charm, I thought. That day, fortunately, it proved to be true—a good jump and a good landing. On the way home with Tom, I celebrated with a can of beer and chased it with the rest of the Jack Daniel's.

Unfortunately, even walking in with the news that I would be bringing home an extra fifty-five dollars each month didn't calm Lala when she found that I had jumped that day. "Benavidez, you're not supposed to be jumping. You're going to kill yourself." She was angry. She always called me "Benavidez" when she was really upset with me.

I didn't tell her I jumped three times.

At any rate, I had proved to myself and the army that I was well on the way to recovery from my wounds. Now I wanted to get back into action—back to an outfit where I could be in the field. The walls of that office were closing in on me.

Shortly before leaving for South Vietnam, I had applied for admission to Special Forces. It had seemed like the best thing to do. Difficult as it was for even me to believe, not all of my time in the army had been spent getting into trouble. I had attended schools, including classes to get my high school diploma and the NCO Academy, in the belief that those qualifications on my record would benefit my career.

And it was normal for an airborne trooper to look to Special Forces as another logical step upward. Although the men in Special Forces—the Green Berets as they came to be known to the American public—had been part of the U.S. Army since 1952, they remained a low-profile organization until the war in South Vietnam.

Many Special Forces veterans disliked the spotlight they found themselves in because of the war. But it was true that as a result of the conflict and the publicity, Special Forces, which until Vietnam had been seriously understrength, grew dramatically in the early 1960s.

The American people were almost totally unaware of the Special Forces until they came to the attention of President John Kennedy. It was President Kennedy who authorized the wearing of the green berets and popularized the elite fighting force.

Fort Bragg was headquarters of Special Forces and home for the 7th Special Forces Group. The basic requirements for admission to the Green Berets were that a soldier had to be a volunteer in the army itself, be jump-qualified, request to join Special Forces, and hold at least noncom rank.

In the old days, as the old-timers used to tell us when I was a newcomer to Special Forces in 1967, first-term enlistees and second lieutenants were excluded. But by the midsixties, both were in training as the Pentagon tried to expand the ranks and find replacements for the SF troopers in South Vietnam who were suffering high casualties.

Also in the early years, as many as nine of the ten applicants to Special Forces were weeded out by attrition through diligent application of extremely tough training standards. By 1965, those failing to qualify had slipped to three of ten. Despite what some might call a drop in standards, the men of the Special Forces were proving in Southeast Asia that they were the best fighting force of its kind in the world.

I made inquiries at the personnel office about my Special Forces application. As I had expected, the army bureaucracy had swallowed it without a burp. No one knew a thing about it.

"You still got all your papers, don't you?" a clerk inquired. "Bring them in and we'll see if we can't get some action on 'em. You know, a waiver."

I had no idea where those papers were now. "Yeah, they're there at the house somewhere," I said. "Which ones were they now?" I asked him, just in case I didn't recognize them.

He pointed to a number of bins, all filled to the brim with forms, and called out the three I needed.

"Okay," I replied, picking up the sheets of paper, "I'll take these along so I'll be sure and remember them."

"Right," he said with a grin.

Back at my office, I typed the correct information on the documents, added a few officers' signatures—I was getting good at that—backdated them a couple of years, and headed for the copying machine. After a few creases were put in the "two-year-old" copies, I figured they would pass all but the most intense examination.

And I didn't think they would be subjected to that. Not now. Not with a war going on, and especially not with me knowing personally every NCO in personnel and half the officers. With eleven years in the army by now, there weren't too many strings that I didn't know how to pull. Pulling strings is standard operating procedure for army sergeants.

A month passed and I received the word: Assignment to the Special Forces training group there at Fort Bragg.

CHAPTER 17

S PECIAL FORCES TRAINING is tough. The first phase is mostly physical—to weed out those who lack the commitment to make the grade and wear the green beret. And there was some doubt in my mind that my back would stand the strain of daily four-mile runs, complete with forty-pound backpacks, followed by calisthenics. But I held up through those plus the obstacle course and more parachute jumps. A man's tenacity, courage, intelligence, and ingenuity are all put to the test. Dropped alone into unfamiliar territory with a minimal amount of food and water, he is expected to use his skill at navigating by sun and stars for twelve consecutive days until he reaches familiar ground.

During my time in the forest, I lost my way for half a day at one point. I consoled myself with the thought that although I was lost in the wilderness of North Carolina I didn't have to worry about a gook popping out from behind a pine tree with an AK-47 blazing. That reassured me while I regained my bearings.

I soon discovered that my toughest challenge didn't lie out in the field. The classroom was where my own personal enemy awaited.

A Special Forces soldier receives intensive training in at least one of five basic disciplines—light and heavy weapons, communications, medicine, operations and intelligence, and engineering. In preliminary testing, I qualified for both light and heavy weapons and operations and intelligence.

I decided to go with operations and intelligence; the increases in rank seemed to come faster in that area. The thirty-week course included a massive study load covering raids and ambushes; guerrilla organization; underground operations; the selection, marking, organization, and sterilization of airdrop and landing zones; kidnap and assassination operations; escape and evasion; intelligence nets; agent selection and handling; fingerprint analysis; counterintelligence; security; oceanography; and meteorology.

I tried to buckle down and study, but the job overwhelmed me. It had been a long time since I dropped out of grade school, and that's one mistake that's hard to leave behind. The college level material they shoved at me required the best in study habits, and I didn't even know what the hell study habits were.

I also had other duties. In the training company of which I was a member, there were five classes made up of about thirty-five men studying each of the five basic courses. As a staff sergeant, I happened to be the ranking noncom in the operations and intelligence class; I was responsible for supervising the men just as I would have been in any other company.

It made for a lot of work. Fortunately, I was rescued a few weeks after school began. Leroy Wright, a sergeant first class I knew from the 82nd, transferred into our class after completing his course in light and heavy weapons.

From Rahway, New Jersey, Wright was Black and that made him, in 1967, a relative rarity in the Special Forces. He was an excellent soldier, and most important, he outranked me. It was a relief to turn over the command of our class to him. I desperately needed the extra study time.

But about ten weeks into the course I finally decided my best chance for success was perhaps in the second category for which I had qualified. Light and heavy weapons was more in my line. I requested and received permission to switch.

We studied firearms from the BB gun to the 105 howitzer, and including foreign weapons. A Special Forces soldier must learn to use whatever weapons are available, even taking a component from one weapon and making it fit and operate in another, although the two are the arms of opposing sides. When he finishes the Special Forces light and heavy weapons course, a member of the Green Berets is able to fight effectively with whatever weapon he finds in his possession.

Following completion of the weapons training, I gave operations and intelligence another try. In the class, I met one of the legends of the Green Berets. The men in Special Forces are constantly training and studying, so it was not unusual to find with us a man who in 1967 was already a grizzled Special Forces veteran.

Stefan "Pappy" Mazak was born in Czechoslovakia. Many of the early recruits into Special Forces in the 1950s were foreign-born. A small man, no more than five feet two, Mazak had first seen action as a member of the French Maquis, resistance fighters during World War II. Following the war, he had served in the French Foreign Legion. As a member of Special Forces in 1960, he had displayed extraordinary heroics in the Congo, in rescuing Whites threatened by rampaging rebel troops. Later, in Vietnam, he would add luster to an already incredible reputation.

Pappy spoke terrible English and had a difficult time reading the texts. We worked together. He was a man whose tenacity I admired and I was encouraged by his determination to see the job through.

Through the spring, summer, and fall we trained. I was constantly in the field. When a particular part of my training was completed, I participated in the teaching of the skills I had learned to those who came behind. And in so doing, I learned even more. In addition to being difficult, the making of a Green Beret is thorough.

Although I made it through, I was in constant pain. My back never seemed to let up. I tried not to show my discomfort, but at times when I was particularly tired, I gave in to it and walked with a noticeable limp. No one ever spoke to me about it, but my buddies must have been aware of it. It made me even more determined not to let them down; at times, I probably performed my duties with a little too much zeal to compensate for it.

In March 1968, with training completed, I looked forward to my first assignment in the Special Forces. And with my knowledge of Spanish, I anticipated assignment to one of the SF groups working in South or Central America. Although they got none of the publicity received by the troops in Southeast Asia, they were performing a valuable service, teaching counterinsurgency techniques to U.S. allies in the southern half of the hemisphere.

One afternoon in the noncommissioned officers' club, I learned that an acquaintance of mine, another Hispanic named Herrera, had broken both legs in a parachute jump. I knew he had been scheduled to go to Caracas, Venezuela, as a military advisor to that country's army. That seemed like a nice place to go; I decided to see if I could salvage some good fortune for myself from another man's bad luck.

I visited him in the hospital the next day. He was trussed up in traction, and it was obvious he wasn't going anywhere. After some small talk, I brought up the subject of his assignment.

"I heard you were going to Venezuela," I said. "That's right—I was," he replied. "Not now. Looks like I'm going to be laid up for about six months."

"How about me taking your place? Any objections?"

"No, I guess not. Somebody's got to go. Might as well be you. Call Special Assignments in Washington; tell them you want to take my place."

When I walked out of the hospital, I was already mentally packing my bags. I stopped back by the club and announced that my next stop was Caracas.

"Lala," I said when I got home, "how would you like to go to Venezuela?"

She was excited but skeptical. "I'll believe it when I see the orders." Smart woman.

Two days later, I went to see another buddy of mine, Bobby Alexander, who was a personnel sergeant in Special Forces. I explained to him about Herrera's misfortune.

"Bobby, will you phone Washington and see if you can get that assignment for me?"

He agreed to make the call right then; I waited anxiously as I watched him dial. Within a minute he was through to Special Assignments.

He explained the situation to the listener on the other end, pointing out that I was thoroughly qualified to take Herrera's place in a Spanish-speaking country like Venezuela.

"Yeah, I said Benavidez," Alexander replied in answer to a question from the other end. "That's right—Roy Benavidez." He turned to me with a shrug and a slightly puzzled expression.

A full minute of silence followed while Bobby listened. The puzzled look turned to a frown; he turned to look at me. I began to fidget. I had no idea what was going on, but whatever it was, I didn't think I liked it.

"Well, Ben," Alexander said, finally hanging up, "they say you ain't goin' to Venezuela."

"Why the hell not? I don't know of any reason why I shouldn't go."

"Yeah there is—a good one. According to Washington, you're going to Vietnam, boy."

CHAPTER 18

I WAS GOING back to a war in South Vietnam that was very different from the one I had left. When they had carried me out of Southeast Asia two years before, the conflict was still pretty much a fight between Vietnamese, but by March 1968, as I boarded a plane in Houston bound for San Francisco, the Americanization of the war was complete. I was actually looking forward to taking an active role—no longer having to abide by what seemed by now to be the totally arbitrary rules that had hamstrung us advisors a couple of years earlier.

The war had changed America too. Outside of what I saw on television—the marches and protests—I was pretty unaware of what was going on in some American cities. Fort Bragg was not exactly a hotbed of dissent. I got a look at the other side in San Francisco. All of my life, I had been led to believe—and I still believe—that the uniform of the U.S. soldier was a source of pride for the wearer and a symbol of service and patriotism for each citizen.

I was unprepared for the treatment accorded us in the City by the Bay. It all began shortly after we arrived at San Francisco International. There were nine of us—all Special Forces—on our way to Travis Air Force Base where we would be processed through to Hawaii and on to South Vietnam.

We got off the plane and headed directly for the bar for a pick-me-up before boarding the military bus which would take us to the airbase. Following a couple of drinks, we went to the lobby to await the arrival of the bus.

We stood near a large column, surrounded by our gear and chatting quietly. I was talking to Dan Chapa when we both became aware of motion around us. I looked up and saw a half-dozen hippies circling us. They stared at us—and we stared back. These were the first genuine hippies I had ever seen in the flesh.

They were bona fide "flower children," in uniform as much as I was—Haight-Ashbury irregulars. With their long hair, granny glasses, beads, grubby blue jeans, and sandals, they were quite a sight—it was difficult to tell male from female. And if they had restricted their activity to just looking, there wouldn't have been any trouble.

They didn't really say anything directly to us. They would just look as they walked around us and then amble off to have what appeared to be a conference. At a safe distance from us, we could hear an occasional comment like "baby killers." Then they would return and pace around us. I didn't know about the others, but I was getting nervous. A couple of times, one of them spat on the floor, coming a little too close.

"I'm going to whip someone's ass," I kept telling Dan in Spanish. And one of the circlers—a skinny guy with a red headband—would bob his head at me like he knew what I was saying.

Finally, I told Dan in Spanish to tell the rest to try and cut the skinny one out from the rest.

CHAPTER 18

"What are you going to do, Ben?" Chapa asked.

"We're going to create a little scene," I answered. He smiled and passed the word around.

On his next pass by the nearest column, Red Headband found a Green Beret blocking his path. I saw his eyes widen, and he wheeled to backtrack. But that way was blocked too.

I stepped in as he stood with his back to the column. Without a word, I grabbed him by the crotch and squeezed—hard, just like I had those bulls back when I was a kid. My companions circled around, partially shielding the two of us from view.

"No! Please! No-o-o! Don't!" he wailed.

"I'm sorry, but I have to go!" I yelled back at him, my face only inches from his.

"No-o-o! Stop it!"

"You don't understand—they need me in Vietnam!"

For about thirty seconds, we stood there, him screaming and me explaining that my country needed me.

Some of the other guys chimed in: "Roy, he don't want to see you go."

"He's sure gonna miss you, Roy."

We were attracting attention, so I decided I better let him go. When I released him, he hobbled for the door, followed by his friends who had scattered at the start of trouble.

"Hey," I called to him as he went through the door, "I'll call you when I get back." I thought about Colonel "Iron Mike" Healy, a Special Forces veteran and legend, who when he addressed us once back at Bragg, clenched his fist and told us that: "When you grab them by the balls, their heart and brain follow."

My buddies were roaring with laughter.

But we all sobered up a bit when a police officer approached us. I hoped my ability to get into trouble hadn't surfaced again.

He was a young cop, and he just stood looking at us for a minute. "Look, Sergeant," he said finally, looking right at me, "what you just did was wrong; you and I both know it. But I'll tell you this—I don't give a damn. I served in Nam too." Then he turned and walked away.

I waited in San Francisco for three days for a flight out. Although it rained a good bit of the time, I was able to get out and see a little of the city, knowing it was going to be the last of the U.S. I would see for a while.

I also thought of Lala and the baby. Denise, who was now over eight months old, would probably be walking and maybe even talking by the time I saw her again. That day I had come in with the news that I was going back to Vietnam, Lala knew something was up before I had said a word. Being left alone while your husband goes off to war is a far cry from heading for a comfortable billet in South America but she didn't complain and went about preparing to move the trailer back to El Campo.

Again, my first glimpse of South Vietnam was from the window of an airliner. But this time, instead of Saigon sprawled below, the giant American base at Cam Ranh Bay rose up to greet me. I would be processed here and assigned to a Special Forces team somewhere in the countryside.

As we stepped through the door and into the perpetual heat—God, I had forgotten that steam bath of an Asian atmosphere—I felt like I had never left. There was a tension in my body now that hadn't been there only a few minutes before—an awareness of being back in a hostile land. And this despite the fact that I was surrounded, not by Vietnamese, but by thousands of my fellow Americans.

But it didn't take long for me to realize that these Americans were not the same as the ones with whom I had served just two years before. Those men had been dedicated professionals intent on doing their jobs. The soldiers I saw upon my arrival in '68 were boys, mostly draftees among a scattering of volunteers. It was obvious from their appearance and behavior that many were far from professional. There was none of the spit and polish that I had become accustomed to during my career, and while the hair of some of the young men may not have approached in length that of their brothers who protested back in the States, it seemed much too long to me, a crew-cut soldier of the 1950s. The army's standards had changed, and moustaches, longer hair, and sideburns were now accepted. But not by some of us.

It was the abundance of hair that prompted another Green Beret sergeant and me to take it upon ourselves to restore the clean-cut image of the American soldier. Ted Goble was a big Texan from down around the Gulf Coast town of Bay City. He stood about six feet three or four and weighed in at around two hundred and forty pounds.

We'd go through the tents, a Mutt and Jeff team, and when we found a man with hair we thought too long, we would order him to go get a haircut. There were protests sure enough at our rather high-handed tactics, but no one was willing to outright defy two Green Berets, especially when one of them was the size of Goble.

One fellow who protested a little too much found himself lifted by the collar off the ground like a disobedient puppy. Goble slung him under his arm and took off to find the man's sergeant. I walked along behind, enjoying immensely the sight of Goble striding among the tents with his burden.

"I gave this man an order to get his hair cut," Goble told the sergeant when he found him, "and he damn well better get it cut."

The sergeant looked at the bug-eyed soldier tucked under Goble's arm and then at Goble himself before answering: "I think you better go get a haircut, boy—and quick."

For a couple of days there, Goble and I kept the barber busy.

Finally, I was flown up the coast to Nha Trang for a short orientation and eventual assignment to a unit in the field. One of the first stops after landing was the NCO club to catch up on the news of buddies who had come ahead. And there was always news—much of it bad.

Because of their active role in the warfare raging in the countryside, the men of Special Forces absorbed more than their share of punishment. Green Berets were being pulled out of Fort Bragg as quickly as possible and transported to Southeast Asia to replace the men wounded and killed. Finding instructors for classes at Bragg was becoming difficult because they were being sent into combat.

The need for men was so great they even sent me, an undersized veteran with a bad back, into combat.

At night, as we lay on our bunks in the transit billet, we could hear the choppers roaring in and out nearby; we listened to the cries of medics and the wounded they tended. It was becoming apparent to me that this was a hotter war by far than the one I had left.

It was difficult to sleep. I spent a lot of time in the NCO club, drinking in the rumors along with the beer, and trying to slow the pump of my adrenaline. Whether a man was on his way home or just arriving, he had his share of tales to tell about what was about to happen, should happen, or had happened.

Of course, the men who were on their way home received the most attention. They passed word on to us about conditions in the field and filled us in on who wouldn't be returning home.

It was there that I learned that Mazak was dead. He had bought it just a few days before I got there. How, I didn't know. Pappy had been with B-56, a reconnaissance unit northwest of Saigon. The details of many a Green Beret's death were concealed by a curtain of secrecy stamped "classified." Pappy's was no different. Much Special Forces heroism went unknown and unappreciated—except by their own.

B-56, I learned, was in the thick of the action, sending out recon teams to locate and observe enemy activity. As Lt. Col. Ralph Drake, the commanding officer of B-56, would say later, his men "were meeting themselves coming and going on operations." The unit had taken a lot of casualties and was in desperate need of replacements. Several of my buddies, including Jerry Cottingham and Ray Sipsky, men with whom I had served in Fort Bragg, were there. I decided that I wanted to go to B-56.

"My God, Roy, why do you want to go there?" Ed Stys, the sergeant major in charge of personnel at Nha Trang, eyed me like he was measuring me for a straitjacket. We were having a drink at the NCO club.

"Why not?" I stared back. "I have friends there. It's intelligence and recon. That's what I trained for at Bragg."

"Those guys are gettin' chopped up every day. You don't want to get yourself killed if you can help it. Don't be crazy."

"Come on, Sergeant Major, that's where I want to go. I want to be where the action is."

We had been friends in the 82nd; he knew both me and Lala. He also knew about the injuries I had received in '66. Hadn't I had enough action then, he asked. Why did I want to be a hero?

"I don't want to be a hero, Sergeant Major," I replied, beginning to get pissed. "I just want to be with my buddies. We know each other and we can work together as a team."

"Hell no," he said, shaking his head. "Forget it. I'm not helping you."

I turned away and continued sipping my beer. The sergeant major's refusal to assign me to B-56 was bringing out my stubborn streak. We'll see, I thought to myself.

When I recalled that conversation much later, it was with the thought that maybe the sergeant had a point when he questioned my sanity.

Later that evening, Colonel Drake came into the club to talk with the men assigned to his unit. They were leaving the next day for Ho Ngoc Tao and B-56.

I watched him sitting with the men who were now his troops. What the hell, I thought, and walked over to him.

"I'm goin' to B-56, Colonel."

The colonel looked up at me; I wasn't prepared for his comment: "Is that right?" he said, popping me on the belly with the back of his hand. "Then you're gonna have to trim down a bit, sarge."

It was true I was a bit soft around the middle. But the important thing was that he hadn't turned me down. I looked over at Stys; he ignored me, watching the foam in the bottom of his empty glass.

The colonel was unable to get a chopper out the next morning, and Cottingham and I went over to the personnel office. I knew I could just get on the helicopter with Drake and the other guys;

no one would stop me. But I hated to stiff-arm Stys that way. If I could, I wanted my assignment to B-56 to be official.

"All right, Roy, go ahead," Stys finally said after another argument. "But goddamn it, if you get killed, I don't want Lala blaming me for it. I tried to keep you from going to that outfit."

It wasn't bravado that made me insistent on going to B-56. I was as scared as anyone about going into a combat situation. Hell, I was more frightened than some; I knew what it felt like to get shot at. But I felt more comfortable and maybe just a little more secure knowing that I would be among friends.

The fact that B-56 had been taking a beating lately didn't really mean that much. Most Special Forces units were hard hit at one time or another. Being assigned to another unit would not have been any kind of assurance of safety.

At about two o'clock that afternoon, we lifted off for Saigon in a C-47 instead of a helicopter. The twin-engined workhorse was used a lot for transportation in Vietnam—most of the time by the CIA.

It was dark when we arrived at Tan Son Nhat Airport. The Colonel proceeded to commandeer a helicopter; we piled onboard and were soon airborne again. There were seven of us crowded together inside with all our gear. It was a tight fit.

Listening over a pair of headphones to the air traffic controllers in the tower, I figured we were breaking a pretty fair number of regulations pulling out in the dark like we did. The controllers were cursing a blue streak wanting to know who authorized our chopper to take off. But there wasn't a hell of a lot they could do. Ho Ngoc Tao was only about fifteen or twenty miles east of Saigon; we were there in a matter of minutes.

CHAPTER 19

THE VILLAGE OF Ho Ngoc Tao is located near the Song Be, a river that loops along on its way to Ganh Rai Bay southeast of Saigon. The bends in the river suggest the rough shape of a fishhook, giving the region its unofficial name. Because the "Fishhook" area was near the end of one of the exit points of the Ho Chi Minh Trail, it figured prominently in American intelligence reports.

The Special Forces camp itself was some distance from the village and was in the midst of a flat plain, spotted with ragged clumps of trees. The absence of cover needed by an attacker seeking to get close to the camp made its location a strategically logical one.

We replacements were immediately put to work training—rappelling from helicopters and practicing insertion and extraction techniques we would need when we were on a mission. In Special Forces, if there was no immediate assignment, you trained—and then trained some more.

Because the primary function of B-56 was intelligence gathering, a lot of attention was paid to the practice of inserting and extracting recon teams—quickly and efficiently. A helicopter would take a group of us out into the bush, we would rappel, or if the chopper could land we would unload as quickly as possible.

The aircraft would not be on the ground for longer than five or ten seconds. Our entire team had to be out and into the underbrush almost instantly.

The procedure was reversed when the chopper returned for us. If the terrain did not permit the pilot to land, a McGuire rig was lowered and we would be taken out one by one, dangling from the belly of the helicopter like fresh-caught mountain trout. The McGuire rig was a simple affair. Two lines were lowered from a winch in the open doorway of the chopper. A horseshoe arrangement of webbing connected the lower ends of the lines. The man on the ground slipped his head and shoulders through the loop and the two lines were pulled snugly under his armpits as the helicopter lifted him off his feet.

A bellyman in the doorway of the aircraft—he was called that because that was the part of his anatomy that he lay on as the upper half of his body dangled outside—held on to the two lines to keep them from twisting, turning, and possibly separating. When you were swinging thirty feet below the bottom of a helicopter with five hundred feet of clear air between your own backside and the jungle below, that face looking down at you from above became your best friend.

While the exercises were invaluable training for us, they must have been boring for the pilots who had to play fetch with us over and over. On one such occasion, our pilot decided to liven up the day at our expense.

There were five of us inserted that day—Jerry Cottingham, Sipsky, Goble, Jerry Fields, another new recruit named Mattingly, and me. As to who picked the location, I don't know, but I wish he could have been there. I also wish he could have gone first—and last.

We had been inserted near a village. I had no idea where we were. We were to be picked up near the local sewage dump, a huge pit used by the villagers for the disposal of their waste. I think maybe they allowed it to dry and then used it for fertilizer. Whatever their use of it, the anonymous pilot who arrived to pick us up found his own use for the stinking lake.

Instead of dropping down for us to get on, he hovered above and we saw the McGuire rig begin to lower. Mattingly was first and positioned himself in the rig and motioned to the bellyman that he was secure.

The chopper lifted a few feet, hesitated for a moment—I like to think the pilot had an attack of conscience—and then slipped to the side and slightly downward.

I'll never forget the sound of that trooper's scream as he hit the brown pond feet first. He looked like he was going to ski clear across it. But the pilot, who was skillful if nothing else, made the necessary corrections, and his victim sank no deeper than his knees into the disgusting mess.

Halfway across, the aircraft lifted again and the soldier emerged, dripping slime. He looked like a potato chip covered in bean dip. Even over the roar of the rotors, we could hear him cursing as he and his rescuer flew away.

As we watched the pit heave slowly, its encrusted surface shattered into a thousand floating cakes of filth. I think each of us resolved that he was definitely not going next. Shortly, we heard the sound of an approaching chopper. The helicopter arrived, the McGuire rig came down, and we just stood looking at it.

We could see the bellyman shouting down to us, the wind of the rotors tearing the words to shreds. But we knew what he was saying. I squinted up at him. Was the same man on the last pickup? Was this a different one? I couldn't remember who the other guy was. Maybe this was the same one—maybe not.

Another of our group—I believe it was Cottingham—stepped forward and slipped into the rig. The chopper lifted smoothly, taking the man aloft. Within an instant, they were clear of the sewage pit and heading into the distance.

Far from being reassured, those of us remaining realized that for the remainder of the exercise we would be playing Russian roulette, never knowing if the practical joker would strike again.

Only one other of our number got the shit treatment. Unfortunately, that one was me. As I was lifted off the ground, I felt my feet begin to swing like a pendulum below the rising chopper. When I was only some ten feet above the ground, the elevator sensation stopped and I knew I was going down.

At least I knew what was happening—not like that first poor son of a bitch who went in screaming with his mouth open. I reached around the McGuire rig as best I could and clamped my hands over my mouth and nose and shut my eyes. If it hadn't been for the stench that assaulted me through my clasped fingers, it would have felt no different than a plunge into a warm lake. I didn't see anything; I didn't want to see anything.

Again the pilot demonstrated his skill, dipping me only to my waist. The flight back to the camp was routine—if you call a ten-minute flight hanging from the belly of a helicopter and dripping crap all the way routine.

Upon arrival back at the camp, the pilot hovered and lowered me gently to the ground. I slipped out of the rig and ran to one side as quickly as I could, trying to get a glimpse of the man in the pilot's seat. But as soon as I was out of the loop, the aircraft leaped into the air and darted away. Dejectedly, I headed for the showers.

We never found out which pilot was guilty. But we had other things to worry about.

It was shortly afterward that I was officially welcomed back to South Vietnam—I got shot at.

I was part of a reconnaissance operation involving two teams. We went by helicopter—two slicks or troop-carrying choppers and a gunship armed with rockets—to an A-team out in the bush. From there we were to head out on our mission. All of us looked forward to seeing new faces and possibly picking up news from anyplace.

But we arrived at the heavily defended twelve-man outpost at a bad time. One of their members, a man named Henderson, I remember, had just been zapped the day before. Losing a friend was bad enough, but the day we arrived, word had come through to the team that the dead man had just become a father. To say the least, morale was low.

We felt like intruders. So, shortly after our arrival, our two teams joined the chopper pilots at the tiny airstrip some two hundred yards from the camp itself and sat down to prepare something to eat.

It took only an instant to shave off some fragments of C-4, a plastic explosive, mix it with a little wood, set it afire and begin heating some C-rations. The explosive was harmless unless you wanted it to explode. Otherwise, it was great for starting a cookfire.

We were sitting around a couple of the tiny blazes; there was not much talk. The gloom of the camp we had just left had come the short distance with us.

We paid little attention to the trees at the edge of a rubber plantation some two hundred yards away. That is, until the first bullet whistled over our heads and was followed immediately by an all too familiar pop that meant someone had it in their heads to kill you.

"Jesus Christ . . . a sniper!" I heard somebody shout as I hit the ground. We all scattered, trying to find the lowest spot possible.

Two other shots followed, none coming close. But nobody moved—our attacker's aim could improve any second.

"The no-good bastard," said a voice I recognized as belonging to the gunship pilot. "The only chance I had to get something warm in my stomach in two days, and this son of a bitch ruins it." He was sprawled by the skids of his aircraft.

"He ain't gonna get away with it," he exclaimed, and I raised my head just enough to see him jump to his feet and clamber into his chopper. Within seconds, the air was filled with the whine of the helicopter's turbine and the rotors began to turn. It was impossible to tell over the sound of the engines if any more shots were fired. But none of us were moving anyway.

The ship lifted, spun and headed straight for the tree line. For almost five minutes, while we continued to hug the ground, he darted above the plantation, firing rockets into the foliage. Smoke and flame rose to the sky.

Finally, he hovered for a bit over the destruction he had spread below, and then turned and headed our way.

As he emerged from the cockpit, he had the self-satisfied look of a man who has righted a great wrong.

"Think you got him?" somebody asked him.

He shrugged. "Probably not. But I guarantee you one thing . . . I scared the shit out of him. Let's eat."

CHAPTER 20

WITHOUT MY KNOWLEDGE, Colonel Drake decided to try me on my first assignment as the bellyman when we inserted and pulled out recon teams. Although I hadn't mentioned my previous wounds, he apparently was aware of them and was concerned about both me and anyone with whom I might be teamed. He didn't want to send a man out who might not be able to perform.

In later years I found out that the man looked upon me as less than a fearsome warrior, the image I guess I held of myself. In correspondence almost two decades after my final tour of Vietnam, he said that in looking back at those early days of 1968, he recalled me as a "teddy bear."

His comments were made with the warmest of feelings, but I am grateful I was not aware of those sentiments at that time. Being thought of by your commanding officer as the equivalent of a child's stuffed toy did not fit my own macho self-image.

Part of the fault for that roly-poly image lay, I'm sure, with my own appetite and the talents of our mess sergeant, a man named Gordon. I loved to eat Gordon's cooking; we all did. And the colonel was constantly on me to keep my weight down.

I was in a hootch with Floyd Mousseau, Sipsky, Cottingham, Brian O'Connor, McAlvey, Jerry Fields, and a couple of others. At one end of the barracks, we set up our own little version of an NCO club.

It wasn't much—a few chairs, a table, and a television to catch the broadcasts out of Saigon. It was our own little corner in which to relax.

The one thing we lacked when we set up our "club" was something to keep our beer cold. If we were going to fight a modern war, we wanted to do it right. We had to have a refrigerator. So Fields and I scrounged one on a trip to the big army base at Bien Hoa just north of our location. It was on that trip that I earned a nickname that was to stick for a long time.

While there, we met at the NCO club some members of an A-team just in from the boonies. They hadn't had any decent food at their camp for a month or two and were determined to take as much of it back with them as possible.

Fields and I joined them in a raid on a mess hall during which we loaded a jeep with everything from choice cuts of beef to fresh vegetables and eggs. And wonder of wonders, we even found a storage area where appliances, including refrigerators, were stored.

A little deception on our part during which four of us masqueraded as base officials to the two Vietnamese guards keeping an eye on the materiel netted us not one but two refrigerators. Our SF buddies had a gasoline-powered electric generator at the A-team encampment, and, what the hell, they needed to keep the lettuce fresh.

When I got back to B-56 and the story of our escapade got around, Jerry Cottingham tacked a sign up on the door of my tiny cubicle that proclaimed me as the "Bean Bandit." I suppose the name also had something to do with a couple of stereotypes of Mexican culture—the frijole-eating peasant and the Mexican as a bandito. The Frito Bandito was big on American television at the time.

In another year, before and after that spring in Southeast Asia, the name, with its hint of an ethnic slur, might have caused trouble. But not then. We were all brothers, molded by our training into a togetherness those outside Special Forces could not imagine. In times of crisis, we were taught to act as one, each fulfilling his role in complete confidence that the others on the team would be doing the same.

And that togetherness carried over into our day-to-day associations, with each of us knowing we had the respect of our comrades. It was an accepted fact that the rough joking of soldiers like us was always tempered with an equally coarse affection. No offense given, none taken.

Within our camp, in addition to the Americans, there were numerous members of the Civilian Irregular Defense Group program. The CIDGs were civilians, guerrillas, who fought with us against the VC.

The CIDGs were created in 1961 by the U.S. Mission in Saigon in the belief that a paramilitary force needed to be developed from the minority groups within South Vietnam in order to strengthen and broaden the counterinsurgency effort of the government. At first it had been made up primarily of Montagnards, the all-inclusive name for the many tribes who lived in the Highlands of Vietnam. Initially, their role had been a defensive one, protecting villages from Viet Cong attack. But by 1968 the CIDG program had matured, and its members were part of the offensive capability of the Special Forces which administered the entire operation.

Sadly, minorities apparently are treated as minorities no matter where they are. The people of the mountains were looked down upon by the ethnic Vietnamese as uncultured barbarians. The CIDG program was not incorporated into the South Vietnamese army in part because the Vietnamese wanted nothing to do with these people.

Back in America, television commentators referred to actions in the field in which "members of the Special Forces and their mercenary forces" saw action. I have often wondered why the CIDGs were branded as mercenaries because they were paid for risking their lives, and why the rest of us, including the ARVN, were not. I know I never turned down a paycheck from Uncle Sam.

Thus, many a Green Beret came with a preconception of CIDG troops as unskilled, unorganized, and disgruntled peasants. They soon came to recognize them, however, as close-knit religious and ethnic minority groups with a fierce loyalty to each other and anyone, including Americans, who treated them with respect and consideration.

On one occasion, I found myself in a wrestling match with one of the CIDGs in our camp. He was a big fellow, proud of his physique. I often saw him working out with the weights.

The confrontation came about when an interpreter told me that this man thought he looked like me. I turned and looked at my look-alike. He seemed pleased by his resemblance to me.

Speaking to the interpreter, I said that "I'd rather have a sister in a whorehouse than look like him."

CHAPTER 20

I thought I was making a joke and meant no harm. I was just trying to treat him like one of the guys, but American humor did not always make the cultural leap that well. As soon as the translation was complete, I knew I had made a mistake.

The man looked shocked and pulled himself up to his full height, glared at me, and spoke rapidly to the interpreter.

"Now wait a minute . . ." I began.

"He says you have offended him," interrupted the interpreter.

"Why? What's the matter? Has he got a sister in a whorehouse?" With that comment, my chance at any apology was gone.

"Look," I said after the translation of that brought the man to an even greater boil, "he looks like a pretty big boy. Why don't we just wrestle if he wants to get back at me?"

Another wait for my words to be translated. The offended man brightened noticeably.

"He wants to wrestle you, Sergeant Benavidez. He thinks you good wrestler."

We soon had an audience, surrounded by Vietnamese who wanted to see one of their number take on an American.

We squared off in an open area; there was no grass, and the ground, pounded by thousands of boots, was rock hard. We circled, feeling each other out. I initially meant to make a good show of it, allowing him to walk away with plenty of face saved. Unless the government had wasted a lot of money training me for the Special Forces, I didn't think I would have much trouble in taking him.

But as we circled, he reached out and slapped the green beret from my head. Without thinking, I moved in and snatched him in a double arm lock and we went down together. I slipped my leg over his shoulder while I pulled hard on his arm and twisted. It was over quickly.

I felt badly about my too-quick victory. I clapped him on the shoulder and told him he was a very good wrestler. Then I invited him over for a cold beer from the refrigerator in our hootch.

It was after that little incident that Brian O'Connor, a young radioman in our group, saddled me with another nickname, calling me "Tango Mike Mike," phonetic radio lingo for the letters which he said stood for "The Mean Mexican."

CHAPTER 21

I N SPECIAL FORCES, time did not take on the molasses-and-quicksilver nature related by so many other veterans of Vietnam, Korea, and World War II—those long days or weeks of maddening inactivity followed by frenzy when the surge of adrenaline was given a boost by the sing-song of bullets snapping by and the thump of artillery and mortar blasts.

For the Green Beret, there was plenty of the latter, but when we weren't actually getting our asses shot at or off, we were in constant training to prepare ourselves for just such an event. Many a member of the Special Forces died in the jungles of South Vietnam, but very few died from lack of proper training and preparation.

Actually, only three events stand out in my mind as I recall the times when I thought my number had finally come up, and on two of those occasions, the weapons were in the hands of Americans.

I was part of a routine recon patrol, and we lifted out of Ho Ngoc Tao early one morning in two slicks; a dozen or so of us completely sterile, without the tiniest insignia on our tiger fatigues to mark us as Americans. In fact, I was carrying my favorite weapon, a Russian AK-47. It made good sense to carry the enemy's own weapon into combat. If you ran short of ammunition, find a dead gook, lift his supply, and pick up where you left off. Let the Russians pick up some of the tab.

Our destination was Cu Chi, home of the American 25th Infantry Division. From there, just northwest of Saigon, we would leave on the actual mission. The nature of the war in Vietnam was such that no one really ever knew for sure who was a friendly. As a consequence, the other side devised some ingenious methods of penetrating the security of American installations. So it was the responsibility of someone from our end to notify the guys at Cu Chi that two choppers loaded with unidentifiable people would be sitting down shortly in their backyard.

That someone screwed up, and so we came flying in unannounced and unexpected, and—without so much as a flyover—touched down at the end of a runway. As soon as we hit, the team was out of the chopper and unloading equipment.

That's when all hell broke loose. Jeeps loaded with soldiers waving mounted machine guns careened across the tarmac toward us. Troops on foot with weapons at the ready were not far behind. We stood dumbfounded, not knowing what was going on. Why some itchy-fingered son of a bitch didn't open up on us is still beyond me.

Within seconds, they were close enough for us to hear the shouts and curses—some even in fractured Vietnamese. It was impossible to make out any distinct commands in the general turmoil, but there was no doubt that we were in trouble. The soldiers who make up the Special Forces are among the bravest and best fighting men in the world, but stupid they aren't. We dropped every weapon we were carrying.

"Get your ass on the ground! NOW!...goddamnit!" were the first words I finally made out. The speaker was a youngster—he couldn't have been a day over nineteen—and he was waving his M-16 like he was leading a parade down Main Street.

I'm a good soldier; I follow orders. I was face down with my arms and legs spread before he got the last words out. With my cheek turned to the hot asphalt, I could see that the others had been just as obedient. My God, I thought, we're about to be blown away by a bunch of jumpy GI kids. The cold steel of a rifle muzzle was hard against the back of my neck.

None of us had spoken; there had been no time for explanations. I suspect that if one of us had stepped forward to attempt to explain, he would have been killed instantly. With our faces greased with camouflage, we weren't recognizable as white, black, brown, or chartreuse. We had ourselves a problem.

I couldn't see what was going on, but the clamor of voices resulted only in chaos. No one seemed in command and the time we lay there in the heat dragged.

"Well, hello, Benavidez. How're you doin'?"

A face as black as coal was a foot away looking down at me. Piano-key white teeth split the face in a wide grin. Johnson, a sergeant I had served with in airborne at Bragg, crouched beside me with his elbows resting on his knees.

"If you want to, you can get up now," he said. I got to my feet—slowly because I wasn't taking any chances. Around me, the other members of our team were cautiously standing. Our "captors" still looked nervous. Johnson had taken charge, and, especially since he recognized me, had taken the tension in the air down a few notches.

Impulsively, I grabbed the Big black man in a bear hug. We must have made a strange pair, standing there embracing within a circle of armed men. I considered it a double miracle that he had been there and that he had recognized me through all the grease on my face.

"Mind telling me what you idiots are trying to prove, dropping in here like this?" he asked after he managed to disengage himself from me.

Within minutes the confusion was eliminated and the tension gone. The soldiers drifted away, and we went about sorting out the gear that was by now scattered all over the place. The rest of the mission was a milk run after that; just fly in, perform our recon duties, and then back out. We never found out who dropped the ball in communications. Just as well; someone would probably have gotten a good ass kicking.

April of '68 was a busy month for B-56. I was drawing less duty as a bellyman and actually going in as a full-fledged member of a team. On one such mission, Fields and I, plus an interpreter, were inserted near a crossroads out in the countryside. Our only objective was to take a prisoner—anyone who looked like he might have some information about enemy activity in the area.

Shortly after dawn, we were dropped near the intersection of two trails. Within seconds, we were into the underbrush and the chopper was out of sight. The area was not heavily wooded; most of the terrain was tall grass with scattered clumps of trees breaking what was a monotonous landscape.

Despite our apparent isolation, we communicated from our separate hiding places with hand signals—and we waited.

During the course of the day, a dozen or more peasants passed our way. None interested us. They all were farmers, carrying shovels or other tools. We knew that they could easily be guerrillas, carrying out their daily routine of growing food for their families and taking up arms at night. But, if possible, we wanted someone we could reasonably assume would be a source of information.

As the day wore on, it began to appear that we were going to learn nothing. Frustration, along with boredom, set in.

Suddenly, we were in luck. A peasant carrying a rifle was a prime candidate for interrogation in our minds—and around the bend heading our way, came our man. He sauntered down the path, his sandals slapping the hard-packed dirt, with his weapon slung over his shoulder as if he didn't have a worry in the world. Until that moment, he probably hadn't.

He passed my position first. It was over fast; I stepped into the trail behind him, and with one quick chop to his neck, sent him sprawling. Five seconds later, the trail was again empty, and peace had returned to the tiny crossroads.

We pulled our prisoner back away from the road into the trees. Within a few minutes, he revived, and our interpreter began interrogating him. Of course, he knew nothing. He was a farmer. The rifle, of Chinese manufacture, was necessary because the Viet Cong had been active in the area. A man needed to protect himself. That was all bullshit; it was hard enough with any Vietnamese to determine his loyalty, but there was no doubt in my mind we had our hands on a genuine VC.

We hadn't expected to extract any information from him. That wasn't our job. Pick up and deliver; that was our mission. We had no idea if any action was even planned for that area. We knew nothing. If we were captured, there wasn't a damn thing we could tell anyone.

As for our captive, let the experts back at camp work on making him talk. But it had been a long day—a hot day sitting in the weeds slapping at insects. And his wide-eyed innocence pissed me off.

"Let me try a little Mexican persuasion on him?" I asked Fields, who was getting a little nervous. He had already radioed for the chopper to come get us out. I could see he was more interested in listening for the telltale slap of the rotors. We were beginning to feel like we had overstayed our welcome.

"Huh?" he cocked an eyebrow at me. "What're you talkin' about?"

"Watch." I rummaged around in my rucksack until I felt the smooth roundness of the small container. Fields' eyes widened when I pulled out the bottle of Tabasco sauce.

"I don't believe you, Benavidez. You ain't goin' to do that, are you?"

"Ask him one more time if he's going to tell us what we want to know," I told our interpreter.

My Vietnamese was good enough to know he was getting the same results as before; while the two talked, I gave the bottle a good shaking, mixing the contents like you're supposed to do.

"Hold his mouth open," I told my two companions. "Make sure he doesn't bite; no telling what you could get from the little bastard." Fields just kept shaking his head, and the interpreter looked mystified. "Don't worry," I reassured Fields, "it won't kill him."

The man, whom we had bound hand and foot, began to wriggle. I think he thought we were going to poison him. After the first couple of drops of the fiery sauce hit his tongue, he was sure of it. The Vietnamese peasant's diet is, if anything, pretty bland. At any rate, the man had never tasted the bite of the peppery liquid they brew in the swamps of south Louisiana.

I emptied half the bottle while he screamed and struggled.

CHAPTER 21

Fields shook my shoulder: "For Christ's sake, Ben, you're going to have every gook within ten klicks down on our neck if he doesn't shut up."

"Okay," I relented. "I don't think he could talk if he wanted to now anyway." I put the top back on and stared at the half-empty container. "I shouldn't have done that; this stuff isn't that easy to get, you know."

Fields handed a canteen to the interpreter who began pouring water into the moaning man's mouth. Water doesn't do much to put out the fire of Tabasco, but it was better than nothing.

"You are one crazy Mexican," Fields muttered, shaking his head again.

I extended the bottle toward him. "Here, want some? Good for you—keeps you alert."

"Unh-uh! I'd tell you anything you wanted to know. I ain't as motivated as him." He scanned the sky. "Where is that slick?"

In answer, we heard the faint slap of rotors in the distance. "About time," Fields grunted.

Our prisoner clambered to his feet, leaves and branches snapping and crackling in the silence as he stumbled and thrashed to maintain his balance.

It all seemed to happen in slow motion. I saw Fields flinch and watched him wheel around toward the sudden sound. I was in direct line between Fields and the prisoner. Reflexes took over as I saw his weapon swing upward. I reacted and hit the ground.

Even then, I felt the hot breath of the bullets as they brushed within inches of my scalp as I fell. On full automatic, Fields had let loose. Behind me, I heard a choked grunt followed by the thump of the prisoner's body hitting the ground.

I looked up and saw Fields standing, wisps of smoke curling from the rifle muzzle, with a puzzled expression on his face. He had the look of a man who had just realized that he had made the wrong turn at an intersection—not someone who had just about blown away his buddy, not to mention probably killed the prisoner.

Our interpreter, who luckily had been standing to the side, was backing away, apparently trying to decide whether to run like hell to get away from the crazy Americans.

Fields finally looked down at me: "Ben . . ."

But the chopper was upon us and there was no time to talk. The interpreter and I grabbed the prisoner and lifted him into the helicopter. He seemed to be alive although he had a good chunk of meat taken out of his belly.

During the short flight back to a B-team camp where we were originally scheduled to deliver him, we gave him what medical help we could. A stretcher was waiting when we got there, and he was taken away. I never knew whether he lived or died; I never knew if the information the brass was looking for was obtained. And I never knew if any field operations were undertaken as a result of our efforts.

That's the way it was. Each individual event had to stand on its own. You had to be satisfied with your individual performance within your own little segment of the war, because you sure as hell couldn't be certain of its effect on any of the overall picture.

Fields and I had not spoken during the flight back. But back on the ground, on friendly terrain, I let him know how I felt about the situation. But I didn't get far.

"You no-good crazy son of a bitch, do you know you almost killed me?" I screamed as we stood beside the chopper after our prisoner had been taken away. A couple of mechanics watched—curious, I suppose, at this exchange between two Green Berets. Fields said nothing, just hanging his head.

"Look at my head—you even singed the hair off it!" I had more to say—I wanted to say more. But I felt my stomach churn and there was nothing I could do about it.

I vomited all over the front of Fields's fatigues, spraying him from head to toe. I felt better after that.

On another occasion, we got into some heavy action on a recon mission and the slicks moved in to extract us. The jungle was too thick and the enemy had the landing zone under heavy fire. So we had to rely on the McGuire rigs to pull us out.

Thank God the forest was thick, because it hampered the vision of the gooks on the ground as they tried to draw a bead on us while we dangled in the rig some thirty feet below the belly of the chopper. It's a terribly vulnerable feeling, hanging there, knowing that the pilot is pulling you out of there as fast as he can, but never fast enough.

The pop of small-arms fire seemed far away as it was drowned out by the roar of the helicopter engine and rotors, and it was impossible to hear the hiss of the bullets as they ripped by—but you knew they were there.

I remember that I began to twist in my rig, and I had the thought—what if these ropes rub together and part, dropping me to the jungle below? If the fall didn't kill me, the men waiting below surely would.

That's when I looked up and saw Leroy Wright, my buddy from Special Forces school back at Bragg. He was the bellyman on the chopper, and he was leaning out as far as he possibly could, pulling the two lines apart, separating them so they wouldn't cause a problem. He was Special Forces all the way, risking his life to enemy fire to make sure a friend had a fighting chance. It was an act I would remember later.

CHAPTER 22

APRIL WENT PAST in a whirlwind of activity—missions and training and training and missions. We would watch choppers leave the pad, not having any idea where they were off to, what the mission was about, and most of all, totally uncertain as to which of our friends would return.

But when one went well, extremely well, it was the greatest feeling on earth even if you weren't involved in it.

A hot and sunny Sunday morning toward the end of the month, I was near the chopper pad when an unmarked slick buzzed the camp. From the way it dipped and swooped, you could sense the thrill of victory filling its occupants.

When it finally settled to the hard-packed surface of the pad, we already had a small greeting party formed to see what was up. I remember seeing Brian O'Connor and Floyd Mousseau—"Frenchy," they called him—in the little group. They had just returned the night before from a little in-country R&R in Vung Tau and even after a good breakfast they looked like shit. But although they were still suffering hangovers, they couldn't resist the curiosity created by the incoming chopper.

I didn't realize at the time that only minutes before, while they were dipping into their eggs and swilling coffee, they had received the first word about an upcoming mission which would change our lives forever—and end more than a few. In fact, they had been on their way to the briefing room when they spotted the aircraft.

But the arriving helicopter was the center of attention now, and as it rocked to a landing and the rotors sliced overhead, Mac, the bellyman, jumped out followed by a team in steriles and a prisoner. He wore the uniform of the NVA and was middle-aged. By God, I thought, as I looked at the way he held himself, dignified despite his bindings, that son of a bitch is an officer.

"We got 'em out! Shit—we did it!" screamed Mac over the sound of the winding-down chopper. He turned his back to us, holding his shirttail out with both hands like a cape. The rip in it was obviously a bullet hole. Looking back at us, the excitement danced in his eyes. "That was fuckin' close," he laughed.

Colonel Drake was there, along with the camp's intelligence officers, and they, the team, and their booty left for debriefing. We stood around for a few minutes enjoying that chill of victory. Even for those of us not on the mission, the experience was as sweet as if it had just been ourselves who cheated death again.

Mac and the chopper crew began unpacking and he pulled the coiled rope of the McGuire rig from the deck and it fell into three or four pieces—shot through. "I was sitting on that," exclaimed Mac. "They were trying to shoot my ass off too. My ass, my shirt— that was close." We could understand his excitement. "But close don't count."

He dropped what was left of the rig on the ground, laughed again, and stopped. Suddenly rage replaced the joy in his face, and he spun around, pounding the side of the chopper with a short but powerful karate jab.

"Welcome home, Mac," I said. "C'mon, the cold ones are waiting for you." He and the rest of the crew got into the jeep and headed for the club. I went along, glad for the opportunity to do a little celebrating. Behind, O'Connor and Mousseau resumed their interrupted trip to the briefing room. If I had known what was being planned in that little shack—and my eventual role in it—I think my own attitude at the time would have been considerably more somber.

While I hoisted a few with the returning crew, Colonel Drake had left the newly arrived prisoner with the intelligence officers and joined O'Connor and Mousseau.

They were going to be part of a twelve-man team, he told them. The initial gathering point for the mission would be Quon Loi which was also headquarters for the First Brigade of the First Infantry Division. Some five minutes flying time west was the Special Forces base at Loc Ninh. Loc Ninh was about ten miles closer to the Cambodian border than Quon Loi. That was just one of the reasons Loc Ninh was chosen as the launching site for the operation. The team would leave Quon Loi early the morning of the mission, hop to Loc Ninh, and wait there for the order to move in. They would be able to lift off from Loc Ninh with a minimum of questioning eyes marking the exact time of their departure. This was the real reason for using the Loc Ninh base.

There would be three Americans. O'Connor and Mousseau were two of them and the third was Leroy Wright, who had already been briefed and was at the launch site making preparations. He would serve as team leader. Seven CIDG soldiers and two Vietnamese

Special Forces warrant officers would make up the remainder of the team.

Considerable enemy activity had been spotted in the area, Drake said. There had even been reports of gasoline trucks—with Esso and Shell logos plastered on their sides, no less. Attempts to obtain photographs from helicopters had proved unsuccessful; it looked like putting men on the ground was the only way any hard information was going to be obtained.

"Our guess is that a large NVA unit is on the move south," Drake noted. "You men go in and just nose around."

They pored over the maps of the area, noting the locations marked as logical enemy staging areas for troops and vehicles. Although not marked, trails snaked throughout the area. It would also be the team's job to map them as they went along. They would take the trails to the main roads over which they suspected the NVA to be moving materiel—and then observe.

"Of course, if the situation warrants it, catch somebody or something," Drake added. "Preferably an officer or truck and driver. If you grab something, let us know and we'll give you the support to get out. You make the decisions when you get down there."

They had a week to train for the mission. The two men nodded—satisfied. Most of the team had worked together and should mesh well.

The days that followed were filled with intense training. Wright returned and took part in the daily exercises. My time during those hot, sweltering days was taken up with the "normal" training we went through. I learned that I would also be going to Quon Loi and then on to Loc Ninh as part of the SF contingency that would provide support for Wright's team. I was not privy to the exact nature of their mission—there was no need for me to know. The fewer who knew, the better—it was a normal part of Special Forces operating procedure. I would simply be on hand to do whatever was needed.

The rest of us paid little attention to the specific training Wright's team was undergoing. If we had paid attention, however, we would have noticed a difference, a few touches that took their work a few notches above the norm. There was extra work with special weapons; they were loading themselves down with extra communications gear and plenty of AK-47 ammunition. Included in the mounting list of equipment were Chinese rocket-propelled grenades; U.S. light antitank weapons (LAW), miniature one-shot disposable bazookas; Swedish, Russian, and Chinese small arms; and a couple of modernized World War II grease guns, the kind tankers carried in that conflict.

Four separate communications links were set up in case the team was forced to split up. There were extra language drills, communication classes, evasion and escape tactics, McGuire rig and land ladder extractions, and vehicle capture and destruction practice. The three Americans and nine Vietnamese CIDGs engaged in solving mock problems with a few actual local recons thrown in to provide some realism. All in all, they were doing everything possible to prepare for a walk in someone else's front yard.

At the end of a day, there was always time to unwind at the club. The atmosphere there was always like that of a football locker room after a particularly good practice. The teams would come after a full day, ready for a little relaxation. We would walk through the doors with the looks on our faces that reflected the intensity that training always produced—focused, serious, and sharp.

But soon, a jovial spirit would settle over the place. One-armed bandits over in the corner sang, rang, and jingled. Pinochle games which had raged for days or weeks went on at a few tables. Often a new player would join, taking the place of a man who had gotten hit, but the games themselves went on—like the war itself.

It was a time for brotherhood. Forgotten for the moment was the big "F"—Fear. There would be time enough for that in the morning. For now there were stories, anecdotes of past battles, and, of course, the practical jokes. There was a carefree air about the place because we knew there were some of us who tomorrow would be "going in to bring back a live package," heading out "to nose around," or "clear the parking meters"—all euphemisms for the heaviest game in town.

The day before Mousseau, O'Connor, and the rest of the team were scheduled to follow Wright to Loc Ninh, I saw O'Connor at the chopper pad. We were loading supplies onto the aircraft for transport to the launch site. I was carrying a double load of ammo cases, one on each shoulder.

He took one of them and we dumped both onto the deck. I wiped the sweat from my face and looked him over.

"You boys are looking smooth," I said. "Happy hunting."

"Yeah," he grinned, "we're about ready." He glanced at the other gear I was toting. "Are you going on this flight?"

"Yep," I replied, jerking my head toward the packed chopper, "if there's enough room." We joked for a while until the whine of the turbine signaled departure. As the rotors began their first, lazy rotations, we wished each other "Happy hunting" again, hugged, and I hopped aboard.

As we lifted off, I could see O'Connor, now standing with Mousseau, both holding their berets on against the wind blast, watching us.

CHAPTER 22

The ride was quiet and Quon Loi soon was in view. Since the base was not all Special Forces, we had our own compound. Part of the job of the First Brigade was to support the airstrip and artillery units. We came in without buzzing and landed at the back of the strip. Jeeps were waiting and after off-loading and stowing all the equipment, we were whisked away to the compound, avoiding any contact with the other non-Green Beret units.

The following day was full of training, continuing to hone skills already razor-sharp. Late that afternoon, bone-tired, I walked into one of the tents in our compound to find a hot poker game in progress. My exhaustion vanished at the sight of the bicycles being flipped around the table. Leroy Wright, Dave Graves, and Jerry Cottingham were the players; soon there were four.

Leroy was hot; the hands kept falling his way along with our money.

The game was interrupted when we heard a jeep crunch to a stop outside. Wright pushed back his chair, snapped his fan of cards closed, clasped them in an exaggerated motion to his chest, and headed for the door singing a Beatles song.

"You say yes and I say no—you say stop and I say go, go, go," he chortled as he stepped through. Graves, Cottingham, and I looked dejectedly at each other.

"Hello, hello," we heard Wright, still singing, call out.

"Hey, Leroy, how's it hangin', brother?" I recognized O'Connor's voice.

"High, mighty high right now. Yessiree—right up there," laughed Wright.

There was a moment of silence broken by Mousseau's "O-o-o-whee, I guess so. Tell you what, we'll unload while you go back in there and win us some beer money with those cards."

The three of us exchanged looks again. Wright slipped back in, sat down, smiled that infectious grin of his, and said, "Now, where were we?" Where we were was at the end of that hand. My pair of sevens wouldn't have gotten the admiration of those guys outside, so I folded, and Graves called Leroy. Wright apparently thought he had taken us for enough, so he flipped his full house—aces and kings—face up.

"Shit," said Cottingham.

O'Connor and Mousseau walked in just as we were sweeping Wright's winnings into his hat.

"I am sorry, fellows," said Wright, "but my boys are here now and they are jealous—jealous."

"Hey, men, sorry to break up the party," laughed O'Connor.

"Yeah, I'll bet you are," I retorted.

"Bet! You bet!" exclaimed Leroy, jumping to his feet with cash-filled beret in hand. "How much you wantta bet this time?"

We all broke up. Leroy was in good humor, as well he should be.

"Tango Mike Mike," said O'Connor, "is today tamale?" It was a standard joke between us.

"Ha," I replied, "every day is tamale," in the ritual response. "Hey," I continued, "how about Leroy spreading his earnings around and buying us some grub and beer? I'll even go with him to get it."

"Hell, you better stay in your cage until you clean up," said O'Connor, noting the paint job still on my face from the day's work. "With that grease on, you'd scare the hair off a monkey."

"Let's get this briefing out of the way," interjected Mousseau, "and we'll all pick up some. Where's the shop at, anyway?" He was referring to the Vietnamese restaurant in the nearby village where we could pick up some beer and eats.

"Out yonder," I said, waving in the general direction of the front gate. "It's not far—at least not as far as I walked today."

"How is it out there, brother?" questioned O'Connor, with the first serious look on his face since he'd entered the tent.

"There's a lot of traffic," I shrugged, "but it could be worse. Listen, you boys go get briefed, and we'll wait for you."

There were a few beers drunk that night. Other teams came in from the countryside, and there was a good feeling in the compound because everyone came back in one piece. Someone broke out a stag flick, and a good time was had by all—an easy, peaceful evening.

Wright, O'Connor, and Mousseau left the party early. Tomorrow was Thursday, May 2nd, and they had a busy day ahead. I took my leave soon afterward, having decided to spend the night at the forward site, Loc Ninh, along with a few others. A slick got us there in short order and I was soon in the sack and fast asleep.

NVA soldiers

Captured Viet Cong guarded by CIDGs

May 24, 1969, Fort Devens, Massachusetts, Roy drives for visiting General Westmoreland (right). *Photograph Department, Norwich University. Northfield. Vt.*

CSM George W. Dunaway (left), Sergeant Major of the Army, congratulates SFC Roy Benavidez at Brooke General Hospital on receiving the Distinguished Service Cross. Roy was still recovering from his many wounds, his left hand still in a brace. Second from left is SFC John M. Prosser, SF Liaison, Fort Sam Houston, and at right, SFC Emmett Reese, SF Procurement NCO—both veterans of Vietnam.
U.S. Army photograph

General Westmoreland talks with Lala and Roy and his brother, Roger, at Brooke General Hospital, September 10, 1968, after presenting Roy the DSC for gallantry in action. *U.S. Army photograph*

Michael Craig, the door gunner who died in Roy's arms

Brian O'Connor in his "native Fiji outfit"

Brian O'Connor and Roy after presentation of the Medal of Honor, February 24, 1981

At the White House, President Reagan served the Benavidez children some of his famous Oval Office jelly beans under Roy's watchful eye—and to the amusement of Secretary of Defense Caspar Weinberger.

Roy is flanked by Secretary Weinberger and President Reagan after presentation of the Medal of Honor at the Pentagon, February 24, 1981

Roy responds to the celebrated Reagan charm in the Hall of Heroes at the Pentagon.

President Reagan puts the pale blue ribbon of the nation's highest award for bravery around Roy's neck, with the assistance of an aide and Secretary Weinberger.

Chow with the troops at Fort Polk, Louisiana, July 1981.

Roy with General "Slim Jim" Gavin and Rudy Hernandez at 35th Annual Convention of the 82nd Airborne Division, Houston, August 1981. General Gavin was commander of the 82nd during WW II. Hernandez won the Congressional Medal of Honor for his service in Korea. *Photo by Tad Hershorn*

This display at Wharton County Historical Museum records Roy's military service and honors. Shown with Roy is Mrs. Eve Bartlett, Director of the Museum. A glass case contains a West Point saber, with the inscription: "Presented to M/SGT. Roy P. Benavidez on 9 October 1981 from United States Corps of Cadets. M/SGT. Benavidez, we will not only remember you as a great American soldier, but also as the Epitome of our Motto: Duty, Honor, Country."

At West Point, October 1981. From left, front, Ab Webber, Brig. Gen. Joseph M. Franklin, Commandant, U.S. Military Academy, Roy, Cadet Donna K. Peterson; back, Cadet Archie L. Davis III, Cadet Charles R. Noll, Cadet Warren Phipps.
Photo by SP5 M. Hordeski. USMA

Roy threw out the first ball to open the 1982 season at Houston's Astrodome.

With the Roberto Gonzalez Post 1065, Catholic War Veterans, Mission, Texas, 1981
Photo by Luis Garcia Jr.

Armed Forces Day, 1983, in Washington, DC. Roy and Lala with their children, Noel, Yvette, and Denise, and Sarah Purcell of "Real People."

With Green Berets (Lt. Col. Ralph Drake in light sport coat beside Roy) at National Guard Armory dedication, 1983, in El Campo.

Roy (standing, center) with the Alamo Silver Wings Airborne Association, San Antonio, July 4, 1985

With other Hispanic Medal of Honor recipients in Washington, DC, in 1984, to design a stamp promoting Hispanic heritage. From left, seated, Mr. Rodolfo Hernandez, Dr. Lawrence J. Korb, Hon. Caspar W. Weinberger, Mr. Jose Lopez; standing, Mr. Alejandro R. Ruiz, Mr. Cleto Rodriguez, Mr. Louis Rocco, Mr. Silvestre Herrera, Col. Jay Vargas, USMC, Mr. Lucian Adams, Col. Joseph C. Rodriguez, USA (ret), Mr. Roy P. Benavidez.

In May 1986, Major General Gerald Childress, superintendent of New Mexico Military Institute, congratulated Roy after presenting him with an honorary Associate in Arts degree from NMMI. Roy addressed the corps of 750 cadets and attended the regimental review in his honor.

At the Shamrock Hilton in Houston, April 1986, Vice President George Bush told the public about the achievements of Hispanics in the defense of the nation, and about the exploits of Roy Benavidez which earned him the Medal of Honor. Bush was the principal speaker at a banquet saluting Hispanic pioneers as part of the Texas Sesquicentennial celebration.
Photo by Efrain

PART IV

NO
PERMISSION
TO
DIE

CHAPTER 23

DAWN OF MAY 2, 1968, slipped lazily over the Highlands and down into the lush valley of the Mekong and toward the tiny outpost of Loc Ninh. Within minutes, it burst into a blinding brilliance that banished the coolness of the night. Seconds later, ten miles to the west, Cambodia felt the sting of another sweltering Southeast Asian day.

I was not awake to see the beginning of what was destined to be the most momentous day of my life. There was no need for me to be up early. I planned a late breakfast. Until then, I slept on. The mounting heat outside would awaken me in plenty of time. I knew that from experience.

But others were up before first light. Back at Quon Loi, Wright, Mousseau, O'Connor, and the rest of their CIDG team were already at the chopper pad waiting as two slicks and accompanying gunships warmed up. It was O'Connor, as the lone American survivor of the mission, who supplied me later with details of the day's events.

In full camouflage and loaded with communications gear and weapons, they climbed aboard—Wright, O'Connor, and half the team in one, and Mousseau and the remainder in the second. As the first rays of the sun slashed into the compound, the choppers tiptoed off the pad and roared off to the west.

After a five-minute flight, they dropped down onto the tiny strip at Loc Ninh. The pilots shut down their machines, and the men waited for the word to move out. Instant coffee was broken out, the choppers' JP4 fuel drains were tapped to kindle a fire, and soon cups of the hot brew were handed around. Then the radio came to life, and it was time to get underway again. Engines coughed as the two troop-carrying slicks and the two gunships took to the air.

This was to be a long, twenty-minute ride, deep into the enemy stronghold and far from where the team could expect to get conventional support.

O'Connor remembers that the cool morning air blowing through the open doors brought tears to his eyes and dried them before the drops could touch his cheeks. The rising sun burned away the morning mist below and they could see the blackened pockmarks of combat in the jungle below.

Within minutes, the landscape changed. Nothing but green—the brightest green imaginable—lay before them.

Wright tugged at O'Connor's sleeve and pointed off to the right. Squinting, O'Connor made out a slight rise with two separate villages nearby. They had traveled over ten miles and were at the twenty-kilometer mark.

"They say the first twenty are the toughest," mused Wright. "Guess we woke some sleepyheads, though." He poked his head out the door and shouted into the slipstream: "Sorry, boys—catch us if you can!" He wore that infectious grin of his when he turned back. The tension loosened with the smile.

CHAPTER 23

The aircraft yawed as the pilot changed direction; from now on, the choppers would pursue a zigzag course, even changing formation as the men at the sticks stitched their way over the deceptively calm terrain. Ground observers would find it impossible to predict their final destination. Sitting in his treetop post, a lookout could not even be sure the two helicopters that suddenly appeared and vanished overhead were the two reported by a comrade sitting in a similar position to the east.

Wright and O'Connor pored over the map, attempting to pick up each landmark; it was a difficult task, made worse by the erratic movements of the slick. Fortunately, it wasn't in either's MOS (Military Occupational Specialty) to keep the wheeling aircraft on course. Somewhere, high above at five thousand feet or so and, as far as they could tell, out of sight, a command and control helicopter, the C&C, was in contact with the team's pilots and directing them on the proper vectors that ultimately would bring them down at the landing zone.

Wright pointed below to a small circular bend in a tiny stream. O'Connor recognized it as the rendezvous point in the event they had to E&E out.

The last landmark before the landing zone passed below and the two choppers suddenly descended, picking up speed. The jungle leaped to meet them—no longer a lush, violently green carpet, but millions of leafy arms stretching to drag them out of the air. At top speed and only a few feet from disaster, the pilots sent the slicks speeding over the canopy like crazed bobsled drivers.

Wright signaled his men to get ready, and they moved into position. The chopper shuddered in abrupt deceleration, sharp enough to produce elevator float in the passengers' stomachs—then they were on the ground. O'Connor had a fleeting glimpse of a slash in the lush undergrowth as a crescent-shaped, smiling jungle mouth swallowed the two slicks.

Seconds later, the jungle spit the chattering machines out, and they whipped away, their mad dash over the treetops hardly interrupted. Behind, they left a silent, empty clearing.

Almost invisible, nestled next to a vine-encrusted tree, Wright surveyed his team. With the speed that comes only with endless hours of practice, they had exited and dived into the edge of the clearing, already well concealed before the first chopper slipped away.

O'Connor and Mousseau gave Wright a thumbs up, and the team leader radioed an "insertion completed" to the departing pilots.

Breathless from the adrenaline rush pulsing through their bodies, they lay motionless for a few moments, and then edged farther back into the dense jungle. For thirty minutes more, they lay quietly—watching, listening, sniffing the torpid air like the animals of prey they had become.

Time passed slowly—it always did while a team was on the ground. O'Connor and Mousseau watched intently the opposite side of the LZ. Nothing moved. Above, two large birds rode the early morning wind currents rising from the rapidly heating earth.

The shadows from the surrounding trees were long, early-morning lines on the open ground. But the jungle was dark, very dark. That would work to the team's advantage. Also, the damp ground muffled the sounds of their movement. O'Connor shivered from the chill of the dank air and the moisture seeping into his clothes from below. He ignored the discomfort; it wasn't even eight o'clock yet and he knew that the equally unpleasant steam bath that passed for daytime would be there soon enough.

Looking around at each other's faces was like looking into a mirror. Tight-lipped, eyes sharpened to every movement, ready for anything, they were a Special Forces team that had clicked into gear.

Wright crawled over to the other two Americans. Pointing to the map he pulled from his pouch, he whispered, "Here we are. We'll move in and work our way around to the trail."

Progress was slow as they made their way into the thickening jungle, Wright leading the way, and O'Connor bringing up the rear with the radio. Although the others cut a tunnel through the network of vines, the radioman was still forced to hump his way backward most of the time. Sweat poured in torrents from all of their bodies. The cool of the morning was soon forgotten, and the massive amount of equipment carried by each man added to their misery.

Periodically, Wright called a brief rest, and the men dropped to their knees, exhausted from continuous hacking at the clinging foliage.

Finally, without warning, Wright's next step took him through what had seemed the impenetrable wall of green. He found himself standing in the middle of a trail running through the jungle like a tiny vein in the body of the emerald giant.

Retreating quickly into the shielding darkness, he hand-signaled down the column that the first objective had been reached. Mousseau moved past the leader and, crouched low, weapon at the ready, slipped down the trail.

Ten minutes later he returned and whispered to Wright that he had seen three—maybe five—enemy soldiers down the trail.

Wright motioned O'Connor forward. "They might be coming this way," he told the radioman. "Frenchy couldn't tell for sure which way they were headed. Get back to your position, and be ready to lead us back out of here if we have to get lost quick." As O'Connor turned, Wright added in a tight whisper: "Remember, no noise."

O'Connor slipped quickly back to his rear position. There was relatively little concern among the team over the spotting of the enemy. O'Connor's own thoughts were that they were probably only a small group on a stroll deep within their own sanctuary. The way the chopper boys maneuvered and buzzed with their crazy throwoff tactics, the team could have landed—or not landed—anywhere within a fifty-square-mile area. There was no chance the NVA that Frenchy sighted were looking for them.

There was always the chance they were point for a company. That could spell trouble. O'Connor shrugged his pack into a more comfortable position. They'd soon know for sure.

Silently O'Connor waited, unable to see much beyond the man in front of him. Time ticked away with the drops of perspiration that dripped from the end of his nose. He was poised to lead the way back into the trackless tangle behind him.

Suddenly, the quiet erupted with the sound of crackling branches—like an animal scrambling through the dense foliage. Then a thick guttural scream, muffled, yet clearly heard in the silence of the jungle. O'Connor identified it as the sound of a man, not an animal, gurgling as a knife slipped into his throat. A short burst of gunfire—the distinctive chatter of an AK-47—finished off the destruction of the forest's hush.

O'Connor had stiffened at the first sounds, ready for flight or fight. But, screened out by the surrounding vegetation, he found his pulse racing as the unseen drama unfolded somewhere ahead him, near the path.

Who had an AK besides himself, he wondered. Mousseau was carrying an M-3 grease gun and the point had a Sten gun. What was going on? Don't move yet—wait.

Finally, the signal was passed back by Wright—move out fast!

Back down the tunnel hacked out minutes before. Only this time the Special Forces team tore through the jungle, heedless of the jagged and torn branches reaching out to trip them.

O'Connor saw the bend ahead at the top of a rise he remembered passing earlier—a perfect spot for an ambush. Stopping, he dropped the AK to hip high. The men behind him made no sound, but he knew they were poised for action.

The radioman lunged forward, turning the corner, expecting the worst. His finger relaxed on the assault rifle's trigger—nothing but the trampled evidence of their previous passage lay ahead. His heart continued to hammer in his chest as he resumed their retreat—still unaware of what had happened back at the path.

O'Connor was almost past the gully before he remembered it being there. Swerving, he leaped into it, rolling over to come to rest on his stomach, the rifle searching the wall of green behind him, covering his comrades. The remainder of the team tumbled after him, hitting and rolling exactly as he had done, each coming to rest in the same position.

Like damn mechanical toys, thought O'Connor, turning all that practice into perfect performance when reality demanded it. There was no such thing as too much training. It always paid off.

Wright crawled to O'Connor's side. The team leader was not even breathing hard. "How's it look?" he asked.

"Looks clear, sounds quiet," responded O'Connor. "What's up?"

"Aw, fuck, a few woodcutters. One of them squeezed off on the way down."

Mousseau rolled over to join them. He looked like he had just butchered a cow. His knife still hung from around his wrist.

His words tumbled out in a rush: "They stopped right in front of us and started cutting. They almost got Chin in the head. The bastards looked right at me."

Taking a deep breath, he added emphatically, "We had no choice."

"No sweat," shrugged O'Connor.

Before leaving the scene, Mousseau and Chin, the point, had hidden the bodies, hoping they would not be found in the dense undergrowth.

"I've got a feeling we're gonna find out right quick what's going on around here," mused Wright. "They ain't just cuttin' firewood."

O'Connor had arrived at the same conclusion. Those guys were clearing the trail for someone coming up behind. And with a little luck, the rest of them would be far enough behind to give the Green Berets time to set up.

Wright got on the radio and informed the C&C of their unexpected encounter. He looked over at O'Connor with raised eyebrows as the voice from high above ordered the team leader to take his men back toward the LZ and attempt another route to bypass any oncoming NVA. They both knew that returning to the landing zone was a risky maneuver. The place could be crawling with the enemy by now.

Wright hesitated after he broke contact, his lips pursed in thought. "Okay," he said, "let's head back."

CHAPTER 24

RETRACING THEIR STEPS, O'Connor recalls that the small Special Forces troop approached the LZ cautiously. Every ear searched the familiar sounds of the jungle—the birds in the trees, the whisper of hot air through the dense foliage—searching for the faintest sound that would betray the presence of intruders like themselves. Only a few short meters from the position they had occupied, Wright halted, signaling his men to stillness.

Voices . . . clear unmistakable sounds of men thrashing through the underbrush, calling to each other. The commotion came from the far end of the LZ, an area less heavily wooded than the vicinity where the Green Berets waited.

Wright signaled O'Connor to his side. "Maybe they'll make it easy on themselves and try to avoid this heavy stuff," he whispered. "I think they're heading for the trail though." It was time, he added, to make radio contact with the C&C and put in a standby request for extraction.

"If they find those dead men, they'll be on our asses in no time," replied O'Connor, agreeing with his team leader's assessment of a situation which was close to getting out of hand.

Crouching by O'Connor with the handset cupped to his mouth and speaking as loudly as he dared, Wright repeatedly called to the C&C helicopter he knew was somewhere high overhead. There was no answer.

"Shit," he spat, handing the instrument back to his radioman. "Let's get out from under here and try another antenna."

Silently, they crept away, heading in the opposite direction from the thrashing enemy soldiers. Soon, a slight increase in the light filtering down to the jungle floor indicated a break in the canopy overhead. Peering through the undergrowth, O'Connor found himself with a clear and commanding view of the LZ. Listening intently, he could just make out the voices at the far end of the clearing and the sound of machetes cutting a path. There was no note of alarm in the enemy calls as they began to fade, moving away toward the trail the Americans and their CIDG comrades had so hurriedly abandoned.

It was at this point that Wright decided against renewing his efforts to call for the standby. His men had not been detected and there was a good chance the dead soldiers would not be found right away.

The Americans were not able to make out any of the words called back and forth by the still invisible enemy troops, and the CIDGs gave conflicting reports of what they had heard. The team's interpreter indicated his frustration at trying to sort out the confusion.

It was either, he said, a squad-sized group of North Vietnamese or a large detachment of woodcutters.

"What do you think?" asked Wright.

The man shrugged his slight shoulders. "It sound to me like they maybe six to twelve NVAs. I think they looking for us or a downed helicopter. But I'm not sure."

O'Connor nodded. The man had worked as an interpreter with him many times and he had always found him reliable. Anyway, it would pay to assume the worst and plan accordingly.

Wright checked his watch while Mousseau and O'Connor broke out the maps. There was still time to try an alternate route to the objective. O'Connor wiped the sweat from his eyes as he focused on the maze of jungle and tiny trails laid out on the chart.

The conference ended abruptly as voices again drifted to them from the far tip of the crescent-shaped LZ. The sounds grew louder. O'Connor looked to Wright. The slashing knives were now on the same side of the clearing as the Special Forces team and coming closer. The decision had been made.

With a new antenna mounted on the radio, Wright made contact with the C&C. Explaining the situation, he requested immediate extraction. Tense minutes passed before he had a response. They were to continue with the mission.

With only raised eyebrows indicating his surprise at the orders, Wright grunted with what O'Connor took to be a certain sense of satisfaction. "Let's go," the team leader said. "We'll take a short cut and get out of here before they sweep through."

With O'Connor accompanying the point man, Mousseau in the middle, and Wright bringing up the rear, their tiger-striped fatigues blending perfectly with the bush, the column of heavily armed men soon left the increasingly crowded area of the LZ behind.

Their route took them to the edge of a small open field. A narrow road ran alongside. They would have to cross the field and the road to get to the cover of the jungle on the other side. Maybe no more than a hundred yards distant, the security of the trees seemed like a mile away to O'Connor as he crouched at the edge of the open area.

Slipping one by one out of their cover, the team members made their way quickly to the roadway—and came face to face with a dozen NVA troops.

Both forces froze in their tracks. The North Vietnamese had been walking down the road, and the trees at the edge of it and the field had shielded each group from the other's view until it was too late.

An officer was at their head. The CIDG point man immediately walked toward him, talking loudly and gesturing broadly with both hands.

O'Connor couldn't understand what he was saying but silently thanked God for the quick-thinking soldier. Ducking his head to hide his own face, O'Connor shakily pulled a map from his pocket and walked back to Mousseau where they apparently studied the document, using it to mask their round eyes from the enemy.

"The shit is about to hit the fan," murmured Mousseau.

"Don't I know it," whispered O'Connor, his head cocked toward the scene being played out at the head of the column. He was ready to act at the slightest indication of a hostile move by the other side.

The team's interpreter walked by them as he made his way toward the NVA officer and the still-talking CIDG. He paused only long enough to quietly tell the Americans that the point man just about had the officer convinced that the Special Forces team was another patrol like themselves.

"Tell him to tell them we're looking for the chopper that was shot down," Mousseau whispered as the interpreter moved on. "Tell them we heard it go down."

Before the interpreter could reach the two men standing in the middle of the road, the point man suddenly turned and, pointing to the jungle hugging the roadside, began shouting orders to the other members of the team. O'Connor realized that the NVA thought the tiny Vietnamese was in charge; the man was ordering "his" men to search the surrounding jungle.

The Green Berets moved to obey their new leader. Before he had taken three steps, O'Connor heard Mousseau's voice in his ear: "I think they may have seen your face. Get ready to take the ones on the left and I'll try to get those on the right. Wait until the point gets clear and we'll move only if things look bad." O'Connor nodded his understanding.

O'Connor heard the NVA officer shout, gesturing for the return of the point who had moved to follow the team to the jungle's edge. The South Vietnamese walked back toward the officer, still shouting orders to the Green Berets. O'Connor couldn't get over the poise of the man. They just might get away with their necks because of the acting of this gutsy soldier.

O'Connor didn't have to look to see what Wright and the rest of the team were doing. He knew they would be slipping into the undergrowth, preparing to set up a defense perimeter should the situation go sour.

Without warning, the interpreter, standing only yards behind Mousseau and O'Connor and watching the point approach the NVA troops, whirled and shouted, "They know!"

At his cry, the quiet little road suddenly turned into a blood-spattered battlefield. Weapons on full automatic chattered insanely as the Americans and the point man laid down a withering pattern of flying steel.

During the entire drama, the enemy troops had made no attempt to disperse, preferring to stay close to their commanding officer. Their lack of training was evident. Ten of them, including the officer, fell almost immediately, screaming and clawing at their bodies as the bullets ripped them to shreds.

But somehow, even as they fell dying, two of the North Vietnamese managed to fire a rocket-propelled grenade in the general direction of the Americans. O'Connor heard the fiery hiss of the RPG as it sailed wide and high into the treetops overhead and burst with a roar among the branches.

With their weapons still bucking in their hands, the three back-stepped, trying to cut down the two enemy soldiers still on their feet, and at the same time, reach the sanctuary of the perimeter now established behind them. O'Connor felt a leaf brush his ear and knew he had reached the jungle's edge. But miraculously two NVAs were still on their feet, returning fire as they dashed for the opposite side of the road.

Now, with their three comrades safely out of the line of fire, the full fury of the Special Forces team was unleashed against the surviving North Vietnamese. Murderous gunfire cut them down even as they tried desperately to find safety in the grassy field.

O'Connor looked up to where the smoke from the grenade wreathed the crown of the tree above him. Far from feeling relieved at the miss, O'Connor realized that the dead NVAs might as well have sent up a signal flare as their last act.

There was no longer any doubt about continuing the mission. Wright was on the radio in seconds, urgently requesting an extraction.

"How about it?" asked Mousseau as he stepped to Wright's side, licking his lips. The excitement of the battle danced in his darting eyes. O'Connor knew he had the same look on his own face.

"They're on their way," replied Wright, as he dug into the pouch at his side and removed a folded handful of documents. "I told them to expect a hot one." Handing the papers to O'Connor, the team leader told the radioman, "Burn them. They're no good to us anymore."

Using a chunk of C-4, O'Connor and Mousseau built a small fire. Within seconds, the documents were ash. Moving out moments later, the team headed back toward the landing zone and the anticipated rendezvous with their rescuers.

CHAPTER 25

ACK AT LOC NINH, eight helicopters sat ready on the landing strip—four UH-1C gunships equipped with rockets and machine guns and four slicks. The pilots and crews gathered around a radio, listening intently for reports on the mission in progress to the west.

Less than an hour had passed since Wright's team had been inserted into the Cambodian jungle. The two pilots who had made the insertion, Warrant Officers Larry McKibben and Jerry Ewing, were in the forefront, along with their copilots. Because they were a part of the mission and had only minutes before completed the run in and then out, they would be called upon to pull the team out when and if an extraction was called for.

The radio crackled and the group strained to catch the scratchy words. It was Wright's voice.

"What'd he say?" someone asked.

"They've made contact," came the reply. "Something about three NVA. He's requesting extraction."

A moment's hesitation and then reaction. Like quail flushed from cover, the men leaped to their feet and scattered toward the waiting choppers. But before the first engine popped into life, the man at the radio shouted above the commotion. "Hold it! C&C told them to continue with the mission. Come on back."

Reluctantly, the chopper crews trailed back to the radio to resume their vigil. For a few moments, the tension that had been building like water behind a dam had been released in a torrent as they had sprinted toward their machines. Now, they forced themselves to suppress their anxiety and just wait.

The minutes passed slowly; the radio was quiet. Without warning, Wright's voice again came through, and this time there was no doubt. Hot contact! They were under fire by enemy forces, and he was no longer requesting extraction—he was demanding it.

The cluster of men literally flew apart as each dashed to carry out his duty. Within seconds, McKibben and Ewing were at the controls of their slicks. The pilots of the four gunships, divided into two fire teams, soon had their ships cranked and prepared to lift off, but McKibben's helicopter refused to start as the pilot frantically flipped switches.

It was quickly determined that the ship's battery was dead, and a second would have to be found. But time was short, and as the rotors of the two choppers of the secondary team were already beginning their slow rotation, they were ordered to take off and make the recovery. Warrant Officer Hoffman and his copilot, Roger Waggie, were in the front seats of one and Warrant Officer Armstrong and Warrant Officer James C. Fussell were pilot and copilot of the second.

Six helicopters chattered into the air and slipped off into the western sky as the ground crews frantically lifted the battery from the gunship piloted by Jesse Naul and hauled it over to McKibben's craft. Within seconds, it roared to life, and with the battery back in Naul's chopper, the two were soon in hot pursuit of the others.

Five miles out from the LZ, which now had become the pickup zone, or PZ, the peaceful and quiet jungle of early morning erupted with gunfire. The door gunners returned the fire, spraying their rounds at the unseen enemy below.

A command-and-control helicopter was on the scene high above the action, and its commander vectored the slicks commanded by Hoffman toward the PZ. At half a mile from their objective, the slicks and their accompanying gunships ran into a virtual wall of fire.

Onboard Hoffman's lead chopper, Waggie winced as he felt the thud of bullets punch into the slick's belly. The door gunners were firing madly, making no attempt to select targets. The entire jungle floor seemed alive with enemy gunners. Out his window, Waggie saw one of the gunships suddenly lurch and begin belching smoke.

A cry of anguish over the roar of the chopper's engines and guns jerked Waggie's attention back to the interior of his own aircraft. Turning, he saw his crew chief, Specialist 4 Class Michael Craig, stagger back from his door gun and fall to the deck. A Special Forces sergeant who had boarded to assist in the attempt to load the team on the ground bent over him. A bad shoulder wound, he said, looking toward the pilots.

"It's too hot; I'm going to abort," said Hoffman, as he banked the helicopter to the right. "Tell Armstrong to follow us."

Waggie tried to raise Armstrong on the radio, but the frequency was jammed by the C&C and the pilots of the other choppers as they tried to get through to the wounded gunship. His instruments shot out, the pilot, Warrant Officer Curry, had turned his crippled ship west and was flying away from Loc Ninh, deeper into enemy territory.

A mile behind Hoffman and Waggie, Armstrong, Fussell, and the crew of their Huey were flying directly into chaos. A gunship was going down, the lead slick was apparently breaking off its approach. And the C&C, in its effort to assist Curry's gunship, had dropped all attempts to vector Armstrong to the PZ.

By now, the intense radio traffic was bringing people to the scene of what had started out as an extremely secret operation. An Air Force FAC somewhere overhead began giving Armstrong vectors on his final approach. With the remaining gunships ripping the jungle to shreds below with rockets, grenades, and the pinwheeling miniguns pouring out an unending hail of bullets at six thousand rounds a minute each, the slick pierced the wall of fire and slipped into the jungle clearing.

Brian O'Connor watched with relief as the helicopter roared in over the treetops. They would soon be out of there—and with no casualties. But it had to be quick. The noose around their neck was tightening. Their position would soon be discovered, and then there would be hell to pay.

To his dismay, he realized the slick was coming to earth over three hundred feet from their position at the far end of the clearing. They would have to cross all that open space to reach it—an impossible task with the woods crawling with NVA.

From the woodline nearest the chopper, a half-dozen men emerged, walking casually, waving the aircraft lower. The helicopter responded, sinking toward the gesturing soldiers.

Oh my God, realized O'Connor, they think that's us.

The CIDG members of the team reacted first, opening fire on the men on the ground. In answer, a door gunner on the helicopter traversed his weapon and opened fire on the Green Berets' position, sending them diving for cover as the machine gun slugs tore into the trees and surrounding brush.

"Tell those sons of bitches to stop firing," shouted Wright as he fumbled with the radio, trying to make contact with someone—anyone—to warn the chopper off. But the helicopter was still descending and Wright's warning was going to be too late.

O'Connor and Mousseau began sniping at the ground troops who were getting much too close to the approaching slick. One of the enemy dropped. The enemy, in turn, opened fire on the helicopter, and the spell suddenly broke.

The door gunners on Armstrong's chopper turned their guns on what they had thought were their own men, and in seconds, the "friendlies" lay dead.

From their vantage point, the SF team could see a column of over thirty NVA making their way through the trees to where the slick still hovered. Wright cautiously stood up behind a tree to get as much height as possible for the radio he held. Getting through to C&C, he shouted for them to "Get them into the air!"

But the slick remained at the far end of the PZ, a sitting duck for the approaching enemy soldiers.

Turning to O'Connor, Wright ordered: "Get a LAW to Mousseau. Fire it into the middle of that column."

With the explosion in their midst of the antitank weapon, the NVA troops knew their attack was no longer going to be a surprise. They broke screaming from the tree line toward the helicopter.

Only ten feet above the ground by now, the door gunners fired directly into the mass of men. It was impossible not to hit someone.

But the return fire was also massive, and both men manning the helicopter's machine guns fell back, severely wounded.

Up front, Armstrong suddenly cried out as a bullet plowed into his head. He slumped forward, held upright by his harness restraints. Fussell grabbed the controls, only to find they had been badly damaged by the incoming fire. All the hydraulics had been shot away. Flinching back as a bayonet lanced through the window by his face, Fussell pulled his pistol and shot the grimacing face of an enemy soldier between the eyes.

Despite the damage inflicted, the slick staggered into the air. The team on the ground watched it limp over the treetops, still being pounded by the ground fire as the enemy continued their attempts to bring it down. They could hear clearly the orders being shouted by the NVA units deep in the jungle.

Wright pulled his team together under a tree surrounded by a high stand of brush to plan their next move. As more and more voices joined the chorus out in the bush, the situation for the tiny band was becoming desperate. The two CIDGs who had been guarding the rear during the abortive extraction attempt reported through the interpreter that they had heard vehicle movement, possibly tracked, crew-operated heavy weapons.

Skeptical, Wright radioed to the FAC or C&C for confirmation. It was not long in coming.

"Well, there's some big shit out there all right," Wright grimaced, the sweat streaming down his black face. "I think there's time for one more extraction try. We'd better get it right this time. We're goin' to have to make sure the PZ is secure and we're visible this time."

Taking out the map, he instructed Mousseau to take the five CIDGs in his group and set up a position in a stand of trees near the center of the inside loop of the crescent-shaped PZ. Once he was in position and prepared to cover the rest of the team, they would advance past him and his men to set up a similar position some sixty feet beyond near another stand of trees and a giant anthill.

"That way, we'll leave about fifteen to twenty meters between us for a slick to set down and we can provide flank support. Got it? Okay, let's go."

Mousseau and his men slipped away, moving cautiously. They scrambled to their objective and took up positions without taking any fire. Then it was the turn of Wright, O'Connor, and the other four Vietnamese.

Following in the footsteps of Mousseau and his men, the six reached the assistant team leader's position and sprinted past it toward the trees and anthill.

Within steps of their objective, the jungle around them exploded with the roar of automatic weapons.

Like a running dog suddenly reaching the end of his leash, Wright spun around and slammed back into O'Connor who was on his heels. As they went down in a heap, O'Connor felt a hammer blow as he took a round in his left arm.

Wright jumped to his feet, screaming to O'Connor: "Get to the hill!" But before he could take more than a half-dozen steps, his body again jerked and he bounced to the ground.

"I can't move my legs," he cried, as O'Connor and the CIDGs, pulling and scratching, somehow got him and themselves to the relative safety of the trees and the anthill. But there were only four of them.

Looking back, O'Connor saw two of his Vietnamese comrades sprawled on the ground, their bodies still twitching in an imitation of life as the NVA continued to fire into them.

Despite his wounds, Wright pulled the radio to him and called for gunship support.

"I'm hit," screamed Mousseau, and O'Connor turned to see ten NVA soldiers break from a tree line near the assistant team leader's position toward him and his five men. To O'Connor's dismay, he saw they were supported by two crew-operated heavy automatic weapons carriers.

The Vietnamese interpreter at O'Connor's side reached for the grenade launcher and began firing the deadly explosives at the carriers while Wright, O'Connor, and the other surviving CIDG in their group laid down a withering hail of gunfire in an attempt to drive off the attackers.

From above, the gunships bore in, their miniguns, rockets, and door guns turning the jungle into a blistering hell of flying steel and fire. For no more than three minutes, the battle raged and then the firing eased.

Taking a quick look from his position behind the anthill, O'Connor saw that Mousseau and his team had moved to a slightly better spot to protect themselves from the tree line from which the last attack had come. The open field of the PZ was littered with NVA. But to the radioman's astonishment, he saw more NVA moving to the edge of the clearing—in spite of the pounding they had received from the gunships.

The crackle of small-arms fire began again from the far side of the PZ, growing to a roar like a forest fire racing toward the Green Berets. Rocket-propelled grenades hissed through the air, exploding in the trees overhead and ripping the underbrush around them.

O'Connor's eyes snapped wide in surprise as five figures leaped to their feet not twenty feet in front of him, and with their weapons on full automatic, raced toward him. Reaction was swift. As he fired into the group, he heard the chatter of the weapons beside him, then a guttural cry as one of the remaining CIDGs took a round through his Adam's apple. The attackers went down, hidden again by the tall grass.

From where the five attackers had fallen, two hand grenades came sailing through the air, landing softly on the side of the anthill and rolling to Wright's side.

"Get down! Get Down!" he cried, grabbing one of them and throwing it back toward its launching point. It exploded in the air, showering the area with shrapnel. With no time to get rid of the second, the team leader squirmed on his side, shielding his men from the grenade which lay in front of him.

The report was deafening and O'Connor saw his leader's legs and the lower part of his body lift into the air as if a giant foot had kicked him in the stomach.

He's dead, thought O'Connor, as he scrambled to the mangled man's side. He had to get the radio. As he reached over Wright, the team leader turned his head. "Give me a gun," he said, his voice little more than a whisper.

There was not even time for astonishment. Another grenade sailed out of the grass, arching over O'Connor's head.

"Lay down! Get down!" It was Mousseau. The explosion set O'Connor's ears to ringing. The assistant team leader and one of his men had crawled to a few feet from where the two CIDGs lay dead in the grass. Mousseau and the soldier with him half rose to their knees and opened fire on the wounded NVA—one of the five who had just gone down—killing him just as he was about to lob another grenade.

"Just came over to borrow this," shouted Mousseau, as he pulled a LAW from under the body of the CIDG nearest him. He turned and the two scrambled back to their position, diving into the trees as the gunfire from the tree line began again.

The enemy troops were apparently improving their position; every square inch of ground around the four seemed to be taking a hit. O'Connor reached over Wright's shoulder, using his knife to try and sever the strap holding the radio to the team leader's body. The slap and sting of near misses forced him flat again, but he managed to pull the handset free.

"Dog! Dog!" shouted O'Connor, trying to raise the C&C. "This is Fox Terrier, come in." But only the excited clamor of the pilots circling out of range answered him—each asking for a clear frequency. His voice was only one more in the chaos on the airways. Beside him, Wright, who had been handed a rifle by the interpreter, fired steadily.

"Goddamnit, get off the air!" screamed the radioman, forgetting any pretense to proper radio procedure. "We're gettin' killed down here, and you sons of bitches got your fingers up your asses. Where's our air support? We need help!"

That did the trick. The C&C cut the other voices off; the FAC broke in and told O'Connor to switch to a clear frequency.

"We have a downed aircraft out here, Fox Terrier," came the FAC's voice. "Hold on; we have support on the way. Just stay calm."

O'Connor twisted his face toward his team leader, afraid to even raise up enough to face him. "Guess what, Leroy? We're to stay calm. They're . . ."

Wright's head jerked up. He looked like he just had a sudden thought. Then he flopped flat, his eyes gazing full into O'Connor's face. O'Connor, the unfinished sentence dying in his throat, stared at the neat hole in his team leader's forehead.

He brought the handset back to his mouth, calling to the FAC. Wright had such a puzzled look on his face. "Bird Dog, this is Fox Terrier. We need that TAC support fast." His eyes never left Wright's face.

"Roger, Fox Terrier. They're less than two minutes out. Hang in there. Can you ID targets for us?"

A shattering pain in O'Connor's left ankle broke the spell. Instinctively reacting to the sudden flash of agony, he rolled, reaching toward the foot which suddenly seemed to be on fire. Someone slapped him on the right thigh. Another one. He felt the blood flowing down his leg, warm and wet, just like he'd wet his pants.

Retrieving the handset, O'Connor managed to answer: "Sorry, Bird Dog. I just took a couple of hits. I'll do the best I can."

He was confused now, unable to make out north from south. The FAC oriented him, and O'Connor proceeded to point out what enemy concentrations he could make out.

"We got two teams down here," he gasped. "I don't know where we are."

"Roger, Fox Terrier, I have contact with your ATL. We'll be marking targets with smoke. Just stay on this frequency."

O'Connor felt a tugging on his sleeve. The interpreter was at his side, pointing toward Mousseau's position. O'Connor saw the man's left arm was mangled, hanging to his shoulder by a shredded tangle of muscle and tissue.

Turning his head, he saw Mousseau waving. "Ammo! Ammo— grenades!" the ATL shouted.

O'Connor grabbed the ammo pouches from the dead CIDG who had taken the hit in the throat, then, rolling to the two dead CIDGs, he stripped the men of their remaining ammunition and grenades. Crawling another six feet toward Mousseau, he threw the clips and grenades to a CIDG who, in turn, tossed them to the American.

Mousseau pointed to the sky and then turned his palm down toward the earth. O'Connor knew what he meant. The jets were coming.

Rolling back to his position, the pain in his arm, ankle, and thigh slicing through his body, O'Connor again picked up the handset. He tried to ignore the passive stare of his dead fellow Green Beret.

Looking up, he saw the smoke rise over the trees.

"On target, Fox Terrier?" It was the FAC.

"Roger, Dog. Right on the money."

"Okay, lay low. They're coming in close."

And close they were. Like howling demons, the jets—Air Force F-4s—screamed down out of the clear sky. They streaked low over the jungle in a pinpoint attack. Hugging the ground, his eyes screwed shut, O'Connor felt the earth shake as high explosives, fragmentation, and white phosphorous bombs exploded only yards away. The heat was tremendous. He could have sworn his hair was on fire.

Again and again they came and the jungle floor trembled with the force of their attack.

"How was that, Fox Terrier?" It was the FAC calling to him in a voice remarkable for its calmness.

O'Connor looked up at the destruction in front of him. Fires burned here and there on the other side of the PZ. Trees lay flat like giant footsteps had quickstepped through the enemy's position.

"Beautiful, Bird Dog, just beautiful," was the best O'Connor could manage through gritted teeth.

The tree line, or what was left of it, was quiet. Unsure of how long it would remain that way, O'Connor and the interpreter quickly moved to patch their wounds, injecting themselves with morphine to ease the pain. O'Connor applied a tourniquet to the interpreter's arm—it would be a miracle if he kept it. The remaining CIDG in their group watched for enemy movement.

O'Connor glanced in the direction of Mousseau, who was dressing a head wound he had received.

The FAC came back on the air, asking for additional targets. O'Connor gave him what information he could. Mousseau whistled; he had propped himself against the piled up bodies of two CIDGs. He pointed skyward with the radio still in his hand.

The F-4s came in again, but their sweeps were farther away, and their strikes were shorter in duration. They're running out of ordnance, thought O'Connor. They would soon be leaving the area.

"They're coming in!" came Mousseau's cry.

O'Connor reached for the radio. Maybe the flyboys had just enough left for one more hit.

"Bird Dog, this is Fox . . ."

The burst of automatic fire caught O'Connor full in the stomach. He flew backward, the radio blown from his hand, shattered. Dazed, the taste of blood in his mouth, the radioman crawled to the shelter of his team leader's body, grabbed the rifle lying there, and began firing, waiting for the ammunition to run out.

Mortar rounds arched into the PZ, and rockets and grenades filled the air. Unbelievably, the NVA firepower seemed even more fierce than before the airstrikes. It was just a matter of time now, O'Connor knew.

Above the continuous roar, he picked out the distinctive chop of approaching helicopters. Maybe it was a strike force coming in to try and pick up what was left. As the pain coursed through him, he realized that in his case, there was not going to be much to haul back.

To his surprise, one lone slick flew into the PZ. Miraculously, it dropped to within ten feet of the ground without taking a hit. A rucksack of some kind sailed out the door. A lone figure followed it—a man dressed in tiger fatigues.

Special Forces, thought O'Connor, as he saw the man hit and roll. Who the hell is that idiot?

CHAPTER 26

TAP ... TAP ... TAP ... tap. . . .

I rolled over and opened one eye against the glare of the morning sun beaming in through the opening in the tent, unaware of the troubles of my comrades and the test I would face in the coming hours. Another droplet of water slipped from the canvas flap at the doorway to continue the soft tattoo on the slatted wooden floor. It must have rained sometime during the night.

The morning wasn't far along and already the heat was becoming unbearable. I got to my feet, slipped into my jungle fatigues, and headed down the path between two rows of tents.

As I stepped past the last two, I saw the jeep parked in front of one of them. A small, attentive group of men were gathered around the front of the vehicle listening to a chaplain delivering a sermon in a quiet voice. A white cloth was spread across the hood with a cross standing in the middle.

I stopped a moment, removed my bush hat, and made the sign of the cross. I don't think he was Catholic; it didn't matter. He was a man of God, and out here where death was constantly at our elbow, it was always comforting to be reminded that God was also at our side.

The chaplain spoke of faith in the face of the trials to be confronted that day, whatever form they might take. And he reminded his listeners that no matter what sacrifices they made, there was One who had gone before who had made the supreme sacrifice. On Him they could lean and rely.

The service ended, and I walked away, hearing his final words as I turned a corner: "May the peace of God go with you."

All thoughts of the service vanished as I saw two men running hard ahead of me down the narrow pathway. They turned left at the mess tent, heading for the airstrip. Something was up. I thought they were pilots, but I couldn't be sure; they were too far ahead of me.

At the intersection, I decided against following them and instead went around the mess tent into the Special Forces communications tent. If there was action out in the field, the operator there monitoring the network radio would be picking it up.

The static from the radio greeted me as I stepped through the door—except that it wasn't static. I could hear the chatter of automatic weapons coming from the speaker and the thump of mortar rounds landing. And the voice of someone cursing and crying for help in English.

The radioman looked up at me, his eyes wide and helpless. We were alone in the tiny room.

"Who is it?" I asked, staring at the radio as if it would be the one to answer.

"I don't know," the operator said. "But they're catchin' hell out there. He just now started the screamin' and cussin'."

I wheeled and ran from the tent. They'd be trying to get whoever it was out, and everyone who could help would be needed at the airstrip. As I ran, I tried to think who it could be. I knew that Wright and his men had left that morning—at least I knew their mission had been scheduled—but there was no way for me to know how many teams were out. One thing I did know: One team was in bad trouble.

People were milling around the airstrip, gathering around the radio to listen to the excited conversation in the air, and then walking away to look expectantly at the western sky. I joined the group around the radio.

It was difficult to make sense of the talk among the airmen over the combat zone. We could tell that one of the gunships had gone down—Curry's—and then we heard the report that McKibben had picked up the crew and was returning to Loc Ninh with them.

Within minutes, we heard the familiar flutter of a returning chopper. It came in straight and low, landing with a jolt that must have rattled the teeth of everyone inside.

It was McKibben with the downed gunship crew. His passengers piled out. I did not see any injured among them. But McKibben's chopper was pretty badly shot up, and he shut his engine down to refuel and make a damage check before heading back into the area of operations.

As the whine of his turbine died, we could hear the approach of another helicopter. This time it was Hoffman and Waggie, also coming in hard and fast. As the aircraft rocked to a halt, I saw the bullet holes. There didn't appear to be a single section of the chopper that hadn't been chewed up. It seemed a miracle it could still fly.

Then I saw Craig. He was in bad shape, that was obvious. I helped lower him to the ground and cradled him in my arms. He was conscious and gasping for air, struggling to live. It was obvious he was dying.

"Where are the medics?" I called. "He needs help quick." But they hadn't arrived yet. "Hold on, Mike," was all I could say. "We're going to take care of you."

"What do you think, Sarge?" It was Waggie, kneeling by my side.

I turned away from the wounded man so he couldn't hear me. "I don't think he's goin' to make it."

Craig stiffened in my grasp and I turned back to him. He stared at me—through me. "Oh my God, my mother and father. . . ."

And he died.

"Goddamnit," cursed Waggie from beside me.

"Cool it," I snapped at the warrant officer, dropping protocol. Waggie stared angrily at me for a moment and then got up and went back to inspecting the damage to his chopper. I knew he wasn't angry at me for the way I had addressed a superior officer. He was pissed at the war, God, the enemy, himself, the army—everything and everybody that had a hand in the death of a soldier who couldn't have been over twenty years old.

I lowered the body gently to the hard ground and got to my feet. Waggie was standing next to the fuselage, his back to me. I stepped up behind him.

"What's going on in there?" I asked. "Which team is catching it?"

He didn't turn. "It's that Black soldier's team."

Oh, shit—Wright, O'Connor, and Mousseau. It was getting worse by the minute.

I heard cursing from McKibben's slick about sixty feet away. It had failed to start again. Someone called for the battery from Hoffman and Waggie's chopper, and I watched with mounting excitement as the ground crew moved to jump-start McKibben for the second time.

He was going back in. All I had to do was stand by and watch him and his crew go. Or—and the thought sent a chill through me as I looked at the battered fuselages of both slicks—I could go with them. After all, they would need a bellyman.

But I also heard the voices of the chopper crews, snatches of conversation that burned their way into my brain as I stood there in the hot sun.

". . . Never saw ground fire like that before. . . ."

". . . If there's not at least a battalion of NVA down there, you can kiss my ass. . . ."

". . . Battalion, hell, there's between six and ten thousand of 'em out there. . . ."

". . . There's armor, I know that. . . ."

The howl of the turbine on McKibben's slick drowned out the rest. It was just as well. As the blades began to slice through the soupy air, I knew I was going to be on that chopper when it took off. Before reason returned, I ran to the slick and climbed aboard just as he lifted free of the ground.

"What the hell you doin', Sergeant?" It was McKibben staring over his shoulder at me.

"I'm going with you, sir," I said buckling in. "You need a bellyman."

He shrugged and turned back to his instruments. Loc Ninh was soon behind, and I had time to think of what I had just done. I must be crazy, I thought. Minutes later I knew I was crazy; I heard the first snap and crackle of small-arms fire from below. I crossed myself for the second time that day.

Both door gunners cut loose, and I grabbed a set of headphones in order to listen in on the conversation between the pilot and the

C&C, FAC, or whoever was directing traffic out there. I couldn't tell who was telling what to whom, but I did hear McKibben's request for a status report on the area and the reply: "I don't think you can get in there. They're almost overrun."

"What's goin' on?" I asked McKibben through the microphone on my headset. I could hear the others, but I could only talk to the pilot in our aircraft.

"It's too hot. I don't think we can make it."

"Just get me close as you can," I replied. "I'll get to them."

As I listened again to McKibben's exchange with the voice I now took to be the C&C, requesting vectors to the PZ, the realization stole over me that I had probably talked them into letting me commit suicide. But I knew I had a duty—to my country and to my buddies. It didn't occur to me to be scared. I was going in! No doubt about it now!

Looking around the interior of the slick for something to take with me, I found a pack filled with medical supplies. That I knew I would need. As to weapons, there were none to be had. All I had on me was my Special Forces knife, a wicked Bowie-style weapon, great for hand-to-hand combat but not much use against armor and machine guns.

There was a web belt with ammo pouches. McKibben said that after he dropped me off, he would fly toward the SF position to orient me and drop them the ammunition.

We flew into the firefight like a runaway roller coaster, madly banking first one way and then another to throw off the enemy gunners raking our craft from below. I continued to make the sign of the cross like a madman. That and hold on were the only two things I could do—until the chopper suddenly dropped and I felt myself thrown forward against my seat belt.

Through the door I saw tree trunks level with the chopper. We were in a clearing. Unbuckling, tossing the headset aside, and without stopping to think—if I had I probably wouldn't have budged—I tossed the bag containing the medical supplies out the door and rolled out after it.

I fell about ten feet to the grass below. It was the first of many shocks that day. I hadn't realized that the pilot was that far off the ground. I rolled like a good paratrooper and came to a crouching position as the chopper banked and headed for the tops of a tree line that looked to be over a hundred yards away.

I didn't realize it then, but the next six hours were going to be the longest—and the most frightening—of my life.

CHAPTER 27

LOOKING AROUND IN the tall grass, I soon found the sack with the medical equipment. The air around me vibrated with the roar of combat; it seemed to come from every direction. Thank God McKibben had flown out over the team's position. Otherwise, I wouldn't have known which way to go.

Although from the sound, there certainly were a lot of people shooting guns all around me, no one seemed to have singled me out yet as I crouched there, my fatigues blending with the waving grass. I knew that was all going to change in about two seconds. I took a few deep breaths, swallowed hard, crossed myself one last time, and took off in a running crouch in the same direction taken by McKibben as he had made his exit.

I had covered between twenty-five and fifty yards when I felt a thorn snag my right pants leg at the calf and send a small flash of pain through the muscle. A few feet further, I dropped to the ground and began calling the team leader's name as softly as I could.

"Leroy . . . Leroy, can you hear me?" There was no answer.

I reached down to scratch the sting in my leg where the thorn had slashed me and discovered, instead of a tiny pinprick, a rip in either side of my pants leg and a bullet hole completely through the fleshy part of my calf. I knew then that I was running on adrenaline when I mistook a bullet wound for the jab of a thorn.

"Ben . . . Is that you?" It was Mousseau, the assistant team leader of the mission.

"Yeah, Frenchy. Hold on, I'll be there in a minute." Forgetting the bullet wound in my leg, I ran forward again, falling to the ground and rolling the last few yards to Mousseau's position as small-arms fire slashed through the grass around me.

I lay flat with my face pressed to the earth, the scent of the grass pleasant after the ever-present stench of JP4 in the chopper and the bitter odor of smoke from explosives and burning underbrush which had greeted me upon my arrival. Getting back to my knees, I looked around, stunned at the sight that greeted me.

The team's "position" barely qualified as one—a few trees bunched together and some high grass made a poor defense against grenades, mortars, and automatic weapons fire. The immediate terrain was as flat as a table top.

And there was blood everywhere. The six men bunched together seemed to a man to be wounded. I crawled to Mousseau who had half propped himself up against the trunk of a tree and examined his wounds. He had taken a round in his shoulder and his head was a mess. Shot in the eye, one side of his face looked as if someone had sledgehammered it. But he was conscious and able to fire his weapon. I made the rounds of the remaining five CIDGs. Their wounds were patched up as well as could be expected.

The firing had died down from the other side after I disappeared from the enemy's view. From what I had heard back at Loc Ninh of the NVA's strength on the ground here and their tremendous fire-power, the fact that these men were still alive was a flat-out miracle.

The other side could have overrun these guys at any time. There was absolutely nothing over here that was capable of withstanding an all-out assault. Looking toward the far side of the PZ, which was still ablaze in spots, I could see no signs of the enemy. They evidently couldn't see us either. Uncertain of our strength, they hesitated to move, being content for the moment to fire occasionally at suspected movement or sounds. Also, the intense pounding they had received from the air had dampened their enthusiasm.

I managed to get the men moved around into a bit more effective defensive situation. I positioned them so that they could cover the part of the PZ where, according to Mousseau, the remainder of the team lay.

Getting on Mousseau's emergency radio, I contacted McKibben. "You better come in and get us pretty quick," I said. "We're in pretty bad shape down here." He rogered and I told Mousseau to get his men ready to go.

I caught a glimpse of O'Connor behind a mound of dirt and gave him a thumbs up. He nodded his head.

"O'Connor, are you okay?" I called.

"Ammo," he replied.

"Okay. Who's alive?" He raised two fingers. Only two out of the four. I couldn't see Leroy, and I didn't hold out much hope that he was the other one.

"Can you make it over here? We're goin' out." He nodded again, and I saw him pull another man toward him. Together, they began to half crawl and stumble toward us. I couldn't see much of the other guy, but I could tell he wasn't black—Leroy was dead.

A slick sliced down out of the sky, the door gunners raking the far tree line with machine gun fire. They were answered with automatic weapons. O'Connor and the other man dropped down as the NVA also opened up on our positions. I rose up a bit and motioned the two back.

When the bullet hit, it felt like someone had slammed me in the right thigh with a baseball bat. There wasn't that much pain at first, but a numbness spread quickly throughout the right side of my body. I fell back, expecting another round at any moment. Then the pain began, spreading like a small hot fire through my leg. God, I hoped I would be able to walk.

After a couple of passes, strafing to drive the NVA back as far as possible, McKibben's chopper disappeared. Maybe the enemy would lie low long enough—expecting him to make another strafing run—so he could slip in and pick us up.

I turned back to the radio. "Okay, I'm throwing smoke now," and I lofted a smoke grenade toward the center of the PZ. "Identify the smoke," I called, as green billows coiled up from the grass.

Moments later came the reply: "I see green smoke."

"Come and get us. We'll be ready."

In he came again, door guns still blazing away at the enemy positions. But this time he headed directly for the smoke.

"Everybody!" I shouted. "If you can move, head for the slick. Let's go!" Although the CIDGs couldn't understand the words, there was no way to miss the meaning.

I jumped to my feet, the right leg almost buckling as the pain snatched the breath from me. Pulling and shoving, shouting all the time, I herded the dazed men toward the settling chopper.

The air was alive with the roar of the slick's turbines, the chatter of its machine guns, and the answering hammer blows from the far side of the PZ. Somehow we made it just as the helicopter touched down.

"Get in! Get in! Get in!" I shouted over and over. The men inside pulled them in as fast as they could, yanking some of them off their feet and literally throwing them into the chopper's interior.

"We've got to get the others," I shouted to McKibben, pointing toward where O'Connor and the other survivor lay. "Follow me."

Somewhere along the way I had picked up an AK-47. I ran toward O'Connor, spraying the tree line to the side with the weapon on full automatic. McKibben lifted off and like a puppy at heel followed at my side.

By God, I thought, we're going to make it. Just a few seconds more. I was lightheaded from the pain, fear, and adrenaline surging through my body.

McKibben stopped short of the trees and I hit the ground beside O'Connor.

"Can you walk?" I asked when I saw how badly he was wounded.

"Yeah, I think so," he muttered. He had lost a lot of blood. "But I don't think he can," pointing to the unconscious man near him. I recognized the interpreter who had been assigned to the operation.

"Where's Leroy?"

"Over there; he's dead."

"Is there anything still on him?"

"He still has the SOI and some maps in that green pouch in his shirt."

The Standard Operating Instructions were classified material and couldn't fall into enemy hands. I would have to retrieve them. I crawled to the interpreter's side and shook him. "C'mon, let's go." He stirred and blinked at me.

"Don't leave me," he whispered.

"I won't. Just crawl toward O'Connor. We're goin' to get you out. Let's go."

He started crawling with me alongside pulling. I caught sight of movement in the grass about twenty feet away. Instinctively, I yanked two grenades from the Vietnamese's belt, pulled the pins and threw them toward the motion. Two NVA jumped to their feet and attempted to run. Twin explosions caught them in midstride and sent them tumbling.

Pushing and pleading, I got the interpreter to O'Connor's side.

"Try to get to the slick," I told the radioman. "I'm going to get the SOI." Seeing he had nothing but a .22 caliber pistol, I handed him the AK-47. "Go ahead, I'll be right behind you."

Turning from the two men as they struggled toward the waiting helicopter, I ran to Wright. Crouching beside the dead man, I reached inside his shirt and pulled out the pouch. I felt the moisture on my cheeks and realized I was crying.

I won't leave you behind, Leroy, I thought. I owe you that. Grasping him under his arms, I tried to lift him to my shoulders.

Another baseball bat crashed into me, catching me full in the back. I dropped Leroy and pitched forward, feeling the blackness reach out for me. Before I lost consciousness, maybe even as I was falling, I heard the roar of a massive explosion behind me. The slick, I thought, as the blackness closed in.

CHAPTER 28

THE THOUGHT CAME to me: That has to be the brightest, bluest sky I've ever seen. It reminds me of a summer day back home when the heat of a Texas summer burns every trace of cloud away. I just need to move a bit from this uncomfortable position on my back so I . . .

I felt a red hot spike bore into me. I think I screamed; I don't know for sure. The pain cut through the daze and confusion and brought me back to the realization of where I was. The silence of the daydream vanished as the roar of combat washed over me again.

One thing I knew. I was hurt—bad. That last blow had been a bullet in the back. Forcing myself over onto my stomach, I managed to get to my knees. It was difficult to breathe, and the entire left side of my shirt was soaked with blood. It only took a moment to find the source. There was a ragged hole under my left armpit. It was the exit wound. God only knew what damage had been done to my insides as the round had gone through my body.

A wave of dizziness rolled over me and I almost pitched forward again. The pain was terrible. If I didn't get up now—right now—and get to the chopper, I was going to join Leroy here among the other dead.

The chopper! Where was the chopper? I was staring crazily at the trees in front of me. It's behind you, you idiot, I thought—in the clearing. Shaking my head to clear the cobwebs from my brain, I staggered to my feet, and turned to run for the waiting slick. I would have to leave Leroy; there was no time left. And I didn't think I had the strength to carry the body of my friend.

I stopped dead in my tracks, forgetting in my horror that I was exposing myself to the enemy. The helicopter was a smoking ruin, lying on its side at the edge of the tree line. Debris from the downed slick, including the rotor blades, had been flung into the center of the PZ. Men were still clawing their way out of the wreckage. That last explosion I had heard had been the helicopter slamming nose first into the ground.

I managed to run the short distance to the craft's side. Elated at their success in bringing the chopper down, the NVA were pouring a murderous hail of gunfire into it, trying to finish off the survivors.

I saw McKibben through the cockpit window. He was covered with blood, slumped over dead against his straps. The engine had broken free, and one of the door gunners had been crushed as part of the transmission had crashed into the cabin. His eyes wide, almost ready to pop right from his face from the tremendous weight resting on him, he stared at me as I dived for shelter beside the smoking fuselage.

Fernan, the copilot, came around the nose, waving a .38 wildly. A tree limb had slammed into the window beside him, and a bloody stub of a branch protruded from his ear.

McKibben had been shot, he told me, and had lost control. There had been nothing he could do; it had happened too fast.

He was almost babbling, dazed and obviously in great pain from his wound.

"Put that gun down before you kill someone," I told him. He stopped and stood looking at the pistol as if it was the first time he had ever seen one. The effort to speak bent me over in a coughing fit, and I began to spit up blood. It felt like my guts would be next.

Hearing cries from inside the slick, I moved to the door and helped what looked like the last man crawl out through the mangled opening. About ten feet away from the crash, I saw O'Connor lying on his back in the grass. Alongside lay the interpreter. They apparently had never made it to the chopper.

A CIDG member of Mousseau's segment of the team was crouched at my feet. He appeared to be only slightly wounded, compared to the others. Reaching down, I grabbed his collar and pointed toward O'Connor.

"Radio, radio," I said. He nodded and crawled toward the radioman.

When he reached the Green Beret, he attempted to unstrap the radio. "Connors, Connors," I heard him call. "Radio—radio."

To my surprise, O'Connor rolled over and looked at me.

"O'Connor, are you okay," I shouted.

"I think so," came his reply.

Looking around, the desperate nature of our situation was clear. There were eleven of us, including six surviving CIDGs, O'Connor, Mousseau, Fernan, and the other door gunner whose name I didn't know.

Mousseau, the door gunner, and three CIDGs had made their way to the broken tail section and were returning the enemy's fire.

The smell of JP4 was everywhere, the slick was smoking badly now, and I feared the whole mess was going to blow up in our faces.

I sent the remaining CIDGs to join O'Connor. "Get to the front, away from the chopper," I shouted. "Try to set up a perimeter over there." I pointed to a small clump of trees.

"We need ammo and weapons," he responded.

"Never mind that. This thing's either gonna blow on its own or someone's gonna do it for us. Get the guns and ammo from the dead."

Mousseau must have heard me. He and his men began crawling toward another stand of trees off to the side away from the chopper's tail section.

One of the CIDGs left O'Connor's side and ran to me, carrying two radios. I saw that O'Connor still had one emergency set with him. As he crawled away, he called back, shouting that the black one was for a Vietnamese monitor in the C&C and probably wouldn't be much good.

I followed Mousseau's group and found them clustered together around three trees, hidden by the waving grass. We were no more than forty feet from O'Connor and the others. Looking back, I saw that we weren't as far from the downed helicopter as I would have liked. The men around me were in bad shape, however, and they had dragged themselves as far as their strength could carry them. The constant pain was draining me also. But I thought, what the hell, this'll have to do.

We heard the whoosh of the incoming mortar rounds and hit the ground, hugging it tight as the explosions blossomed around the smoking ruin of the slick. Over and over, the earth heaved as the enemy searched for us.

After awhile—it's difficult to measure time accurately when death is dancing all around you—the barrage eased and I grabbed the emergency radio and contacted the FAC. I wiped my forehead with my hand, and it came away stained red. Scores of tiny shards of shrapnel had lodged in my scalp, and the bleeding threatened to blind me.

"For God's sake, we need help," I called. "Bring in some air support." The FAC asked for target identification, and I called for strikes as close to our position as I dared. Within minutes, the F-4s closed in and began dropping their loads. The gunships were pinwheeling overhead, hammering the jungle below them with machine gun fire.

While the enemy was laying low under the pounding, I got out the medical kit and began giving morphine shots all around. I gave myself two. Mousseau and one of the CIDGs were in extremely bad shape. The CIDG's belly was ripped wide open, and his intestines were hanging out. Insects were buzzing all around the wound, and the stench in the sweltering heat was terrible. While I bandaged him, he begged me in Vietnamese to kill him.

Mousseau was only half conscious from loss of blood. All I could do was try to make him as comfortable as possible.

The air strikes didn't seem to be having much effect on our tormentors. As soon as the fighters and gunships would move away, the fire from across the way would increase, seeming to grow more ferocious with each passing minute. The sounds around us were like a great wind whipping through the grass and the leaves above our heads.

The air support returned for another run, and I took the opportunity to crawl to O'Connor, dragging the medical supplies and the radio with me. Part way there, I felt another kick in my butt, and I knew I had been hit again. I dropped flat and lay still for a few minutes. The morphine kept it from hurting too much, but I lay there anyway, crying, feeling the tears cut through the blood and dirt that had formed a crust on my face.

I moved on toward O'Connor. He must have seen me take the hit, because when I reached his side, he asked me how bad was it.

"Shit, man, I don't know. I been hit so many times I can't feel nothing anymore."

I gave O'Connor another shot of morphine—it was his third he said. He was cross-eyed from the dope.

"Go easy on the ammo," I told him. "Just wait for anyone that tries to make it across toward us." He nodded.

While the air strike continued, one of the CIDGs and I crawled forward until we found a couple of NVA bodies. We dragged them back to O'Connor's position and piled them in front to form a human barricade. I saw another body lying several feet away and motioned the CIDG to follow me and help. Before we had crawled five feet, we came under intense automatic weapons fire and tried to make it back to O'Connor.

I took another hit in my leg, and the CIDG screamed as a bullet plowed into his stomach. I dragged him the remaining distance to O'Connor's side. The radioman was lying flat, and I saw an ugly hole over his left kidney where a piece of shrapnel had torn into him. I looked for the radio, but couldn't find it. I shook O'Connor.

"Where's the radio," I exclaimed. But he only groaned. I caught a glimpse of it under his body and pulled it free. The signal was weak; the batteries were giving out. Just like us, I thought.

I managed to contact someone—I was no longer sure who I was talking to, but I managed to point out the direction from which the latest burst of fire had come. Within seconds, a blast of rocket fire from overhead took out the attackers.

"I think I got another morphine Syrette in my back pocket," muttered O'Connor. I fished out two, gave him another injection and myself one. All the time, I was talking, babbling through the pain and morphine haze, telling him that it was going to be all right, that we were going to get out.

Taking some fresh dressings out of his harness, I rebandaged his wounds, put one on the CIDG's abdomen, and tightened the tourniquet on the interpreter's arm.

Getting on the radio, I called again for more air strikes. Someone, a faint voice forcing itself through the dying radio, asked for our position. I looked at O'Connor; I wasn't sure anymore where we were.

"Which way is that helicopter?" I asked him.

"I think it's due west," he said.

I shook my head. The morphine was making it hard to think. But that didn't seem right. I just didn't know, and if I called in the strikes wrong, we'd be roasted by our own planes. I was out of smoke, so there was no way to mark our position.

"Never mind," came the voice from above. "We've got you spotted. Get down; they're goin' to be comin' in low and close."

"Cover me," I said to O'Connor. "I'm going back over to Mousseau. Try to hang on a little longer."

I began crawling; the forty feet separating the two mauled clumps of men stretching out like forty miles. I could hear the pop and crackle behind me as O'Connor and his men attempted to suppress the enemy fire. The bullets hissed and whined around me like a swarm of angry bees. There was no way our pathetic little band could lay down enough firepower to hold them off.

By some miracle, I reached the trees under which Mousseau and his men lay. The Vietnamese with the stomach wound was still crying loudly for someone to kill him.

It was impossible now to tell from which direction the fire was coming. The NVA had apparently succeeded in surrounding us. We were in the middle of hell. Every movement brought a hail of gunfire. Men were crying and screaming for help. I was one of them. We were going to die. There was no doubt of that now.

Suddenly, the scream of the jets rose above it all. In they came, low, their afterburners scorching the treetops below. The roar of rockets and bombs falling almost on top of us rocked us from side to side as we lay cowering in the slight cover. The heat from the airplane engines and the continuous explosions was tremendous. There seemed to be no end to the pounding as we were showered with burning branches, hot metal, and dirt.

Again and again they came. Smoke and fire and the insane howl of the jets seen and felt through a narcotic haze. I wouldn't have been surprised if a demon with a pitchfork in hand had appeared in the midst of the flames and welcomed me personally to hell.

Just as quickly as they had appeared, they were gone. Overhead, helicopter gunships moved in, circling our position and spraying the scorched jungle below. I saw one of them lurch and plummet into the trees near us. Minutes later, the wounded crew members crawled to us. Come to help us, they would now die with us.

"Get away! Get away!" I shouted into the handset I still clutched. "You'll give us away." As if the gooks needed directions to find us.

I don't know if anyone heard me, but the wagon wheel of choppers dispersed.

"Okay, get ready, we're coming in to get you." I stared dumbly at the radio. What had he said? How in hell could they get us out now? Around me, the firing had died down; the massive air strikes had taken their toll—for the moment.

But I knew that the enemy would soon regroup and be back on the attack. They had come back at us like mad dogs each time the fighters and gunships had left. The scene around me looked like the site of a massacre. It was difficult to tell who remained alive. We couldn't withstand another assault, and I think the other side realized it.

After the continuous roar of the jets and the circling gunships, the stutter of a single helicopter just out of sight over the treetops seemed oddly out of place. The lone slick whipped through the smoke into the center of the PZ and settled to earth some twenty to thirty meters from us. Warrant Officer Roger Waggie was at the controls. Our ride was here, and it was the most beautiful sight I had ever seen.

Overhead, the gunships appeared again and began firing into the jungle around us. It was now or never. We had to get moving.

"All right, goddamnit!" I shouted above the roar of the choppers and machine gun fire. "We don't have permission to die here. Let's go!"

A Special Forces medic, a Sergeant Sammons, jumped from the slick and ran to our position. He and I began to push, pull, and carry as many of the wounded as we could to the waiting chopper. Precious seconds were ticking away, and despite the covering fire from above, the enemy was firing point blank at the craft. I saw two of the men we helped aboard lurch forward and crash to the deck, shot in the back. They were picking us off as we climbed aboard. The door gunner, Warrant Officer Bill Darling, was laying down a blistering barrage over our heads, trying to buy just a little more time.

I turned and ran back, looking for anyone who might still be alive. Half-blinded by the blood still running into my eyes, the morphine, pain, and loss of blood were turning the surroundings into a dreamy swirl where all I could see was the ground directly in front of me.

I found Mousseau lying in the grass. He was still alive. I managed to get my arms around him, hoisted him over my shoulder, and headed back toward the chopper.

I staggered under Mousseau's dead weight. I was so intent on just taking one step after another, I didn't notice one of the NVA bodies stir as I passed. Halfway to the slick, my head exploded, sending me reeling forward, a fireworks display of lights erupting within my skull that guttered out immediately, threatening to plunge me into the blackness of unconsciousness.

I don't even remember dropping Mousseau, but I must have because when everything suddenly clicked back into place, I found myself standing upright and Mousseau was gone from my back. I hadn't gone down. Whirling, I saw the enemy soldier standing not three feet from me. Almost no time had passed; he was just pulling his rifle back from slamming the butt of the weapon into the back of my head.

There was a look of surprise on his face that I was still standing. His astonishment was replaced by a snarl as he leaped forward again. Dazed and reeling from his first attack, I was helpless to avoid him. I recognized the AK-47 just as he clubbed me in the mouth with it, snapping my head back. Again the lights flashed before my eyes, and this time I went down.

I was beyond thinking; reflex alone sent my right hand to the Special Forces knife at my belt. I had no other weapon. Forcing my fingers to close around the haft, I pulled it free.

His eyes widened further at the sight of the eighteen inches of razor-sharp polished steel in my hand. Immediately, he brought his weapon down, pointing the bayonet fixed to the end at my belly. Why he had not used it on me at the beginning of his attack I didn't know, but as I watched the needle point making tiny circles in the air before me, I was grateful that it had not been his first choice.

He hesitated for only a fraction of a second, but that was all the time I needed to begin scrambling to my feet. Then, like the single fang of a deadly reptile, the bayonet snaked out as he lunged forward, attempting to disembowel me with one thrust. I twisted to the right and felt its honed edge slice into my left forearm. I clamped the arm down onto the blade, trapping it, and somehow regained my footing.

"Shoot him! Shoot him!" I shouted at the wounded O'Connor, not realizing at the time that he had too much morphine in him to see anything but a haze.

Then with a scream, I forced the much smaller man to his knees as I slammed my knife into his side with all the force I could muster. He only grunted as he felt it cut deep into him.

Frantically, he tried to pull the bayonet free, slicing my arm to ribbons as he sawed it back and forth. But it was too late. Again and again, I plunged the Bowie-style knife into his ribs, still screaming at the top of my lungs.

Like lovers in an embrace, we knelt while the sounds of the battle still raged around us. I felt the life leave him as he began to sag against me. Pushing him away when I felt his grip on the rifle loosen, I looked him in the eyes. Only a few moments before they were bright with the insane light of combat. Now they stared dully at me, and blood flowed from the now slack mouth.

"You rice-eatin' son of a bitch!" I spat at him as I slammed him face down into the grass. My knife was still embedded in his ribs. I tried to pull it free, but it had lodged tight in a bone, and in my weakened condition, I couldn't retrieve it.

Mousseau was lying beside the dead NVA. Somehow, I managed to lift him and the enemy's AK-47 at the same time. With the limp assistant team leader over my left shoulder and the automatic weapon cradled in my right arm, I resumed my trip back to the slick.

As I approached the chopper, I saw two NVAs leap from cover near the tail of the aircraft and charge it. The door gunners were blasting away over my head, and didn't see the new danger. Even if they had, their guns couldn't traverse enough to cover the rear.

Bringing the AK-47 up, I opened fire and cut the two men down as they ran toward the open doors. Warrant Officer Darling, the door gunner, was startled at the sudden burst of gunfire virtually under his nose. Instinctively, he snapped the barrel of his weapon around toward me, pointing the smoking muzzle into my face. For the frantic moment before he recognized me, I thought I was going to die, blown away by one of my own comrades.

I heaved Mousseau in through the door. Turning, I saw the medic, Sammons, trying to help O'Connor cover the last few yards to the chopper. Intense fire had pinned them down, and they were crawling, O'Connor leaving a trail of blood through the tall grass.

I ran toward him, but he motioned behind him, shouting that his interpreter was still back there.

"Okay, okay," was all I could get out through my ruined mouth. I didn't know how much more I could take. And the slick had been on the ground almost two minutes—it seemed an eternity—and was not going to be able to remain much longer. It was taking a terrific pounding. Normally, during an insertion or extraction, the time spent unloading or loading was measured in seconds. If I didn't find the man quick, they would have to leave me behind.

Firing into the brush as I ran—I didn't want any more surprises—I retraced the short, bloody trail left by O'Connor and found the interpreter within seconds. Lifting him to my shoulder, I ran back and dumped him in the chopper.

I decided I should take one more look around to make sure we weren't leaving anyone behind. That's when I picked up the three NVAs, thinking they were my CIDG comrades.

I got to the slick just as Waggie applied power. The skids were beginning to tap dance on the blood-soaked, trampled grass as it prepared to lift off. Turning my back to the door, I felt the weight being lifted from my shoulders. I could hardly see because of the blood flowing into my eyes, so I must have sensed movement out there in front of me.

With my back to the helicopter, I lifted the AK-47 and began spraying the undergrowth. Unseen hands clamped onto the collar and back of my shirt and dragged me up and back into the shadows of the slick as I dropped the still-chattering weapon.

CHAPTER 29

AFTER THE TERRIFYING experience with the body bag at Loc Ninh—and with my identity firmly established once again—the medics prepared me for the flight by chopper to the hospital in Saigon. The preparation wasn't much—there wasn't much time if any of us were going to live—but at least I got my face cleaned of some of the clotted blood so that I could see fairly well again.

As they loaded me aboard the chopper I noticed Mousseau lying on another stretcher on the floor. He watched me with the only eye he had left. As the chopper lifted from the Loc Ninh pad, I reached toward him, and we clasped hands. We sailed through the Vietnamese skies holding desperately to life and to each other.

Minutes away from the doctors in Saigon, I felt his fingers dig into my palm, his arm twitching and jumping as if an electric current was pouring through his body into mine. I forced his face into focus and saw his eye widen, staring full into my face, and pain and fear radiating from him like a heat wave.

He blinked once, the grip loosened, and his face softened as his eyelid drooped. It was like a brightly lit candle guttering and going out as I watched.

No, Mousseau, don't leave me now. We're almost home, man— don't go now.

I struggled to lift my head and call out to the pilots, the only two in the chopper with us. I don't know how the pilot heard the gurgle that escaped my lips above the roar of the engine, but he glanced over his shoulder at me twisting and turning, flopping like a landed fish.

"My God, he's strangling!" I heard him yell to the copilot. "Get back there."

The copilot was at my side in a second. "Free his windpipe," ordered the pilot, and I saw the knife blade in the man's hand.

A knife! The son of a bitch thought I was suffocating and was going to give me a tracheotomy or maybe cut my throat in the attempt.

"Unh, uh! Unh, uh!" I spluttered, still unable to speak, as I pushed him away as he brought the blade to my throat. I pointed to Mousseau. It took him only a split second to realize that it was Mousseau who needed help, not me.

He knelt beside the dying man, his back to me, blocking my view. For a long minute he crouched there, while I squeezed Mousseau's hand over and over, praying for another miracle.

The flier turned to me, reached down and pulled Mousseau's limp hand from my grip. He finally looked at me, shook his head, placed the dead man's arm under the blanket and pulled the blanket over his head.

I closed my eyes. As the copilot crawled over me, back to his seat, I felt the helicopter begin to descend on its final approach to Saigon. The tears came, and I cried until unconsciousness ended my misery.

The days that followed my arrival back in Saigon are blurred by the narcotic haze of heavy doses of pain medication. One operation followed another as doctors struggled to keep me alive. The one bright spot came on the day when, bandaged like a mummy and with tubing stuck into every part of my body where a doctor could find an opening, I recognized a familiar face in a bed across the ward I shared with other wounded soldiers—O'Connor! He was alive.

He looked to be in about as bad a shape as I was. Neither of us could move or talk, but each morning we would wiggle our toes at each other to prove that we had made it through another night.

I opened my eyes one morning . . . afternoon? I couldn't tell one from the other, or even if it was still 1968. But anyway, there stood Colonel Drake over my bed. He smiled when he saw I was awake.

"I knew my little Indian buddy could make it," he said, and my eyes filled with tears. With my mouth stitched and bandaged shut, I couldn't talk, but I reached for him with my good right arm. He took my hand, and I went back to sleep.

Sometime during those endless days and nights, I was moved to another ward—or maybe O'Connor moved. Or maybe he died. I didn't know, and no one told me. I was consumed with my own battle to live. Twice they opened my side up, searching for bullet fragments. They found one lodged near my heart—they decided to leave it alone. An attempt to remove it would likely kill me.

Colonel Drake continued his visits. After the doctors had removed enough cotton from my mouth to allow me to mumble a few words, I managed to ask him if the papers and a camera I had found on Wright's body had been recovered.

He straightened and looked at me with disbelief. "Goddamnit, Roy, here you almost get yourself killed and all you want to know about are some papers and a camera."

Well, I thought, that had been part of my mission as I saw it. Knowing that those classified items had gotten into the right hands would help make the misery I was going through a little more bearable. I told him so.

"Don't worry, Roy, it's all been taken care of. You just get well and get out of here."

I nodded. That's all I wanted to know.

A Red Cross volunteer, a wonderful lady who came in every day, wrote a letter to Lala for me. I knew she had probably received a telegram announcing that I had been wounded. But I also knew the message had not told her much. In the letter, I told her I was as well as could be expected, and that I would be home as soon as I was able.

Then one day they told me I was going to Japan where I would eventually be processed on to the States. By then, I was able to stand—barely—for very short periods of time. I was not what you would call mobile by any stretch of the imagination.

On a stretcher I was transported to a waiting helicopter on the hospital grounds for the trip to Tan Son Nhat. Then it was on to Tokyo, another hospital, and a long stay there.

One day slipped into another, made bearable only by the knowledge that at least I knew I was going to live. And unlike the first time I left South Vietnam on a stretcher, this time I was aware of who I was and what had happened to me. It made a big difference in tolerating the constant pain.

Then they came for me again with a stretcher and I heard the familiar engine of a chopper waiting on a lawn to take me to another airplane. I insisted on walking the few feet to the helicopter door.

A helpful medic attempted to help me on board and in doing so, he clasped his arms around my middle to lift me the few inches to the chopper deck. I almost passed out from the pain as he squeezed hard on the foot-long incision and those wire stitches along my side.

The scream came out as a high-pitched whine which was swept away in the roar of the helicopter, and I struggled to get free from this guy who was only trying to help me. But the more I fought him, the harder he tried to pick me up and put me aboard. He probably thought I was a psycho case who was afraid to fly again.

With as much strength as I could muster—which wasn't much—I took a swing at him with that all-purpose right arm and knocked him back and away from me. His grip loosened, and I stumbled against the side of the chopper. I set my back against the hull, and opened the front of my robe just as my helper recovered and headed toward me again.

When he saw that my entire midsection was covered by bandages, he stopped short and the realization of what he had been putting me through dawned on his face.

"God, Sergeant!" he shouted over the noise, "I'm sorry."

"Forget it," I managed to gasp. "I'm getting used to it." He probably didn't hear my muttering, but I didn't care. I just wanted to get the hell out of there.

Gently, he helped me aboard, and within hours I was asleep, sedated, out over the Pacific, and on my way home.

My final destination was again Brooke Army Medical Center in San Antonio. And wonder of wonders, Mrs. Garcia was there again at my side.

"My God, Sergeant Benavidez," said Mrs. Garcia, when she first saw me, "I thought we'd seen the last of you the last time you were in here."

"Yes, ma'am, so did I. This time I think I'm in a little bit worse shape than before."

The hospital was my home for most of the next year, 1969. Lala made regular trips to see me, and just like before we would sit in the dayroom and talk, watching the afternoons pass. Relatives came to see me occasionally. My cousin Janie even brought me a bottle of tequila which I hid in my pillowcase and sampled when no one was looking.

The wounds slowly healed. The grand total amounted to seven individual bullet wounds in my legs, stomach, butt, and back. When the shrapnel was added, it came out to about twenty-seven or twenty-eight holes in my body. Half of one lung had been removed during one of the operations and there were a couple of pieces of shrapnel lodged near my heart.

Sprinkled throughout my scalp and face were also tiny pieces of shrapnel which the doctors had not bothered to remove. All of that didn't even include my left arm which my NVA friend had tried to slice off with his bayonet. It took four individual operations to save the arm and make it even half useful to me again.

One hot summer day, the kind you have to live in South Texas to appreciate, I was lying in bed when in breezed a second lieutenant lugging a pasteboard box. He began calling out names in the ward. When a patient answered, the officer would pull out one, two, or even three medals and hand them to the man. Naturally, a Purple Heart was always one of them.

He was passing them out like prizes at a carnival show. It was certainly nothing like I would have expected for these men who had taken a bullet or worse for their country. But this was the Vietnam War, and there just didn't seem to be time for all the niceties of proper protocol.

"Benavidez, Roy P., Staff Sergeant," he shouted.

"Yessir, over here."

"Here you go, Sergeant," and he handed me four Purple Hearts.

He turned to go and then stopped. "Oh, here, I almost forgot. This is yours too," and handed me a small black box.

I opened it and just sat there, open-mouthed, and astonished at the contents. Nestled there in the velvet was the Distinguished Service Cross, the second-highest award presented by the U.S. military—second only to the Congressional Medal of Honor.

"Congratulations, Sergeant." I looked up and the lieutenant was beaming.

I stared back down at the gleaming medal, unbelieving. I had no idea I had been nominated for the DSC. And then the growing delight at the honor melted away. Even the rawest recruit should know that regulations required the DSC to be presented by a general—not handed out like a cereal premium by a second lieutenant.

The officer was turning to leave again. "Hey, Lieutenant," I said, "with all due respect, sir, it takes more than a second lieutenant to award this medal."

He wheeled and fixed me with a glare. He had more medals to hand out and he didn't want any shit from me. "Don't worry about it, Sergeant. You got it."

"Hold it a minute, Lieutenant. He's right—you can't do that." It was the ward master, a male nurse—a sergeant—in charge of our ward. He had walked up to the head of my bed and stood looking across at the officer.

"Can't do what? What're you talking about, Sergeant?" The lieutenant looked a little baffled now.

"That's a DSC isn't it?"

The officer looked down at the open box and its bright contents. "Yeah . . ." he answered uncertainly.

"Lieutenant, the Distinguished Service Cross"—the medic said it slowly and deliberately—"must be presented by a general officer."

"Now just a minute . . ." The young man was clearly confused. I think it was the word "general" that was bothering him.

"Sir, why don't we go check with someone who can straighten this out?" The ward master's voice lowered. "This could be embarrassing for everyone. Why don't you give me that, Benavidez?" And he took the medal out of my hands and handed it back to the lieutenant.

The two walked out of the ward, the lieutenant stammering an explanation to the ward master, "I tell you, Sergeant, I didn't have any idea. . . ."

They left behind silence. My ward mates stared first at me and then at the two retreating backs.

"I'll be damned," a guy across the room muttered. "I ain't never seen nothin' like that."

Twenty minutes later, the ward master returned alone and without the medal.

"Well, Roy," he said, stopping at the foot of my bed, "they'll be presenting that little doodad to you in a proper ceremony."

"Thanks," I replied, still a bit uncertain. A few minutes earlier I had actually had the DSC in my hands, regulations or no regulations, regardless of the rank of the officer who had handed it to me. Now, it was gone. Maybe they would change their minds.

But they didn't. In fact, it couldn't have turned out better. General Westmoreland, by then Chief of Staff of the U.S. Army, was scheduled to make a tour of the hospital and visit the wounded the second week of September, 1969. He would present the medal to me.

I didn't think the general would remember our encounter back when I had been his driver in Georgia, but as I stood at the side of my bed and he held the DSC, he surprised me as he addressed the assembled officers, my family, and the press.

"Many years ago, I met him at Fort Gordon, Georgia," the general said. "I was impressed with his appearance. I was impressed with the self-discipline that he displayed. I was impressed with him as a soldier. And I said, 'Sergeant Benavidez, you should go airborne.' He accepted my advice; I recruited him on the spot. He shortly went airborne and he's still a paratrooper, I believe. Aren't you, Sergeant?"

"Yes sir," I managed to answer, "and I will be one, sir, for a long time."

"You see the spirit that the sergeant has," Westmoreland went on. "This is the spirit that has won for him this very high award."

Interestingly enough, there was no mention in the citation of Cambodia. I was officially commended for action that took place in the Republic of Vietnam—South Vietnam. But that was okay with me. I knew where I almost died, and I knew why the army didn't want to mention it. After all, in 1968, we had no troops in Cambodia, so it would have been extremely difficult for me to have been shot there. I thought nothing—at that time—of the government's decision to shift the scene of action a bit to the east.

I lay in bed that night, holding the gleaming medal in my hand, letting the light overhead play on its surface. It was a wonderful feeling, the fitting end to a terrible experience. Or so I thought.

PART V

PURSUIT
OF
HONOR

CHAPTER 30

AFTER THE CEREMONY at Brooke and my eventual release from the hospital in May 1969, I returned to active duty and was assigned to temporary duty at Fort Devens in Massachusetts, headquarters of the 10th Special Forces Group. I even made a jump while I was there. But the experience convinced me my days of leaping from airplanes were nearing an end—I was hurt too badly to want to endure the punishment.

My tour at Devens was cut short by—of all things—the weather. Fort Devens is in the northeastern part of the state near the small town of Ayer. Members of the 10th SF Group went into the mountains of Vermont and New Hampshire for mountain training. And although the summer days were pleasant enough, the cool nights and mornings made my wounds ache to the point that at times I was almost incapable of functioning. Toward the end of summer, all I could think of was the coming of winter.

So it was with a great deal of excitement that I read in an edition of *The Army Times* that an old commanding officer of mine, General Robert Linville, for whom I had driven in the 82nd Airborne, was taking over as commander of the 1st Infantry Division at Fort Riley, Kansas.

I made a phone call to the general, explaining my situation and telling him that I was again available as a driver. I soon found the orders on my desk for my transfer to Kansas. It seemed to be the best I could hope for. I knew the Kansas winters weren't going to be much better than in Massachusetts, but at least the summers would be pleasant.

The next three years passed uneventfully on the Kansas plains. I did my job, enjoying the warmth of the summer sun and suffering through the icy winters. During that time, I even went on two exercises with the unit in West Germany. But my time in the field with the troops was over, although I hated to admit it. I had to be satisfied with driving officers around.

In early 1972, General Patrick Cassidy, on a tour of Fort Riley, noticed I was wearing the DSC. When he found out I was from Texas, he asked if I would like to come as his driver to Fort Sam Houston in Texas where he commanded the 5th Army. Would I! By May, I was in San Antonio.

It was while I was driving for General Cassidy that those early turbulent days of my military career peeked through the door of the past. During a drive one sunny afternoon, the general, just making conversation, mentioned that he had known of a corporal named Benavidez when he was a colonel in Germany years before.

"That guy kicked a soldier in the balls and put him in the hospital one night in Augsburg. I almost ended up court martialing him." He looked at me. "You don't happen to know him, do you, Sergeant?"

I felt like stopping the car and running like hell, but I kept my eyes on the road ahead. "No, sir, I don't think I do. There's a lot of Benavidezes in the army, and he may have spelled his with an 's' at the end which makes even more of us with the same name."

"Yeah, could be," he replied, and the subject was never brought up again—to my relief.

But it was there at Fort Sam in 1974 that my life took a turn that I could never have anticipated.

General Cassidy was retiring and I would be out of a job as his driver. Because I was a lifer approaching the end of the line, and probably also because my injuries limited the kinds of work I was able to do, the general gave me the option of choosing my next assignment.

A new readiness group was being formed in the 5th Army to serve as advisors to the National Guard and reserve units in the thirteen states covered by the Fifth. Special Forces veterans were being recruited to work with the SF reserves also. That's what I wanted to do. Despite the reservations held by the general that I could handle that type of position, I was finally assigned to the group.

It was when the Green Beret advisors showed up in San Antonio that all the rumors that I had heard in the last five years were confirmed. During those years at Fort Devens, in Kansas, and finally at Fort Sam, old Special Forces buddies had surfaced from time to time. Each one, almost without exception, had brought up the subject of why I had not been presented the top award—the Medal of Honor. Some thought I had, others thought I should have, and a few said they'd heard that I had at least been recommended for it.

But the discussions had almost always been over a drink at the noncommissioned officers club, and I had really never thought more of it than just drink talk. Oh, I had talked to General Cassidy on one occasion about the possibility of my having been put in for the MOH. His answer had not been encouraging.

"Sergeant," he said, "I've recommended a number of men for the Medal of Honor in my time, and I can tell you that getting it is about the most difficult thing you can do. Everything has to be in perfect order. You need sworn eyewitness statements, the cooperation of superior officers, and the ability to wade through a mountain of paperwork. It's a tough job." And he looked pointedly at me. "Especially after some time has passed after the action."

The general had one DSC himself and had made three combat jumps during World War II. Obviously, he knew what he was talking about. Hell, I didn't even know where Drake was, and he was the man who may—or may not—have recommended me for the medal. I hadn't seen him since he visited me in that Saigon hospital. And when it came to eyewitnesses, well, that was another matter in itself.

There were men who, I knew, could verify what had happened that day in May, but the question was, where were they and how many of them were still alive?

General Cassidy did go so far as to put an inquiry through the proper channels for a copy of the original recommendation by Colonel Drake. A look at that, we both figured, would clear up a couple of points. What did the original recommendation suggest as an award to me, and what were the considerations that led to the final decision to grant a DSC?

Within a matter of weeks the reply came, and while I was disheartened, I was not surprised. "Research has not located the original documentation" was all it said. Not at all unusual, I thought. The war in Vietnam was not only one of bullets and bombs, it was one of paperwork—tons of paperwork documenting everything from the acquisition and disposition of a roll of toilet paper to the movement of divisions.

In the early seventies, President Nixon could have silenced and satisfied both the proponents and opponents of the idea of closing Haiphong Harbor. Instead of bombs he simply could have dumped into the harbor all the paperwork generated by the American and South Vietnamese armies during the conflict. Without loss of life, the waterway through which Hanoi was supplied with the weapons of war would have been clogged with millions of tons of soggy documents. The North Vietnamese would be dipping requisition forms out of the water to this day.

Napoleon said an army moves on its stomach. Not so with American forces. Paperwork is the fuel that keeps them moving.

With such a blizzard of forms, both in duplicate and triplicate (not counting photocopies), it was inevitable that a tremendous number would simply disappear, swallowed up and digested without a burp by the huge bureaucracy which supported the action in Southeast Asia.

I should have let the matter drop at that point—and probably would have if I had not been assigned to the readiness group.

When the Green Beret advisors—many of whom I knew—came to San Antonio and I joined them, the matter was raised again and again. It was impossible to forget it.

And when Colonel Jim Dandridge came to town, it was impossible for me not to do something about it. Dandridge was a former SF intelligence officer in South Vietnam, and he was not only certain that Drake had put me in for the MOH, he also knew where the colonel was.

"We're going to call Drake and find out what happened to your Medal of Honor, Sergeant," he said.

Drake was more than surprised to hear my voice on the telephone when we called him at his office in Fort McClellan, Alabama. "Benavidez, I thought you died."

"No, sir, not quite," I answered, trying to keep the emotion from both my voice and my face. I didn't want the officer at the other end of the line or Dandridge, sitting across the desk from me, to see the effect this conversation was having on me. I remembered the concern and compassion this hard-nosed Special Forces colonel had shown for me as I had lain half-dead in that hospital bed in Saigon.

Yes, he said, he had submitted a recommendation that I be awarded the DSC. No, he hadn't suggested that I be awarded the MOH. He went on to explain that the recommendation he had turned in was pretty short of detailed information, particularly when it came to what had occurred in the LZ at the height of the fight. He wasn't even aware that they had given me the DSC.

"All I was able to put together was some sketchy material from a few people, including a couple of chopper pilots. You and O'Connor were gone—I didn't even know if both of you survived—and Mousseau and Wright were dead. And busy as I was, there frankly just wasn't enough time to do any research on the matter."

My heart sank as I listened to the colonel. The flip-style calendar on Dandridge's desk showed the day to be April 1, 1974—April Fool's Day. And I felt as if I had just had the greatest joke of all played on me.

I had become convinced that Colonel Drake had submitted my name for consideration for the Medal of Honor. Too many people had seemed equally persuaded of the fact. But Drake's revelation put the matter into a totally different light, because there was a time limit now involved—a two-year span following any action in combat during which any and all recommendations for awards had to be made. When the two years elapsed, requests for new awards and for review to upgrade existing ones were automatically turned down.

But no matter, decided Dandridge and Drake that day. Dandridge would send Drake by mail a copy of the citation included with the DSC. Drake promised to review it, and if it seemed feasible, would resubmit his recommendation. Only this time it would be for the Congressional Medal of Honor.

And with that I had plunged into a pursuit I had not really sought. It would lead me through the frustrating corridors of power of the armed forces and governmental bureaucracies. It would go on for years. It would make me more friends than I even dared dream I would have. And it also would make me a few enemies who would misinterpret my motives and actions. But the die was cast.

CHAPTER 31

OLLOWING OUR CONVERSATION that April day in 1974, Dandridge mailed a letter and a copy of the citation accompanying the award of the DSC to Drake in Alabama where he was director of plans, training, and security at the U.S. Army School/Training Center at Fort McClellan.

A week later, Colonel Drake set the wheels in motion with a letter to the awards and decorations board at Fort Sam Houston. The letter was everything I had hoped it would be.

9 April 1974
Commander
Fifth US Army
ATTN: Awards & Decorations, AFKB-PA-P&M

1.   SFC Roy P. Benavidez, SSAN 464-46-1557, was awarded the Distinguished Service Cross by GO Number 3572, HQ, United States Army Vietnam, dated 24 July 1968, for action while serving as a member of my command.

2. Recently I reviewed the citation quoted in the referenced GO and noted that two very important aspects of this extraordinarily heroic action were not included in the citation.

    a. SFC, then SSG, Benavidez was on duty at a Forward Operating Base when a patrol from his unit became heavily engaged with a superior enemy force. Benavidez was a member of a reaction company which was on alert at an airfield to deploy in support of patrols of this type. As a member of this unit, SSG Benavidez saw helicopters return from the battle scene after being driven off by heavy enemy fire. The pilot of one aircraft had stated that he was going to succeed in getting the wounded out, "he would not be driven out, no matter what." SSG Benavidez voluntarily boarded this helicopter as it was returning to renew attempts to extract the beleaguered force. This was not in line with his mission at the time, but realizing that his comrades were in critical straits, he acted with unique initiative to offer much needed assistance even though the hazardous nature of the mission and the possible consequences of the action were known to him.

    b. After rendering the valuable assistance to his comrades, noted in the published citation, SSG Benavidez refused to board the first evacuation helicopter to land at the site of the action even though he was seriously wounded. Having assumed responsibility for the patrol, he acted with exceptional valor and heroism in refusing to leave the area until he was assured that all survivors had been evacuated and all possible efforts had been made to recover the bodies of his dead comrades. He repeatedly returned to the perimeter to escort wounded to the evacuation helicopters and to salvage equipment, even though he continued to expose himself to sniper fire. He finally was assisted aboard the last helicopter in serious condition from his numerous wounds and resultant loss of blood.

3. To the best of my recollection these facts were not known to me at the time I prepared the original recommendation for award. Had the completely voluntary nature of these extraordinary and repeated acts of heroism been known to me, I would have recommended SFC Benavidez for the Medal of Honor. I consider these new facts adequate basis for a review and upgrading of his award.

Ralph R. Drake
LTC, GS
Dir, Plans, Tng & Scty

I had no illusions about an immediate response to the colonel's letter; it would take time to make its way through the proper army channels. So I settled down to doing my job, working with the reserves, trying to keep my mind off the subject.

In August, I received a letter from Colonel Drake and my heart sank at the news. "I spoke recently with Maj Badine at DA reference the action dealing with upgrading your DSC to the Medal of Honor," he wrote. "Maj Badine was familiar with the action and stated that it was in process through PACOM. He expressed concern that perhaps your award would not receive favorable consideration because of the date of the original action. He feels that the statute of limitations provision in the regulation prohibits favorable action."

Yeah, I thought, that damn two-year time limit again. Oh, well, I shrugged, it had been worth an . . . then my eyes scanned the next paragraph.

"He stated that the Air Force was sponsoring legislation to extend the statute of limitations, but he was not specific in this regard. Maj Badine will contact me if there is any change or any other action taken on your award."

An extension of the time limit! God bless the flyboys. They had saved my butt once before with their massive firepower. I only hoped their influence on Congress was as great as it had been with the NVA.

At Colonel Dandridge's urging—"Sergeant, if they do pass a law extending the statute of limitations, you need to be ready to go"—I took a five-day administrative leave and drove my old, green '65 Chevy to Alabama to discuss strategy in detail with Colonel Drake.

Drake was ill when I arrived and I was not able to spend much time with him over the three days I was there, but I left with his promise to give me all the help necessary if and when the proposed legislation passed. He would reconstruct the recommendation and resubmit it to the review board.

"But, Sergeant," he had warned, "they're going to want much more verification of what went on down there on the ground. You'd better get busy and start trying to round up as many eyewitnesses as you can."

Within weeks, the paperwork resulting from Drake's letter began to filter in. There was disappointment but no surprise at the phrases.

"Research has not located a copy of the original for review; hence, no determination can be made as to the novelty of the current documentation which, while relevant may not be material. . . ."

". . . Recommend disapproval of request for reconsideration with advice to recommendor that consideration may be given if and when the two-year time limit on recommendation is suspended. . . ."

". . . It should also be noted that, in the absence of the original recommendation, complete justification will have to be provided. This justification must include witness statements and other data provided for by Army Regulations. It is the opinion . . . that data presented in basic correspondence would be insufficient to support upgrading award of the DSC to the MH. . . ."

No doubt about it, Dandridge and Drake had been right—if I wanted a Medal of Honor, I was going to have to work for it. I knew I had earned it. But this time, there were no enemy soldiers, hidden by dense jungle, to do battle with. Facing me and the people who supported my decision was a giant bureaucracy running on red tape and regulations. Our only weapon was determination—it could be called stubbornness on my part which eventually hardened into an obsession. Sadly, the only results which the army would recognize were cold facts and irrefutable evidence.

Perhaps additional information on the mysterious missing initial recommendation could be pried from the massive records of the Department of the Army by people with more clout than either myself or Colonel Drake could muster.

Congressmen J. J. Pickle and O. C. Fisher, both Texas representatives, joined in the search. General Cassidy, retired by then, enlisted the congressmen in our campaign. However, their letters to the secretary of the army on down were as unsuccessful in turning up any helpful information as ours had been.

But then, in November, came a letter—from the chief of the army's Military Awards Branch—that was a definite boost to my lagging spirit. "On 24 October 1974," I read with delight, "President Ford signed Public Law 93-496, suspending the two-year time limit on recommendations for award of the Medal of Honor and lesser decorations. Headquarters, Department of the Army is now staffing a directive to announce the suspension of time limits."

I wrote letters; I made telephone calls. Using the army's communications system, I put out inquiries as to the whereabouts of anyone that I could remember having been involved in any way in the operation. Lt. Col. Charles Kettles, chief of the aviation section of the readiness group, assigned Captain James Mason, an advisor to the aviation section, the job of tracking down the pilots, door gunners, anyone in the 240th Assault Helicopter Company, the "Greyhounds" who flew the choppers in support of the Green Berets that day in 1968.

The word went out through the Aviation Officers Association that we were looking hard for men who could remember what had happened during that action. We had no doubt that they would remember the event; it remained to be seen how many were willing to recall it.

I made a trip to Houston to talk with the parents of Larry McKibben, the pilot who died trying to pull us out of the jungle. The McKibbens supplied me with the names of the men Larry mentioned in the letters he had sent home. We searched for literally hundreds of men who we knew had become scattered around the world, some of whom had never returned from Vietnam.

In January 1975, a letter arrived from Greensburg, Ohio, from Major John Crist, a member of the Greyhounds. At first there was excitement, but then disappointment. Crist was not an eyewitness, being far from the scene and hearing of the carnage secondhand from returning pilots.

In late January, I located Jerry Cottingham, the man who by recognizing me as I lay there alongside the dead NVA on the airstrip at Loc Ninh, had probably had as much to do with saving my life as anyone. From his post at my old assignment in Fort Devens, he penned a statement and forwarded it to me.

While not an eyewitness either to the battle, he had at least seen the brutal evidence of the butchery as he had helped unload the wounded, dead, and dying at Loc Ninh. "Upon returning to Quan Loi," he wrote, "the total recap of the battle, the project had eighteen personnel dead or wounded and lost two gunships, one UH1D and all of the aircraft had numerous bullet holes. This operation inflicted so many casualties to personnel and aircraft that the project closed down for three days to receive new personnel and aircraft."

That, I thought, proved at least that it had been no picnic in the countryside.

February saw a letter arrive from Iran from Ronald Radke, warrant officer and pilot of a 240th helicopter gunship in Vietnam. I was amazed at how Mason tracked him down halfway around the world. And I was delighted as I read his comments—an eyewitness! Radke had been flying support for Wright's mission that day and had been heavily involved in the attempt to drive off the attacking NVA. On his return to Loc Ninh to rearm his aircraft, he had even seen me board McKibben's chopper.

He had shuttled back and forth between the forward base and the jungle clearing all day, expending his ordnance and returning for yet another run at the relentless enemy. He recounted that upon one of his returns ". . . we counted over forty bullet holes in our aircraft, and at least that many in the other gunship. We were back in the area in forty-five minutes with one slick and two gunships to try another extraction if it could be determined that anyone was left alive in the LZ. To our surprise, Sgt. Benavidez came up on one of the pilots' VHF emergency radios and informed us that they had changed position in the LZ." He ended his account with the assertion that "I believe that if it were not for Sgt. Benavidez's courageous decision to join his men on the ground, no one would have gotten out of that LZ alive."

We continued our search with renewed enthusiasm. I knew there were more of them out there who could help reconstruct the events of that long morning and afternoon. But there were frustrations. Many we contacted refused to help, preferring to keep private their recollections, holding their pain close and refusing to let it loose. Some promised to respond but never did so.

In March, we reached Gerald Ewing in Maryland. Again, his statement brought to life the hailstorm of death encountered by those brave chopper pilots and their crews over that Cambodian jungle, but his story had no detail to speak of about what was happening on the ground. "This letter," he concluded, "does not describe the actions of Sgt. Benavidez, because I did not know at the time that he was the one responsible for helping get the wounded out. I do know that May 2nd was the day I decided never to fly a hostile mission again."

In April, Mason received and passed on to me the statement of another gunship pilot, Jesse Naul, who, like Radke, had provided fire support. We had located him living near Dallas. He had been reluctant to remember and put down on paper his account, but despite the evident pain it brought back, he did so. Naul had seen McKibben make his last run in to pick us up and heard McKibben's final transmission before he was killed. "In talking with Warrant Officer McKibben just before he was hit, he stated that the team members were wounded and that they were attempting (SFC Benavidez) to get them to the aircraft. The ground fire all this time was as intense as any that I had encountered."

Unfortunately, Naul also said that it was only later that evening that he learned that I had been aboard McKibben's slick. In other words, he had not actually seen me.

Five statements. Five men who could put me at the scene of the operation and who could testify to the ferocity of the combat that day. Colonel Drake decided to go with what we had and resubmitted his recommendation for the MOH.

But we didn't rest while we waited for the recommendation to make its way through the necessary channels, and the search went on. I continued to call, write, searching for anyone who could, and, more important, would write an account of what they saw that day.

In October 1975, Captain Mason received the statement of another pilot, Michael Grant. His report was by now a familiar one. He was in on the action in the air, but unaware of what was occurring on the ground although he recalled my radio transmissions.

My spirits lifted somewhat that same month with the arrival of James Fussell's statement. Fussell had been a problem to track down. He had transferred from the Army into the Air Force. But he was important, again, because he could recount in detail the unbelievable conditions encountered in the LZ. He was the pilot on the first slick that unsuccessfully attempted to extract Wright's team. From his comments, it was evident that from the first minutes on the area was crawling with NVA. He was even forced to fire a pistol into the face of an enemy soldier who was trying to bayonet him through the window of the helicopter.

But following the escape, without the SF team, of his chopper from the LZ, he had to return to Quon Loi to treat his wounded. His participation in the rest of the operation was limited to listening to the radio. His recollections were helpful but substantiated nothing about the events following his abortive rescue attempt.

We sent Grant's and Fussell's statements along to join the recommendation and, we hoped, add weight to what we had already submitted.

The months rolled on, unrewarding months. There were no further replies to our inquiries. There was also no word on the action of the authorities reviewing the recommendation. I was beginning to feel the opportunity slip away. From my many trips to the army doctors, I knew they were getting ready to send me into retirement in 1976. It was evident that my ability to perform up to standards was becoming increasingly impaired. And it was only through the communications resources of the army that I had been able to keep up the flood of inquiries.

Nineteen seventy-five rolled over into 1976 and in May came the response I had been dreading. Upgrading of the Distinguished Service Cross to that of Congressional Medal of Honor had been denied due to lack of additional "substantive evidence."

What the hell did that mean? Simple. They wanted an eyewitness, that's all. Outside of the NVAs who had been running around in the bushes trying to blow me and my buddies' heads off, the pilots were just about the only ones I could rely on. Wright and Mousseau were dead, I knew. O'Connor—he had disappeared from the face of the earth. There was no information I could dredge up about him. I assumed he was dead. The CIDGs who had been part of the team . . . forget it. If any of them were still alive, they had vanished into what was now a united Vietnam. Their testimony would be worthless anyway—I needed an American eyewitness. The pilots and crewmen of the choppers were my only hope.

In the early months of 1976, I had located Waggie, the pilot who had miraculously pulled us out of that hellhole. For over two minutes—an eternity in the firefight in which we were engaged—he had maintained his position on the ground while we loaded the wounded and dying.

The hundreds of combat flights Roger made during his tour had taken their toll. A constant patient at the VA hospital, he lived in Salem, Virginia, a victim of the unbelievable stress experienced by so many of the returning Vietnam veterans.

Extremely reluctant at first, Waggie finally, in late April—too late to influence the decision already reached by the review board— wrote a short one-page statement which was the closest one yet to an eyewitness account.

"On the last desperate attempt to extract the team, SSG Benavidez made three trips to load the wounded soldiers on the aircraft. I saw SSG Benavidez kill two of the enemy as they attempted to rush our helicopter. He was in serious condition and covered with blood. He carried a radio and other equipment to the aircraft as he helped the wounded. On his third trip, SSG Benavidez carried a South Vietnamese member of the team who appeared dead to me. SSG Benavidez fell between W. O. Hoffman and myself. I gave him a 'thumbs up' as we took off."

"We can't quit now," I told Colonel Drake. "This could do it for us."

"One more is not going to make a difference, Sergeant," he said. "It helps, but we need more."

Nevertheless, we forwarded Waggie's statement directly to the Senior Army Decorations Board with a request that this new information warranted their reconsideration. Within a month, the answer was back: their decision stood; there would be no upgrading of the medal.

Three months later I was retired from the army, after twenty years and three months of active, often painful, duty. The date was September 10, 1976, and I was more than a little apprehensive when I went out the gates of Fort Sam Houston that day.

I was on my own now. If it was to continue—and how futile it seemed now—the search would have to be on my own. The phone calls, the postage would have to come out of my own pocket. With the approval of my disability, the one thing I did have was time . . . that and the growing conviction that a real injustice was being done.

The real problem was in explaining to others the root of my desire to continue. Why go on? I couldn't explain. Why hadn't they just told me that I didn't deserve the medal and let it go at that? I could have accepted that decision. But that damned phrase, "additional substantive information," whirled through my brain constantly, goading me with the thought that with just one more attempt, I could find the man who could remember and tell it all.

Back in El Campo, I carried on my correspondence, limiting the phone calls as much as I could. Nevertheless, my small savings dwindled. Lala said nothing. She didn't understand, but she was the wife of a soldier and knew that a soldier did what he had to do.

In February 1977, I found William Darling, a member of Waggie's crew that day. From his home in Seattle, Washington, he wrote what, up to that time, was the most comprehensive account of probably the longest two minutes of his life.

Darling had not been part of the action in the first part of the day. Only upon one of the returns of Waggie from the combat area did Darling get the opportunity to get into the fight. Hoffman and Waggie were short a crew chief and door gunner. Darling volunteered to take the position of crew chief while Warrant Officer Smith handled the door gun.

"This [position] put both WO Waggie and myself on the left side of the helicopter, the side in which the eventual loading would take place," he wrote. "After we got airborne, I switched the radio channel to the Special Forces team only to hear SSG Benavidez giving directions and taking charge of the situation. It seems that WO McKibben had been shot and killed, and his aircraft was down in the PZ. . . . We were next to go in; down at treetop level, I could see that all the aircraft were under heavy fire but the gunships were getting it worse. On short final, I could see WO McKibben's helicopter turned almost upside down propped against a tree. I could see WO McKibben still strapped in and blood covering his face.

"As we landed within ten meters (close enough to recognize the Special Forces members easily) of the downed aircraft, I saw the Special Forces start running toward the aircraft. They were coming from my one o'clock position and WO Waggie's nine o'clock position. I was on the machine gun putting out fire from the tail boom to as close as I could to the team (thus I was able to keep track of the load of team members).

"Loading was going very slowly; in fact, it gave SSG Benavidez enough time to make three trips from the downed aircraft to our ship. I saw SSG Benavidez make trips to our aircraft carrying radio equipment, and carrying a badly wounded interpreter under his arm. On one of his trips (the second) he shot two enemy who were behind our helicopter and whom I couldn't get with my machine gun. On his final trip, he was holding his intestines in his arms—I didn't think he would make it back: he was very badly wounded. I was hit at this time which spun me around, giving me my only view of the inside of our aircraft—it was full of dead and dying people; the enemy was picking off everybody just as they were getting on.

"I got back on the machine gun and continued to put out protective fire. By this time, SSG Benavidez was close enough to the aircraft to be pulled in. He gave the thumbs up to the pilots and we took off. We started giving first aid to the wounded, which amounted to little more than putting the live people on top of the dead. SSG Benavidez was near the front of the aircraft—I don't believe he received any attention for the above reason. We had so many seriously wounded that the blood flowed out of the helicopter. . . . I feel very strongly that MSG Benavidez deserves the Medal of Honor in that he was able to operate and take charge of a situation that would have been impossible for anyone else. Even though he was seriously wounded, he repeatedly risked his life to rescue personnel and retrieve equipment. I am proud to know MSG Benavidez."

This'll do it, I told Drake over the telephone. "When they read this and put it with Roger Waggie's statement, it'll all come together—I know it."

Again, only a month passed before the report came back—upgrade denied because the new information "did not add any substantive evidence not previously considered."

It was more than I could take. "What the hell is going on here?" I shouted, storming through the house, waving the Department of the Army stationery around like a battle flag. Lala and the kids listened to my tirade in silence.

"They're not even looking at the statements any more. It's just another nuisance to them. It's just more work for them from that crazy Mexican down in Texas: I don't understand, I just don't understand."

But Fred Barbee did. "Maybe it doesn't have anything to do with the facts, Roy," he said a few days later when I told him about the runaround I was getting.

"What do you mean?" I stopped my pacing about his office at the El Campo *Leader-News*. I had just told him that it looked like the end of the road. I couldn't think of anything else to do that would convince that faceless and nameless Senior Army Decorations Board.

"I've read the accounts of other Medal of Honor recipients just like you have. A lot of them won the medal with less of their 'substantive evidence' than you've given them. I think we're dealing with a matter of politics here."

I still didn't understand.

"Cambodia, Roy, Cambodia. You were in Cambodia that day, Roy. You know it, I know it, and the army knows it. The trouble is, while you and your buddies were getting chopped to pieces, the government back here was saying that no American servicemen were in that country. They still say there were none of our soldiers there. If they recognize you anymore than they already have, they just might have to tell the American people where you were."

"Now, just a minute, Fred." I was suddenly very uncomfortable with the way this conversation was going. "I don't know if I was in Cambodia."

"See, Roy, you're still army too. Don't want to breach security, reveal too much. If you can't say it, why do you think they will?"

There had to be another way, I said. There didn't have to be any mention of any other country.

"Put political pressure on them," Barbee said. "Talk to every Congressman in every district around here. Write to the governor, Senator Tower and Bentsen, get the veterans' groups here to support you, the Rotary Club, Lions Club, anybody who can write a letter."

It was a good idea—except it didn't work. I made a nuisance of myself, buttonholing every officer of every civic club and veterans organization that would listen, urging them to write a letter for me. Texas congressmen—Joe Wyatt, Kika de la Garza, Olin Teague—helped, but their requests for explanations and pleas for assistance got the same blank response.

In April 1977, I even located one more eyewitness. Chandler Carter had been flying in the vicinity of Loc Ninh and had landed there when he heard of the fight over his radio. His statement contained secondhand information because he had remained on the ground at Loc Ninh, but, what the hell, I thought, I'll go ahead and submit it anyway. I knew what the results would be. Sure enough, the army swallowed it and it disappeared without a burp.

By February 1978, it was evident that there was no way around the wall facing us. That was when Barbee, more out of frustration than anything else, I think, wrote a front page editorial which would find the only crack in that wall of silence. We didn't know it, but with his typewriter, he was about to punch through it.

CHAPTER 32

CLOSE MY EYES and can see again the headline that appeared February 22, 1978, in the pages of the El Campo *Leader-News*:

ROY BENAVIDEZ . . . SOMETIMES THE
PATIENCE WEARS THIN
By Fred Barbee

El Campo's Roy Benavidez is a patient man.

An uncommonly patient man.

You see, Master Sergeant Roy P. Benavidez, U.S. Army Special Forces (Green Berets) Retired, has been getting a runaround of bureaucratic innuendo and military double talk for the past three years.

And that's enough to tire a man out.

Any man, that is, but one the caliber of Roy Benavidez, who has a drawer full of Purple Hearts and other medals, including the Second highest this nation has to offer, the Distinguished Service Cross (DSC).

It's this "Second" highest thing that concerns Roy and his many friends and supporters, who range from his wife and children to members of Congress and Army generals.

Unfortunately, none of the above are privileged to serve on a group called simply the "Senior Army Decorations Board." This board, whose members are anonymous and whose actions are not subjected to any sort of public scrutiny, supposedly has reviewed a request submitted first in 1974 by Sgt. Benavidez's former commanding officer, Lt. Col. Ralph R. Drake, to upgrade the Distinguished Service Cross to the Congressional Medal of Honor. The request was based on new and substantive evidence not available when the sergeant was first put up for the DSC.

This faceless Senior Army Decorations Board reportedly (but, in the aura of official secrecy, who knows for sure) reviewed Sgt. Benavidez's case in June 1976 and again in April 1977. In both instances the Board disapproved upgrading the DSC to the Medal of Honor with the same obtuse reason given, that "no new substantive information" had been presented.

One wonders what the distinguished Senior Army Decorations Board used for comparison, since by the Army's own admission, the original recommendation for the award for the DSC and accompanying supportive statements had been lost somewhere in the vast wasteland of military red tape.

Nevertheless, a third attempt was made through Congressman John Young's office in October 1977. The attempt contained a completely documented report of one of the most heroic acts any man has ever attempted, accomplished and amazingly, lived through.

In December 1977 Secretary of the Army Clifford Alexander sent Congressman Young a letter containing what has now become the Army theme song: "I regret to inform you that following a full and careful review the Board (there's that 'Board' again) determined that the information was not new substantive evidence not previously considered.

"Accordingly, the request to upgrade Sergeant Benavidez's award of the Distinguished Service Cross to the Medal of Honor was not favorably considered."

Secretary Alexander's letter went on to say: "It is neither fair nor equitable to subject the members of the 'Board' (same old Board) to microscopic inquiry with respect to their votes of conscience. Therefore it is Department of the Army policy not to reveal exact reasons for or against any specific recommendation." This, in response to Cong. Young's request for "a detailed statement in support of the board's position if they render an unfavorable report."

"I've been told by some high-ranking officers, friends of mine, that Vietnam was an unpopular war and that bringing up anything about it now is also unpopular," Roy said recently in his matter-of-fact way.

"You know, it seems that those who deserted and avoided serving are getting more consideration from Washington these days than those of us who served and did our job," the sergeant added.

What, then, happened on that awful day in May ten years ago in the Republic of Vietnam?

Or, perhaps this particular action on May 2, 1968, actually took place outside the boundaries of Vietnam, perhaps in an area where U.S. forces were not supposed to be. After all, at about that time the American public was being fed information downgrading the amount of U.S. participation in the actual combat operations.

Perhaps that is a contributing factor to the continuing "run-around" given Sgt. Benavidez and his supporters, maybe "we weren't supposed to be there, so officially, let's just ignore it and it'll go away."

I smile now as I remember inwardly cringing at Fred's words suggesting both that the action took place outside the boundaries of South Vietnam and that there was collusion on the U.S. government's part to conceal that fact. Those comments had definitely set me to squirming as I read them. My training to preserve security above all rebelled at the idea of even intimating that we were not where we officially should have been that day. And my faith in the fairness of the system I had served for so many years would not permit me to believe that a decade-long preoccupation with the political repercussions of such an admission would stand in the army's way of doing what I knew was the right thing.

Some would call me naive—others probably just dumb.

Fred's editorial had gone on to recall the details of the action in the jungle that day. The whole piece took up an entire page in the paper. Following his recounting of the awarding of the DSC, he picked up the story of Drake's efforts on my part, beginning in 1974:

> At that time Col. Drake, Benavidez's commanding officer, put into motion a request that should have been routine, but has since developed into what appears to be a glaring example of military pomposity.
>
> The matter suggests several leading questions.
>
> Did the prestigious Senior Army Decorations Board really consider the additional testimony on the 1968 action?
>
> If they did, why did they refuse to upgrade the medal, with every eyewitness who lived through the action citing

the unbelievable display of heroism on Sgt. Benavidez's part that day.

What criteria did this group of anonymous men use in arbitrarily refusing to upgrade the medal?

Is Vietnam really such a distasteful memory in the Pentagon, where it was promulgated for so many years, that they still can't bring themselves to admit a mistake was made by the first Decorations board that considered the medal?

If the Army is really sincere in learning all the facts about this case, why have they never questioned Col. Drake?

What does the treatment that Roy Benavidez has received do for the image of the "Volunteer" Army? Maybe that's one of the reasons it isn't working?

Yes, Roy Benavidez is a patient man.

However, his many friends and supporters aren't so patient. They would like some answers, not more military mumbo jumbo, and although it apparently goes against the bureaucratic and military grain, the American public still has a "right to know."

While uncomfortable with the content of the article, I was also delighted. The questions and conclusions reached by Fred were not new to me. But I had not been able to bring myself to voice them. Why had the army never bothered to question Colonel Drake on the matter? Not one single attempt had ever been made by them to seek out additional information.

Taking a close look at my steadily dwindling financial resources, I decided to make one final attempt before calling it quits. God, how I hated the idea of giving up. Maybe Fred was right. Maybe publicity and political pressure were what was needed.

I mailed somewhere between 150 and 200 copies of the editorial to Texas state representatives and senators and the governors, members of the U.S. Senate and House of Representatives, especially those from my own state, and business leaders across the country. If I went down, I was going down swinging.

A number of newspapers across the country picked up the story and printed excerpts. Politicians and ordinary citizens responded with letters either promising to write their representatives or, if they were elected officials, saying they would look into the matter.

But from the Pentagon, there was silence. And there it would have ended except for a reprint of Fred's article in a Honolulu newspaper that appeared more than two years after the *Leader-News* article.

There, a casual reader, scanning the daily news for the latest on crime, passion, and politics, stopped short as he read of the questions still surrounding events now twelve years old. That evening, he placed a telephone call across the Pacific to Australia, leaving a terse message at a hotel in Sydney.

In the weeks that followed, the slip of paper upon which the hotel clerk had dutifully written the man's words was buried under a mountain of other mail. Then one evening, a dark-haired man sporting a mustache, an American by his accent, arrived to pick up his mail.

"Here you go, sir," said the clerk, with easy familiarity as he handed over the stack. "Got a quite a bit to look over when you get back to Fiji."

CHAPTER 32

"Yeah, it looks like it," replied the American. "Probably be up all night going through it all."

"Well, have a nice trip back."

"Thanks, see you next time I'm in."

"Yessir. G'day, Mr. O'Connor."

CHAPTER 33

I WAS SITTING in the den with my son, Noel, one warm summer evening in July 1980, watching TV as usual, when the phone rang.

Reaching up from my seat on the couch and keeping my eyes on the screen, I picked the telephone off the bar.

"Hello," I answered, still concentrating on the television set.

"Hello," replied the other voice, high and distorted as if the caller were speaking from a great distance. "Is this 'Tango Mike Mike?' "

"What?" I sat up straight. "Who is this?" It had to be an old SF buddy, one who remembered that nickname from Nam. But none of the ones I had communicated with since returning still used it when talking with me. I was just Roy to them.

"This is 'Big Team' calling. Do I have 'Tango Mike Mike' on the line?"

I was speechless. "Big Team" was the nickname—where in the hell he got it I don't know—of Brian O'Connor, but O'Connor was dead . . . wasn't he?

"O'Connor? Is that you?" was all I could get out.

"Yeah Roy, it's me. How're ya doin', brother?"

The emotions boiled over in both of us, and for minutes, neither of us could speak more than a word or two before choking up. It had been over twelve years since we had spoken, twelve years of not knowing if the other were even alive.

The last time we had exchanged words, the air about us had roared with the scream of death calling our names. Later, in the stillness of the hospital, not a word was passed between us as we lay wrapped like mummies. Now, as I listened to his voice on the other end, I realized that I had never considered finding O'Connor. No man could long live with the wounds he had. At his next words, I realized his thoughts were the same.

"Man, the last time I saw you, you looked like you were floating in your own blood. There was no way you could live shot up like that." Then he laughed. "I guess you're a meaner Mexican than I thought."

He was living in the Fiji Islands, he told me, and had been there for quite a while. Didn't say what he was doing there and I didn't ask.

"You're calling from there now?"

"That's right, and I'm writing a statement on what happened that day we last partied with the gooks. When they read what I'm going to write, the shit's goin' to hit the fan. You're going to get that Medal of Honor, Roy. I'm going to see to that."

He followed through on his promise. Dated July 24, 1980, his ten-page, single-spaced, typed statement recited in painful detail the bloody events of May 2, 1968.

His report hit the Department of the Army like a bomb. Suddenly, stony silence from the Pentagon turned into cooperation. Congressmen, who like me had been frustrated at the brushoff they had received from the army, were now urged to waive another time limit which had gone into effect since the one I had slipped past in 1976 had expired.

The days following the announcement that Congress had approved legislation awarding me the Medal of Honor were bittersweet. On Thursday, December 18, it all became official when President Jimmy Carter signed the bill. Now all that remained was to set aside time for the award ceremonies.

That duty would fall to the incoming president, Ronald Reagan. The White House announced that President Carter's full schedule (he was still totally preoccupied with the hostage crisis in Iran) would prevent him from presenting the medal before he left office. That was okay with me. I had waited this long; I could wait a little longer.

In the closing months of 1980, the newly revived process to award Roy Benavidez the Medal of Honor proceeded routinely. Some of my friends thought the bureaucratic red tape was senseless, but I told them to be patient. "I've waited twelve years for this. I can wait a little longer."

And a little longer was all I had to wait! One chill morning in February 1981, the army arranged for thirty-nine members of my family to join me, Lala, and the kids, Noel, Denise, and Yvette, for the trip to Washington, DC, to receive our nation's greatest military award, the Medal of Honor.

We were welcomed graciously at the Marriott Hotel in Washington and ushered to our penthouse suite, which we found decked out in flowers and baskets of fruit and cheeses. The other members of my family were escorted to their respective rooms. The army had taken over an entire floor of the hotel for the occasion. There was even a communications post set up in one of the rooms, and entry to the floor was controlled.

It sure seemed like a lot of trouble to go to for one Mexican, I told Lala.

The most important event listed on my agenda for our first full day in the nation's capital was lunch with Secretary of Defense Caspar Weinberger and John March, Secretary of the Army.

They had asked me to select the menu for the meal. I thought steak and the usual trimmings would be nice. One other thing I had requested—pico de gallo, a hot, spicy concoction whose main ingredient is diced jalapeno peppers. In Texas, they say a jalapeno is not any good if it doesn't make the sweat pop out on your forehead with the first bite. It never occurred to me that some of my hosts might not be too familiar with this fiery dish.

As we sat down with the Cabinet officers and their staffs in the Pentagon dining room, I proceeded to heap my steak with the pico de gallo. Weinberger watched with interest and followed my lead. After one bite, his face turned red and he reached for the water glass.

"Who ordered this stuff?" he spluttered when he got his breath back.

"He did," laughed Secretary March, pointing at me.

I smiled back at the Secretary of Defense and took another bite.

Following the meal, we went back to the hotel. The afternoon saw a flow of old buddies coming to the suite to visit and shoot the bull just like the old days. Colonel Drake was there, along with retired Warrant Officer Tom Carter and his wife, Irene, all the way from Alaska, and Jerry Cottingham, among others.

That evening, after most of the people had gone, there was a knock at the door. There stood Drake again, with someone standing behind him, partially blocked from my view.

Drake suddenly stepped aside, and it was like I was looking at a ghost, a man who should have died almost twelve years before. I recognized him immediately.

CHAPTER 33

"O'Connor!" The words would hardly come out.

"Yeah, it's me, 'Tango Mike Mike.'"

We embraced and held each other, the tears flowing freely.

"You son of a bitch," I finally managed to rasp. "You look a hell of a lot better than the last time I saw you."

"I'll bet. I know you do," he replied. "I almost didn't recognize you without all those tubes sticking out of you."

"Yeah, just a little bit older and a lot fatter." God, it was good to see him after only talking to him on the phone a couple of times. Of course, that first telephone conversation had been the shock of my life. And now, there "Big Team" was, standing in front of me. We talked that night of days long gone and buddies whom we would never see again, but remember always. We talked of Wright, Mousseau, McKibben, the list went on and on. We were lucky, damned lucky, and we knew it.

The session broke up before it got too late. Tomorrow, I had an appointment with the President of the United States.

CHAPTER 34

I WAS AWAKENED early Tuesday morning by my military escort, Captain John Hammond, and joined the rest of the family in the dining room for breakfast. We were again briefed on the order of events for the day. From all those years in the army, I could appreciate the beauty of a well-put-together operation, one in which everyone knew what he and the others were to do.

After breakfast, we were to be escorted to the White House where we would have coffee with President Reagan and the First Lady. Then, we would accompany them in their car to the Pentagon where the ceremony would be conducted in the huge courtyard.

The government was pulling out all the stops. Quite a show was planned. Only Audie Murphy's ticker-tape parade was on a larger scale, I was told. I was under no illusions. They intended to present the Congressional Medal of Honor that day to Roy Benavidez for action in Vietnam—or wherever—but the ceremony was directed just as much toward every Vietnam veteran who was still feeling the sting of rejection by his own country when he returned from Southeast Asia.

As I prepared myself for the day's events, my mind wandered back to that early December evening of 1980 when a very excited voice had exclaimed: "Roy, have I got some good news for you! The Senate just approved the bill! It's on its way to President Carter's desk for him to sign. The Congressional Medal of Honor is yours!"

"Oh my God," I whispered. "I don't believe it." My legs felt like rubber and I thought I was going to fall flat on my face. And maybe start bawling like a baby to boot. I groped for the arm of the couch and managed to sit down, still trembling.

"Roy, are you all right?"

I stared at the telephone receiver.

"Yeah, Ab, I'm fine. I just had to sit down." I heard the chuckle on the other end of the line. "Ab" was A. T. Webber, a Houston industrialist, owner of Webber Steel Products, and a graduate of the U.S. Military Academy at West Point. It was through his efforts and a handful of others who had believed in me while many more thought I was just a crazy Mexican hungry for glory, that this day had finally arrived.

I tried to express the depths of my gratitude, but Ab cut me short. "Forget it, Roy. You deserved the medal—and now you've got it."

He went on to tell me how the Senate had approved the bill, HR 8386, in the closing hours before the 96th Congress adjourned in 1980. Next year a new president would be in office, and if the action had not been taken, a new bill would have had to be introduced into the new Congress. It would have meant more delay in a process that had now gone on for years.

After Ab hung up, I sat in my chair, uncertain of the rush of feelings that flooded through me. My son, Noel, watched the flickering television screen across the room, unaware of the impact the conversation just ended had had on his father.

My eyes strayed around the room, taking in the paneled walls covered with pictures. There was my basic training outfit, photos of Fort Bragg, me all decked out for my first jump—almost twenty years of a life that had known nothing but the work of soldiering.

Glancing from the shots of the trim young man who stared back at me from the walls, I looked down at my belly. Tango Mike Mike, the Mean Mexican, I thought with a sigh, was now just a fat, middle-aged man.

Would the medal make it all right? I wondered. The months and years following the eternity of that day spent in the hell of a Cambodian jungle had been filled with pain. And the pain had taken its toll. Then it dawned on me. Tango Mike Mike was going to become a symbol.

I was a proper and convenient vehicle for the incoming administration to use as a demonstration of a new attitude of respect and understanding toward those who had fought and died in Vietnam. In that regard, I felt that I was, in effect, a stand-in for all of the millions who served over there and the 350,000 who died or were wounded. It was a high honor.

And the trip this morning to visit President and Mrs. Reagan before receiving the medal was solid evidence that a new spirit of patriotism was sweeping the land.

The five Benavidezes arrived at the portico of the White House in a big black limousine. We were escorted to the Oval Office and there greeted personally by President and Mrs. Reagan. Lala and Mrs. Reagan seemed to hit it off immediately and were soon chatting away.

I did my best to relax, but I was in the presence of my commander-in-chief, and twenty-five years of strict army discipline simply didn't permit me to talk to him like we were old fishing buddies. I was the stone-faced master sergeant at first, yes-sirring and no-sirring right and left. But the legendary Reagan charm is real and within minutes I was laughing at little anecdotes he told us and answering questions about my future plans.

Little Noel really set us all at ease. He had spotted a large jar of jelly beans on a table and had strolled over to it. He stood there, as casually as a nine year old can, and walked his fingers around and around the jar, never taking his eyes off its contents.

"Noel," said the president, "would you like a jelly bean?"

My son's eyes brightened with a smile and he nodded yes.

"Tell you what," said Mr. Reagan, "why don't you just take the whole jar? I'm sure I have more."

The boy scooped up the container and held it tight. Within seconds, Captain Hammond was at his side, relieving him of his burden and assuring him that he would keep it safe and secure for him.

"I'm glad you offered them to him, Mister President," I said. "If he hadn't asked for a jelly bean, I was about ready to." And everyone laughed. How about that, I thought, old Roy actually cracked a joke in the presence of the President of the United States. After that, the rest of the brief social event was a breeze.

Then it was time to leave for the ceremony. Lala and I rode with the president and Mrs. Reagan. The children followed in another car. En route to the Pentagon, we were whisked through the capital city in the presidential limousine with a motorcade snaking ahead and behind, with sirens wailing. I stared out the window at the crowds of people who stopped along the sidewalks to watch and wave as we went by. It was literally more than I could conceive that a little ol' barefoot Mexican American farm boy from Cuero and El Campo, Texas, could ever find himself in such company.

That was when President Reagan posed the first question he had asked all day about the action of that day in Vietnam.

"Do you mind if I ask you, Sergeant, what went through your mind that day?"

I looked blankly at him: "What day, sir?"

"When you were bayoneted. You had already been shot so many times and were hurt so badly. What was going through your mind at that time?"

I answered without thinking. "Well, sir, the man got me mad, and I had to kill the son of a bi. . . ." Lala slammed my leg with her shoe before I completed the sentence.

The President began to laugh and turned to his wife. "Nancy, did you hear that?" I didn't catch her reply. Under Lala's withering gaze, I had returned to watching the passing Washington scenery.

We arrived at the Pentagon, and were escorted through the Hall of Heroes, where photographs of Medal of Honor recipients are displayed. It was startling to realize that soon my portrait would join their ranks.

We then went down a flight of stairs and entered the courtyard as the band began to play. Halfway down the stairs, I realized I needed to go to the bathroom. Too late now, I thought, but soon it didn't matter as the impressive ceremony that began to unfold drove all such thoughts from my mind.

The huge open area was crowded with people. Vice President George Bush and his wife, Barbara, were among the many dignitaries present. Many of the workers were waving to us from the windows in the Pentagon. Honor guards stood at attention as the president, Mrs. Reagan, my family and I, and Secretary Weinberger mounted the stage erected for the event.

After a rendition of "Hail to the Chief" and a review of the honor guard by the president and myself, we returned to the podium where we watched a display of precision marching by the Army Honor Guard and a performance by the Fife and Drum Corps dressed in Revolutionary War uniforms. Then Weinberger introduced the president in a short address. During our turn around the courtyard, my leg began to throb. I tried to avoid limping, but upon viewing videotapes of the ceremony later, I saw that I had not been able to hide it.

The president spoke of Vietnam and the sacrifice of the millions of Americans who served there. He spoke of the dead who never returned and the wounded who would bear their scars for the rest of their lives. He spoke of the belated gratitude of a nation for the men and women who had only done their duty. He told of the many humanitarian acts of U.S. servicemen in Vietnam. I felt good as he cited the building of hospitals, schools, waste treatment centers, the housing and medical treatment of children and civilians. Too long I had listened to the term "baby-killer" being the only one applied to U.S. soldiers.

Then I suddenly realized that he was talking about me. He was reading the citation himself. I had been told that it was highly unusual for a president himself to recite the acts for which a Medal of Honor recipient was being honored. Possibly, I was led to believe, it was the first time.

Whatever, I stood as if in a trance as I listened to the commander-in-chief. With each sentence, my mind recalled in all the vivid detail that day so long past now. I heard the chatter of machine guns, the howl of jets as they thundered overhead at treetop level. I could smell the stench of frying flesh and, worst of all, hear again the cries of my dying comrades.

And then the president turned toward me as I stood at attention, and I saw it for the first time. A lieutenant colonel stepped forward, carrying in his white-gloved hands the sky-blue ribbon from which hung the Congressional Medal of Honor. It's a rather tiny medallion, in point of fact, but one which all the riches in the world could not purchase.

As President Reagan placed the medal around my neck, the lieutenant colonel stepped behind me and fastened it in place. This, I thought, is for you guys—Leroy, Frenchy, and the rest who didn't come out of the jungle that day.

I started to step back and salute the president, but before I could move, he reached forward and grasped me in a hug. I was startled—it wasn't exactly military protocol, after all. But I returned the embrace and then stepped back to give him a proper salute. He returned it with his right hand over his heart. I was intensely moved at his personal display of warmth. It was something to remember. I don't think there have been too many sergeants in the U.S. Army who have ever been hugged by the President of the United States.

One small embarrassment marred the ceremony, for me at least. I had been so taken by surprise with the president's bear hug that I accidentally stepped on his toe with my highly shined combat boots. Some of my friends later would say the incident was prophetic.

And so a day for which I had worked so hard and invested so much emotion for years was over in a matter of hours. I was exhausted when we returned to the hotel, and Lala and I both agreed that we were ready to return home and take up a normal life again. One last evening talking over old times with a few of the boys, and the next day we headed toward the airport and the trip home.

I met O'Connor for one last moment at the airport. There wasn't much to say, and we couldn't seem to get our throats clear enough to say it anyway. "Take care of yourself, Big Team," I said, as we embraced.

"You too, Roy. Keep in touch."

We both had tears in our eyes as he walked away and I turned to board the plane.

We arrived back in Texas that evening and were treated to a big reception at the El Campo gymnasium when we got into town about 7:45 p.m. The get-together was conceived and organized by Chris Barbee, managing editor of the *Leader-News* and son of its publisher. Over a thousand people crowded into the gym, which had been opened and prepared on extremely short notice by my friend Lionel Garza, El Campo High School principal. Lionel had supervised the hanging of banners by the students. There was even a banner over Highway 59 going into town welcoming us home—and a phone call from Bill Clements, Governor of Texas. I had to stand at the podium with the telephone earpiece against the microphone so everyone in the place could hear the governor.

It was quite a bash for a town the size of El Campo. It was also the first indication that a return to any kind of normal life was going to be hard to come by.

CHAPTER 35

SINCE MY DISCHARGE from the army and return to El Campo, I had been stamped with the label of a local eccentric, a has-been war hero who lived on past glories. To some in El Campo, there was no doubt as to my future. I would be added to that list of men whose names popped up in the pages of the local newspaper from time to time—soldiers who, even decades after the end of World War II, were still attempting to persuade the government to grant them the Medal of Honor. People would shake their heads in wonder, look up from the paper and ask each other, "Why does he do this, after all these years? Poor soul."

But now my name was to go onto another list: The roll call of honor, joining the 3,411 other Americans who have been accorded the nation's highest award for valor since the Medal of Honor came into existence during the early days of the Civil War.

People being what they are, it probably made little difference to most of the ten thousand or so citizens of El Campo whether Roy Benavidez was awarded the Congressional Medal of Honor. They were involved in the daily tasks of maintaining their own lives, and the news had little impact there. It was only one of the topics of conversation over a morning cup at the coffee shop or at the barbershop—of momentary interest but that was all.

Of course, there were the ones to whom I had turned for assistance during the years of frustration. They were proud and happy that together our efforts had finally succeeded.

And there were those whose civic pride was touched. Little El Campo, quiet, peaceful community in the middle of farm and oil land, its people living in the shadow of bustling Houston, now had a moment in the sun. Network anchormen spoke of our town, the name of El Campo (it actually means "the camp," in Spanish) appeared in the largest newspapers—not in the context of natural or man-made disasters or crime but as a place where patriotic men and women were not afraid to do their duty for their country.

Many people would come up to me on the street, extend their hand, and offer their best wishes. "Congratulations, Roy," they would say, "we're proud of you." It made me feel good.

But there were some who made it clear to me and my friends that the presentation of the Medal of Honor was an injustice and an insult to the many brave Americans who had received the medal—many of them posthumously. Maybe that's the way they wanted me to receive the medal. These folks were in a minority, I know, but their hostility cut me deeply.

It was a shock to be stopped on the street by people who I had known for years and be told, "You really didn't earn that medal. They're just givin' it to you to get you off their backs." Or to hear the sarcastic comment: "Well, you finally got what you wanted."

It was doubly difficult when I was caught in the middle. Standing in a line of about a half-dozen people at my local supermarket to cash a check, an assistant store manager walked up to me.

"You're Mister Benavidez, aren't you?" the young man asked me.
"Yeah, I am."

"Can I help you?"

I nodded toward the empty manager's booth. The clerk who was cashing the checks had stepped away for a moment. "I'm just waiting to cash a check," I said.

"Here, let me take care of that for you," he replied, taking the check from my hand. He went behind the counter and returned with my money under the stares of the others in line.

"Thanks," I said self-consciously and turned to go.

"You really think you're hot shit, don't you?" snorted a young woman in front of me. She was a rather pretty lady except for the look of disgust on her face.

I was becoming touchy and pretty confused by the mixed reactions I was getting. My testy response didn't endear me to any of the people who, like me, had been waiting patiently to get our money and go on our way.

"Well, I got my money, didn't I?" I snapped back and stalked out of the store. What the hell is happening here, I thought—to me and to them?

Then, of course, there was the incident at the American Legion Christmas party that year. I had been a member of the local post for years and had enlisted their help in support of my quest for the MOH—assistance which I thought was less than wholehearted and definitely less than enthusiastic. But I was not prepared for what happened that night. Lala and I, along with her cousin, Lupe Coy—also a member of the Legion—and his wife, Jessie, arrived at the hall, hearing the Christmas music as we entered the door.

People stood about, talking and drinking. There was a festive atmosphere to the large interior. Only days had passed since the announcement that I would be awarded the medal, and a number of fellow veterans came up and offered their congratulations. But even more either ignored me or greeted me with a casual hello. I suppose I expected more of a reception. Again, I realized that I was just Roy Benavidez to them, a local boy, nothing more and maybe, just maybe, a bit less.

Time came to eat at about seven o'clock, and the four of us joined the buffet line for a Christmas dinner with all the trimmings. Picnic tables were set up in long parallel lines, and we took our seats at one of them.

When all were served and seated, the Legion commander, Lt. Col. Merrill Adamcik, a Vietnam veteran, stood up from his place and asked for everyone's attention.

After wishing everyone a Merry Christmas, introducing and welcoming the area commander, past commanders of the local post, the district commander, their guests, and thanking all of those who had a part in putting the party together, he turned and pointed to where I sat.

"I'd like to extend a special welcome to Roy Benavidez and his wife, Lala. Here's a man who is our next Medal of Honor recipient, a man who will put El Campo on the map. I know we're all proud of him."

The applause that broke out died abruptly as a loud voice at the table next to us interrupted.

"Boo! . . . Boo-o-o! He doesn't deserve it! No way! He doesn't deserve it!"

The silence was deafening in the large hall as people shifted nervously in their seats, most at the far side straining to see who was making the commotion. I sat, staring straight ahead, while a few of his table companions tried to shut him up.

They succeeded, and a low murmuring filled the room as whispered comments flew the length of the tables. Everyone suddenly discovered the food sitting before them, and within a minute, the level of conversation returned to normal amid the clink of glasses and tableware. Those around me were still quiet; I felt sick and no longer hungry. But I ate, putting on my best master sergeant's face, oblivious to everything.

A dance followed, and the four of us sat quietly for a while. No one approached us, and finally, I turned to Lala and said, "Come on, let's get out of here."

Adamcik stopped me at the door as we were leaving. "Forget it, Roy," he said. "He was drunk."

"Yes, sir," I replied. "Well, we'll be seeing you." And we left.

To some, my efforts had been no more than an arm-twisting political campaign to pressure the army and the federal government into taking action where none was needed. The Medal of Honor, they said, was intended to be an expression of gratitude from a grateful nation, given freely, spontaneously, and accepted humbly. What hurt the most was that many of them were veterans like myself, although of earlier, perhaps more honorable, wars. Their rejection was like the rubbing of salt in an open wound.

They saw Roy Benavidez out daily taking the sun, walking, and occasionally working up to a short jog. While they went to work to earn a living for their families, Benavidez led a life of leisure, drawing a pension from the government, talking to whoever would lend an ear about an event that happened in a war that was over—that we had not even won, for God's sake. And what about a job? Any man who can walk three to four miles a day ought to be able to work.

What they did not understand was that no amount of pressure or outside influence would force the U.S. Army board which reviews such matters to recommend awarding the MOH to an undeserving individual. And, in addition, they were not aware that the history of the medal is full of the stories of Medal of Honor recipients who did no more than I had done—search long and hard for the eyewitness verification absolutely necessary for final authorization of the honor.

Yes, the Congressional Medal of Honor is awarded freely, and yes, it is accepted with humility and gratitude. But no, it is not always an automatic thing. War is death, pain, boredom, fear, and probably above all, confusion. This was especially true in Vietnam. Men who were your comrades one day were dead or medevaced to hospitals in Saigon or some other base the next day.

It was a war of mobility and speed. There was no program and the players didn't wear numbers. On that one day in May 1968, hundreds of men, wheeling about the sky or lying pinned down and dying in the grass, were intimately involved. But within seconds following our extraction, they were scattered to the far corners of the compass, already preparing for the next day's killing or on their way to the rear for medical treatment. It was no wonder that Colonel Drake, burdened with the responsibility of still another mission which would get underway with the sun's new rising, had little time or opportunity to research the details of an event that was already history.

And I walked, not because of the pleasure it gave me, but to prevent the torn muscles and ligaments—healed now but covered with scar tissue—from stiffening and crippling me for life. As it was, standing or sitting for any length of time extracted payment from me in sleepless nights of pain. I was out there because I had no choice. And I came home and sat, exhausted from the effort, for a half hour, before I could go about any other business.

There was a job—a good one—waiting for me if I said my last goodbye to the army and to my small pension. A friend with an insurance company in Houston had an opening for a claims adjuster. I had prepared for it by attending night school after duty hours while I was still on active duty. My experience as a military policeman would have come in handy.

The drawbacks were that I would be on the road a lot and on call night and day. It would mean putting up with discomfort and being away from my family; my wife and children had seen little enough of me in the past, but there seemed no choice. My army retirement pay, 75 percent of my base pay averaged out over the past twenty years, didn't amount to much. There would have been an additional 10 percent of my pay in the mailbox each month because I was a recipient of the DSC, but because there was a request for an upgrading of that award to a Medal of Honor, it would not be forthcoming.

But before I could report for work, the word came down from the Social Security Administration. I was declared 80 percent permanently disabled. In 1980, it was boosted to 100 percent. The missing lung and fragments of NVA bullets lodged near my heart made the difference.

It was still a difficult decision. Except for the times spent in the hospital and recuperating from wounds, the army had always found work for me to do. Even when it was obvious to my commanding officers that I was unable to carry out my duties in the field, there had always been something to keep me busy.

The prospect of doing nothing scared me. But the thought of turning down the disability pay, finding myself incapable of holding down a regular civilian job, and living off the tiny pension given retired enlisted men frightened me. I knew it would be a long, hard fight with the federal bureaucracy to get the disability reinstated if I lost the status of a disabled veteran by taking a civilian job. That thought—more than any other—made my decision for me.

CHAPTER 36

I DON'T KNOW why it is, but it seems that when I get involved in something, it always gets out of hand and mushrooms into a major undertaking.

On impulse, I jump onto a helicopter to go and help my buddies who are pinned down. The next thing I know, I'm fighting for my life against the North Vietnamese. By the sheer grace of God, I live through the experience and am applauded as a hero.

I'm informed that the award I received for staying alive and doing what I could to help a handful of other men do the same should have been of an even higher nature. At the time, it seemed a matter of just getting a number of eyewitness statements together and upgrading a Distinguished Service Cross to a Medal of Honor. That evolved into a six-year obsession and a running battle with a bureaucracy as stubborn as me.

When that was behind me, I expected to settle down into graceful retirement, my battles finally fought, and just watch my kids grow up. In addition to a small increase in my military pension as a result of being a MOH recipient, possession of the award resulted in a number of appearances at community clubs, schools, and youth organizations such as the Boy Scouts.

I enjoyed the opportunity to speak to youngsters, especially Hispanic ones, about their country and the responsibility to freedom they bear as the result of the shed blood of patriots throughout our history. Having worked so hard to get the medal—and work is what it was—I could appreciate its significance and the responsibility that accompanied it. It was not to be put away in a drawer and forgotten, but used in a way to foster—especially among the young—love and appreciation of the nation in which they live.

That was my goal, and for over two years after President Reagan fastened it around my neck, I spent my time working to achieve that result. I also attended Wharton County Junior College and received my Associate of Arts degree in political science.

But having the Medal of Honor also makes it easier for the spotlight—even when it is unwanted—to focus upon the wearer. I found that to be true in the spring and summer of 1983 when, again, a series of events brought me to the forefront of the nation's attention.

It all began innocently enough with the arrival on February 22 of a letter from the Social Security Administration. After seven years, my benefits were being terminated, it said. I was shocked and at a total loss as to what was going on.

It didn't take long to find out. In 1980 while I was still fighting the government over the MOH, Congress, under the Carter Administration, had passed a number of Social Security amendments, tightening the requirements for receipt of benefits. It was an attempt to rid the system of abuses.

So someone hidden deep in the bowels of the Social Security Administration's bureaucracy (how familiar it all sounded) had decided in early 1983 that Roy Benavidez no longer needed assistance from the government and should go out and get a job like everybody else. But it was not only Roy Benavidez. It was literally hundreds of thousands of people who were arbitrarily trimmed without warning from the system. And for many, it was their only way of surviving.

Fortunately, you could appeal, and I immediately did so. The Congress did have the compassion to allow people like myself who were appealing to continue receiving our benefits while the process went on. The catch was, that if I lost the appeal, I would have to pay the government back whatever money they had forked over in the meantime. The idea made me very uncomfortable.

But I knew how bad a shape I was in. So did my family doctor, Ron Goelzer, to whom I went with the news that the government apparently thought my wounds had healed to the point that I could now look for gainful employment and wanted him to release all medical records on me so that they could prove it.

I sent the documents off to the Department of Human Resources and within a month, got word again by mail from the government. The letter said that "they" had determined from looking at my records that I should be able to lift a fifty-pound weight and work an eight-hour day.

Doing what? I thought, as I looked at the message. I glanced down at my arms and the scars still visible. Yeah, I might be able to lift a weight that size with my right arm—certainly not my left—but not many times and not over an entire day. These guys are nuts, I concluded, if they think the kinds of wounds I received get better as I get older. If they had to spend a day in this body, they'd have a different opinion.

But they wanted me to see another doctor in Houston for a complete examination. Yeah, I thought, this was becoming all too familiar. I went to the doctor and he stuck me, shook me, had me blow into a tube to test my lung capacity, walk on his treadmill, and when he was through, he concluded that I was unfit for work requiring any type of physical exertion over any extended period of time.

As I walked out of his office, I only wished the government had paid me what they just had that medic, because I could have told them the same damn thing. And given them a 10 percent discount besides.

I waited . . . but heard nothing about the result of my appeal. And the fact that every nickel of the Social Security benefits I spent might have to be paid back made the waiting tough. Finally, I wrote the office of Texas Senator John Tower asking for assistance. Soon after, I was ordered to appear before an administrative law judge for a hearing.

For two-and-a-half hours before the judge, with a psychiatrist in attendance, I went over how I was wounded and what the physical effects (and apparently emotional and mental ones from the way the shrink kept eyeing me) had been.

Shortly after my appearance before the judge, I received a letter from him saying he wanted me to see a psychiatrist before he made his final ruling.

Another psychiatrist. Somebody's crazy, that's for damn sure, I thought.

I went to the psychiatrist's office in Victoria, a pleasant city located about halfway between my native Cuero and El Campo. I sat down across from him, leaned my elbows on his desk, and asked him: "Before we get started, I have one question for you. Have you ever served in the military?"

He seemed a little startled, but he answered no, he hadn't.

"Well, how can you question me about my experience? All you know is from books."

Nevertheless, I entertained him with war stories, and he asked me questions about my experiences in combat, and the thoughts I and other veterans had about everything in general.

When I walked out of his office, I knew no more than when I went in. I didn't think I had acted crazy, but I had this thought lurking in the back of my head that being crazy might be the only way to retain my benefits. Well, they could keep their benefits, I thought.

It was at this point that things, as they so often have done in my life, got complicated. In its April issue, the *Reader's Digest* printed the article, "A Medal for Roy Benavidez," a condensed version of my Vietnam experience.

George Schlatter, a producer for the television series *Real People*, read the piece and thought that my story would be right for their Veteran's Day show scheduled for November 9. It would be taped on Memorial Day, May 31.

In May, a reporter from the *Dallas Times Herald* who had covered my story in the past, called me to get my opinion on the trimming of the Social Security rolls. He had no idea that I was one of those targeted for elimination from the public trough. I hadn't gone after publicity on this matter. In fact, I found the whole thing pretty embarrassing, being forced to prove to bureaucrats once more the truth of my statements.

But in the course of the telephone conversation, I let slip the fact that I was appealing the decision to drop my Social Security benefits. I couldn't see the young man's face through the telephone, but the change in tone of his voice was instant. He had wind of a story—a big story. "Wounded war hero denied meager benefits." Oh, my God, I thought, here we go again.

The story was printed, the wire services picked it up, I was asked to appear on a radio talk show on WFAA in Dallas, and a flood was released.

The days of the Medal of Honor were nothing compared to the rush of telephone calls, letters, and visitors who came to my door at all hours of the night and day. They were desperate people: cripples, mothers with small children, disabled veterans, you name it. And they all thought that since I was a Congressional Medal of Honor recipient, there was something I could do about the situation. I tried to tell them that I was in the same boat as they.

However, my situation was not as desperate as that of some of the people who came to see me. If I was finally declared ineligible for Social Security, I could always apply through the Veterans Administration for benefits, although they would not even equal the relatively meager payments of Social Security. But many, no, most of the people who wrote or lined up on the street outside my house had nothing to fall back on.

The White House was stung by the publicity of a Vietnam veteran, and a recipient of the Congressional Medal of Honor at that, being turned out by the Social Security Administration. I received two letters and two phone calls from the Reagan Administration, voicing the president's concern over the matter. There were even news releases to the effect that President Reagan would see to it that the private sector aided Roy Benavidez.

I assumed that meant finding me a job. The humiliation was unbelievable. Well-intentioned people—total strangers—from around the country sent me contributions of two, five, or ten dollars.

During the previous two years, I had spoken out repeatedly on "Duty, Honor, Country" as a patriot—an endangered species in the post-Vietnam era. I felt proud every time I put on the U.S. Army uniform, placed the MOH around my neck and addressed a gathering of schoolchildren. With old-fashioned patriotism in short supply, and with movie and rock stars becoming rich while they subverted the morals of the young, it didn't seem too much out of line for one short, fat Mexican American to stand up and publicly state that he was proud of the uniform he wore, the country he served, and considered it a privilege to wear its highest award. This was done to the amusement of some, outrage of others, ridicule of a few, and with the encouragement of many. But maybe, just maybe, I could become one small symbol of patriotism and inspire some of the young people with whom I came in contact.

Being that type of symbol, even if it robbed you of some of your individuality, was rewarding. But with the Social Security flap spreading, I found myself representing another: the common man, in general, and the veteran, in particular, ground under by the machinery of an unstoppable bureaucracy.

It was a far less flattering image than that of war hero, but there seemed to be little I could do about it. Also, possibly some good could come of it. If instead of a vague idea of a great mass of people suffering under the suffocating restrictions of the new guidelines and procedures, those opposing them could focus on one individual who already had some identity with the public, then maybe the symbol of Roy Benavidez, exploited war hero, would get the job done.

But I knew there would be a price to pay. Many would see Roy Benavidez, the man who cried and held his breath until they gave him his medal, again stomping his feet in a tantrum until the government this time put him back on the public payroll.

Again, events moved fast. Schlatter, or someone on his staff, thought it would be a great idea if, while I was in Washington the end of May shooting the segment of *Real People*, a meeting could be arranged between me and the White House.

Also, as a result of the publicity, I was contacted by California Congressman Edward R. Roybal and asked to appear before the House of Representatives' Select Committee on Aging and discuss the Social Security matter.

The meeting with the White House staff was a real media event. The *Real People* camera crew, one of its on-camera personalities, Sarah Purcell, Lala, my three kids, and I all trooped into a meeting room and sat down with one of the staffers, Michael E. Baroody, deputy assistant to the president.

"Although the president couldn't be here, he wants you to know that he hasn't forgotten you or what you did for the country," Baroody began in a sincere tone. He went on to say it was not the White House's intention that I be "left out in the cold." There were, Baroody said, "plenty of people willing to pitch in" within the private sector if I needed help.

There was no mention of the thousands of other veterans who were faced with the same outlook—or worse, much worse—as

mine. What I heard spelled out in capital letters was CHARITY . . .
nothing more nor less.

When Baroody had finished, it was my turn. "I'm sorry, but I
can't accept it from him or the private sector. I just want what me
and my buddies are entitled to. These same people who are denying
us our benefits are living free at the expense of my buddies, their
lives, blood, and limbs."

Although they were surprised at my response, the *Real People*
executives couldn't have been happier. They had it on camera.
Vietnam vet and war hero turns down president's offer of help out
of concern for other vets.

As for me, I was anything but pleased. After more than two
decades of duty in the armed services, I had just gone on national
television and openly defied, and probably created some embarrassment for, my commander-in-chief, the man who had draped
the Medal of Honor around my neck. And I was certain I had just
stepped on his toes again.

Baroody spoke of the Congressional hearings going on about
Social Security and voiced his hope that many of the problems
such as the ones I had encountered would be resolved. I told him
that I would be appearing before one of the sessions.

As we left the White House and I followed my wife and children
into the car, I wondered if I had done the right thing. I had turned
down certain assistance for them. That bothered me. But they had
offered charity. I couldn't get that out of my mind. I didn't want
charity—I wanted justice.

On June 20, I was back in Washington to testify before
Congressman Roybal's committee. The *Real People* cameras
were there, in addition to the networks. The issue was getting

the exposure it needed. As I sat down in the huge hearing room, I wished again for the thousandth time that it didn't need me to get the public's attention.

Along with me was my lawyer, Tom Burch, a fellow Green Beret and Vietnam veteran. Headquartered in Washington, Tom was also there as spokesman for the United Vietnam Veterans Organizations. He used the opportunity to enter into the record, based upon my individual experience, the plight faced by other veterans who had fought and suffered in Nam and then had the plug pulled on them upon their return.

Tom also entered into the record the *Reader's Digest* article and a number of the countless letters I had received from people lopped from the Social Security benefit rolls.

Then the questioning began from the committee members, all lined up across the front of the room behind a long bench, just like I had seen on television. For public consumption, I again went over the events of the previous months—the receipt of the notice of termination, the appearances before both medical doctors and psychiatrists, and the wait for the judge to decide my fate.

The representatives were sympathetic to my plea that none of us—and I could speak more appropriately for the veterans—wanted any more than what we were entitled to. But as they listened to my story of the fifty-pound weight criteria, (adding their own versions which included ten, fifteen, and twenty-pound weights), they seemed as confused as I about just who determined what in the Social Security Administration.

At one point, I broke in on Congressman Roybal to vent my own frustration: "I would like to make this statement. If, sir, if my comrades and I are denied the benefits that we deserve, then I ask one last favor—to please kneel and join me in prayer to God to save this republic from bureaucratic bungling; there is just no hope."

I was a military man. That was the only life I had known. I couldn't speak for all the veterans. I didn't have that right, but I could speak *as* a veteran. And through looking at my experience, I hoped these lawmakers could gain a little insight of what the system was doing to people who were no different from me.

But Congressman Tom Lantos, another California representative, put me into a category which I had attempted to avoid, that of representing everyone harmed by the present method of doing business.

"Let me ask you, Sergeant, if I may, because understandably, in all of your testimony you have focused on the military, do you feel that it is fair for this government to put civilians—men and women—through the same process that you have been put through?"

I leaned forward toward the microphone. "Well, those civilian men and women, they pay into the Social Security fund, so they are entitled to the benefits."

"What your testimony is," Lantos replied, "is that you are speaking both for veterans and for nonveterans. You are speaking for all Americans who have been so unjustly treated."

Oh my God, Benavidez, I thought. How do you get yourself into predicaments like this? All I wanted was to get my benefits restored so I could pay my utility bills, feed and clothe my family, and have enough left over to take a trip now and then to speak at a school or an Optimist luncheon. Now, here I am, and this guy has me standing up for every American in the country who is being shafted by the Social Security Administration.

Oh well, what the hell.

"Yes sir, it seems like I have been labeled that, so I come before you, the committee here, the chairman, to speak for all the American people who are locked in the same situation."

The session droned on and my testimony soon neared its end. New Mexico Congressman Bill Richardson, after pointing to the many problems I had encountered since returning from Vietnam, had one last question for me.

"I wonder, if you had everything else to do over again, if you knew that these events were going to happen, whether you would go through serving in Vietnam and serving in the armed forces again?"

There was no doubt as to my reply. "Sir, to answer your question properly and honestly, I would say yes . . . yes sir, I would do it all over."

GLOSSARY

AK-47—Assault rifle normally used by the North Vietnamese and the Viet Cong.

ARVN—Army of the Republic of Viet Nam

ATL—Assistant Team Leader

C&C—Command and control; aircraft that circled overhead to direct the combined air and ground operations

CIDG—Civilian Irregular Defense Group

DMZ—Demilitarized Zone

DZ—Drop Zone

E&E—Evade and escape

FAC—Forward air controller

Hootch—Almost any shelter, from temporary to long-term

Huey—Popular nickname for the UH-series helicopters, HU 7A, UH-1C, UH-1D, etc.

LAW—M7s light antitank weapon

LZ—Landing zone

MACV—Military Assistance Command, Vietnam

MOS—Military Occupational Specialty

NVA—North Vietnamese Army

PZ—Pickup zone

R&R—Rest and recreation vacation

RPG—rocket-propelled grenade

Slick—Helicopter used to lift troops or cargo with only protective armaments systems

USOM—United States Operations Mission

TAC—Tactical (air support)

INDEX

Roybal, Cong. Edward R., 336–338

S

Saigon, xvi, xviii, 3–4, 7–9, 12, 14–15, 23, 25, 34, 46, 148, 151, 153, 155, 162, 163, 168, 261–263, 276, 278, 326
Sipsky, Ray, 151, 156, 162
Social Security Administration, 327, 330, 334, 338–339
Special Forces (Green Berets), xvi, 13, 108, 136–143, 145, 147-148, 150-151, 153, 155, 163-165, 167-168, 175-176, 179-181, 183, 207, 209, 211, 213-214, 216, 221, 232, 234, 238, 255, 257, 273, 275, 278, 293, 299
Stys, SGM Ed, 151–153

T

Tam Ky, 21, 23, 26, 46, 52, 61, 63–66
Torres, Frank, 91–93, 104
Tower, Sen. John, 296, 332

U

U.S. Operations Mission, 12–13, 342
United Vietnam Veterans Organizations, 338

W

Wag, ARVN Lt., 37–41
Waggie, WO Roger, vii, 121, 220–222, 235–236, 255, 259, 291–293, 295
Webber, A.T., 195, 314
Weinberger, Secretary Caspar, 190, 192, 198, 310, 318
West Point, 102, 106, 194–195, 314
Westmoreland, Gen. William, 17, 89, 129, 188, 269
Wharton County Junior College, 330
Wright SFC Leroy, 140, 175, 179, 180–185, 203–213, 215–217, 219–220, 223–229, 235–236, 241, 243, 245–248, 263, 278, 287, 290–291, 311, 319

Y

Young, Cong. John, 300–301

ABOUT THE AUTHORS

Roy. P. Benavidez, served twenty-four years in the U.S. Army. He was a member of the 82nd Airborne and 5th Special Forces Group, as well as the Studies and Observations Group (SOG). Roy served two tours in Vietnam. On February 24, 1981, Roy was awarded the Medal of Honor for his heroic actions that took place in Cambodia on May 2, 1968. Later in life, Roy became one of America's most popular motivational speakers and youth role models. For 17 years he traveled throughout the country speaking to Fortune 500 companies, schools, prison inmates, and civic and military organizations. Roy and his wife Lala, have three children and eight grandchildren. He passed away on November 29, 1998, at the age of 63 and is buried at Fort Sam Houston National Cemetery in San Antonio, Texas.

Oscar O'Neal Griffin, Jr., was a U.S. Army Veteran, a graduate of the University of Texas at Austin, former Editor of the Pecos Independent and Enterprise, and a former Houston Chronicle White House Correspondent. In 1963 he won the Pulitzer Prize in local reporting for exposing the Billie Sol Estes scandal during the Lyndon B. Johnson administration. Oscar also served as Assistant Director of Public Affairs for the U.S. Department of Transportation from 1969-1973. In 1974, Oscar and his wife Patricia settled in El Campo, Texas, to run his father's oil company and raise their four children. He died on November 23, 2011, at the age of 78.

www.ingramcontent.com/pod-product-compliance
Lightning Source LLC
Chambersburg PA
CBHW020432130626
46549CB00001B/94